W9-CSU-184

TABLE OF CONTENTS

Introduction   vii

PART I: STUDY GUIDE TO TEXT MATERIAL

Chapter 1: Introduction to Managerial Economics   1

Chapter 2: Decision Making under Risk and Uncertainty   13

Chapter 3: Utility Analysis of Consumer Behavior   24

    Appendix 3A: Income and Substitution Effects   32

Chapter 4: Market Demand Analysis for Decision Making   35

Chapter 5: Estimation of the Demand Function   46

    Appendix 5A: Demand Forecasting   55

Chapter 6: Production Functions and Cost Curves   61

    Appendix 6A: Isoquant-Isocost Analysis   69

    Appendix 6B: Linear Programming Analysis   74

Chapter 7: Cost Concepts for Decision Making   78

    Appendix 7A: Breakeven Analysis   89

Chapter 8: Cost Estimation and Forecasting   92

Chapter 9: Models of the Firm's Pricing Decision   103

    Appendix 9A: Further Models of Pricing Behavior   113

Chapter 10: Pricing Decisions in Practice   118

    Appendix 10A: Illegal Pricing Practices   126

Chapter 11: New Product Pricing   129

Chapter 12: Competitive Bids and Price Quotes   138

Chapter 13: Advertising and Promotional Decisions   148

Chapter 14: Product Quality and Competitive Strategy   156

Chapter 15: Capital Budgeting and Investment Decisions   164

PART II: ANSWER KEY TO SELF-TEST QUESTIONS AND PROBLEMS

Answers to Questions 1 through 300   171

Answers to Discussion Questions   230

Answers to the Quick Quizzes   257

PART III: COMPUTER COURSEWARE MANUAL

Table of Contents   269

Introduction   270

The Benefits of Using the Computer Courseware   270

How to Use the Lotus Templates   272

The Templates   274

How to Modify the Templates, or Make your Own   285

The Fortran Programs   287

EPV - the Expected Present Value Program   288

MULTREG - Multiple Regression and Statistics program 289

INTRODUCTION

This book is designed to help you get a better grade in your Managerial Economics (or similar title) course. It will do this by helping you to improve your understanding of the material in the textbook, and by enhancing your analytical powers. It may even teach you some better study habits, which will be applicable in other courses as well.

Part I of this book is a **Study Guide/Workbook** that takes you through each chapter and appendix, one section at a time. For each chapter or appendix there are the following components:

* Summary of the Chapter (or Appendix)
* Statement of Learning Objectives
* Overview of Each Section
* Reading Assignments (in the text)
* Self-test Questions
* Practice Problems
* A self-graded Quick Quiz to judge your knowledge

To use this book effectively, follow the directions given in each chapter. Start by reading the chapter summary and learning objectives, then the overview of the first main section in the chapter. Then you will be asked to go and read the section in the text, to learn the details and finer points. Then come back to this book and write short answers to the self-test questions on the material you have just read. It is important to write down your answers. It forces you to organize your thoughts, and is good practice for exams. Often there will be a practice problem next, to allow you to apply the material you have just learned. Do the calculations, write down your answers, and check them against my answers, which are found in the Answer Key. Then proceed to the next section of the chapter and follow the same pattern. In this way you will be building blocks of knowledge that will prepare you for the Discussion Questions and Case Study Problems at the end of each chapter and appendix. Finally, take the Quick Quiz to check how well you know the material before proceeding to the next chapter.

Part II of this volume is the **Answer Key**. This is where you look to compare your answers with my answers, to see if we are on the same wave-length. Many of the answers are worked out in full, so you can see where you went wrong, if you went wrong. The answers to the 300 self-test and practice problems are offered in order, followed by suggested short answers to each of 200 or so end-of-chapter Discussion Questions found in the text.

Part III of this volume is the **Computer Courseware Manual**. This is a guide to accompany the files that are available on disk for use on IBM and compatible personal computers. If you have access to a computer, and the Lotus 1-2-3 software package, you can obtain a copy of the courseware files and use these in conjunction with your course and the Study Guide/Workbook. Ask your Instructor, who can request (and copy) the disk from Prentice-Hall, Inc.

The computer courseware is an optional extra. You do not have to use it, and you will still understand the material and enjoy the course without it. But if you do have the hardware and the software required, it will add a whole new dimension to the course, because you will be learning to use Lotus 1-2-3, the most widely-used spreadsheet software in business, in the context of Managerial Economics. The "templates" will help you work through many of the end-of-chapter problems, as well as save hours of your time and preserve arithmetic accuracy. There are two fortran programs for more complex expected-present-value and multiple regression analysis problems. You will find this course-ware to be useful well beyond this course. I urge you to try it.

Your comments and feedback are welcomed. Please let me know if you find mistakes in the Answer Key, or if you have ideas about how the Study Guide/Workbook and Computer Courseware could be improved. Write to me at Bentley College, Waltham, MA. 02254.

Acknowledgements: I wish to thank Andrew Chan and Andrew Mara for their assistance in compiling this volume. Both worked many long hours putting this material on disk file. Many thanks also to Gert Glassen, Supplemental Books Editor at Prentice-Hall, Inc.

Study Guide

Managerial Economics

CHAPTER 1:   INTRODUCTION TO MANAGERIAL ECONOMICS

1.1 INTRODUCTION

Summary

The material in chapter 1 of the text is discussed under four main headings, which are as follows:

1. What is **Managerial Economics** and why do we use **models** in the study of it?

2. **Present-value analysis** of costs and revenues when these occur in the future as well as in the present period.

3. **Expected-value analysis**, used when the outcome of a decision is uncertain.

4. **Decision rules** when costs and revenues occur in the future and are uncertain.

In this workbook we shall proceed through these topics, one at a time, to build and reinforce your understanding of this material.

Learning Objectives

By the time you have completed this chapter, you will be able to:

*   Define, in broad terms, the field of managerial economics.

*   Distinguish between three major types of models, and identify the three purposes of models as they are used in managerial economics.

*   Calculate the net present value of a stream of profits which will arise as a result of a decision to be made.

*   Calculate the expected value of a decision when the outcome of that decision is uncertain and there is a probability distribution of possible outcomes associated with that decision.

*   Identify the appropriate decision rule, for a firm wishing to maximize its net worth, under four different scenarios relating to the length of the firm's time horizon and the state of information held by the decision maker.

1.2 WHAT IS MANAGERIAL ECONOMICS ABOUT?

Managerial Economics is **the economics of managerial decision making.** Managers are better able to solve their decision problems with the aid of economic principles, concepts, and methodologies.

Managerial Economics is based on **Microeconomics,** which offers theories to explain the behavior of individual economic agents, like consumers, producers, and suppliers of labor and other inputs to the production process. Like Microeconomics, Managerial Economics is **normative,** or prescriptive, because it seeks to establish rules which allow the firm to best pursue its objectives. But because Managerial Economics is oriented to the decision problems of business firms in the real world, it also draws upon elements from other disciplines, including accounting, finance, marketing, statistics, and management.

In the real world, firms operate under conditions of **uncertainty.** Certainty means full information, while uncertainty means less than full, or incomplete, information. For example, the firm may expect its sales revenues next month to be "about $50,000" and acknowledge that actual sales might fall anywhere between $40,000 and $60,000. Thus the sales level is "uncertain." We shall use the concept of **expected value** to crystallize this potential range of outcomes into a single value for expected sales.

Models, or simplified representations of reality, are used extensively in managerial economics for three main purposes, which are **pedagogical, explanatory,** and **predictive.** Pedagogical models teach you how a complex system works. Explanatory models explain the interactions within complex systems, and predictive models predict the future values of variables (sales or costs, for example) in a particular system. Models must be judged in the light of their purpose. If a model is meant to be pedagogical, does it help you to understand the system? If explanatory, does the model adequately explain the inter-relationships in the system? If the model's purpose is predictive, does it predict accurately? In managerial economics we use mostly **verbal and diagrammatic models** as an aid to communication and understanding of the material, although mathematical and computer models may also be used, of course.

READING: Now read sections 1.1 and 1.2 in the text. You may wish to underline or highlight the more important definitions, terms and concepts. This will help to keep them in your memory. After you finish reading this section, write a short answer to each of the Self-test questions found on the following page.

Self-test Questions

1. Define, in broad terms, the field of managerial economics.

2. What is the difference between positive and normative economics?

3. What are the three main types of models? Name the three subgroups of the third type.

4. When is it okay for a model to be unrealistic? When is it not acceptable?

5. What is jargon? Why does economics (like all other fields) use it?

     Now, check your answers against mine, which are found in the Answer Key in the back of this workbook. If there are any major deficiencies in your answers, re-read the section in the text and satisfy yourself that you fully understand the material before continuing.

1.2 PRESENT-VALUE ANALYSIS

Section 1.2 of chapter 1 in the text introduces and explains present-value analysis. Before reading that section, read the following overview in order to get the broad picture of what is developed in more detail in the text.

Overview of the Text, Section 1.2

For proper economic decision making, it is important that cash flows be **valued** correctly. When cash flows form a stream over time, the nominal value, or face value, of that stream of costs or revenues will overstate the economic value. This is because a dollar received today is worth more than a dollar to be received in the future. The **present value of a future dollar** is something less than a dollar because a lesser sum received now would grow to a dollar (by earning interest) between now and the future point of time when the dollar would otherwise be received.

     Thus, future cash flows must be **discounted** back to their present value. The discount rate to be used is the **opportunity discount rate**, which is equal to the rate of return one could obtain on those funds if they were deposited or invested somewhere else, at similar risk of default. When both revenue streams and cost streams are expected as the result of a decision, we subtract the costs from the revenues to find the **net present value** (NPV).

Cash flows can be treated either as if they arrive at the **end of each year** or as if they arrive on a more-or-less **daily** basis throughout each year. Cash flows for a particular year are discounted less heavily if they arrive on a daily basis; this is because the funds are available sooner for deposit somewhere and can earn interest before the end of the year.

Annuities are uniform cash-flow streams. The discount factor for an annuity is actually the sum of the discount factors for all the years of the annuity.

The firm has a **planning period** over which it takes into account all cost and revenue implications of its decisions. The end of the planning period is known as the firm's **time horizon**. If the firm considers only the present-period implications of its decisions, it ignores any future cash flows, and hence present-value analysis is not necessary. More realistically, however, the firm's time horizon usually falls in a future period, and thus the firm should use present-value analysis to properly value the cash flows resulting from its decisions.

READING: Now read section 1.2 in the text, underlining or highlighting the more important definitions, terms, and concepts. After completing the reading, write a short answer to each of the following questions.

Self-test Questions

6. What is the relationship between future value and present value? State this relationship in words as well as in symbols.

7. Explain why a sum of money presently held would compound to a larger sum in a future period, and go on to explain why the present value of that larger sum would equal the presently held sum of money.

8. What is the appropriate discount rate to be used when discounting a cash-flow stream?

9. When would you use the daily-cash-flow discount factors in preference to the year-end cash-flow discount factors?

10. What is the firm's time horizon, and what are the implications of the time horizon for present-value analysis?

After writing out your answers, check them against mine in the Answer Key and reconcile any major differences.

Practice Problems

At this point, let's work through a couple of problems together to make sure you really understand present-value analysis.

11.   Turn to the end of chapter 1 and read problem 1-1.

        To answer part (a) of this problem we need to array the cash flows in the order of their arrival and multiply them by the appropriate discount factors, as in the following table. You fill in the gaps. You will find the cash-flow information in the problem, and the discount factors are in appendix B, table B-1, at the back of the textbook. Note that you will use the year-end discount factors because the problem explicitly states that the cash flows will arrive in lump sum at yearly intervals.

YEAR	CASH FLOW	DISCOUNT FACTOR	PRESENT VALUE
0	---------	----------------	-------------
1	---------	----------------	-------------
2	---------	----------------	-------------
		TOTAL	
			=============

Your answer should be $9,856,300. (The full workings are shown in the Answer Key.) Thus this option is inferior to receiving the $10 million immediately.

(b)   Now write a memo to the president of the university explaining why $11.5 million over two years is not as good as $10 million immediately.

(c)   This part of the question requires recalculation of the above table using 12% discount factors first, and then again with 16% discount factors.

Do the calculations, write up your summary answer, and then compare your answers with mine in the Answer Key.

12.   Now read problem 1-4, concerning the Doreen Delights Drinker's Device.

(a)   Using the table on the next page, calculate the present value of each bid using the 9% discount factors found in table B-1 at the end of the text.

YEAR	DISCOUNT FACTORS	COMPANY A FUNDS	P.V.	COMPANY B FUNDS	P.V.
0	--------	-----	-----	-----	-----
1	--------	-----	-----	-----	-----
2	--------	-----	-----	-----	-----
3	--------	-----	-----	-----	-----
		TOTAL	======	TOTAL	======

Work it through and you should get $36,039 for company A and $36,278 for company B. If not, check your methodology first, and then your calculations. If you still can't find the error, compare it with the solution in the Answer Key.

(b) Rework the above calculations using 11% discount factors. Then write down whether you would make a different decision compared to the one implied in part (a) above, and why you'd make it.

(c) Given your (assumed) viewpoint that 11% is the appropriate discount factor, write a short report to management explaining which offer should be accepted and why.

Now compare your answer with mine in the Answer Key. If your answer lacks important details, make sure you understand the material before proceeding.

1.3 EXPECTED-VALUE ANALYSIS

In this section, we will learn how to treat future cash flows which are "uncertain" and how to establish decision rules for the firm which are appropriate to its particular situation. Before reading the section in the text, read the following overview.

Overview of the Text, Section 1.3

When an event or cash flow is uncertain there is a **probability distribution** of potential values for that event or cash flow. For example, next month's sales might be expected to fall within the range of $40,000 to $60,000, with the probability distribution shown on the next page. Note that the probability of each possible outcome is the "chance" that it will occur. Thus there is a 5% chance that sales will be $40,000, and so on. Note that the **sum of the probabilities must equal 1.**

POSSIBLE OUTCOME	PROBABILITY
$	P
40,000	0.05
45,000	0.20
50,000	0.40
55,000	0.25
60,000	0.10
Sum of the probabilities	1.00

For decision making purposes we will want to express the above probability distribution of sales as a single figure which summarizes the information presented. The **expected value** of a probability distribution is the weighted average of the possible outcomes, where the weights are the probabilities. In the following table, you do the calculations to find the expected value of sales.

POSSIBLE OUTCOME		PROBABILITY		WEIGHTED OUTCOME
$		P		$
40,000	x	0.05	=	_____
45,000	x	0.20	=	_____
50,000	x	0.40	=	_____
55,000	x	0.25	=	_____
60,000	x	0.10	=	_____
	Total =	Expected Value		

Your answer should be $50,750. Thus the weighted average of the probability distribution of sales is $50,750. This expected value serves as a summary measure of the probability distribution. Using expected values, we can compare two or more decision alternatives that have uncertain outcomes.

READING: Now read section 1.4 in the text. When you finish, write short answers to each of the following questions.

Self-test Questions

13. Define certainty as distinct from risk and uncertainty.

14. What is the probability that you would get two "heads" if you were to flip two coins?

15. What is the difference between subjectively and objectively determined probabilities?

7

Practice Problems

16. What is the expected cost of manufacturing the next batch of valves, given the following data relating to the past twenty times we manufactured a batch of valves?

COST PER BATCH $	TIMES OBSERVED
800	1
825	4
850	8
875	5
900	2
------	------
	20
	======

17. The values of sales to the first ten customers in the store last Monday were $18.50, $6.25, $2.40, $12.40, $6.25, $8.60, $24.20, $13.70, $9.50, $17.20, respectively. What is the expected value of the first sale next Monday?

After you have written out your answers, check them against mine in the Answer Key and reconcile any discrepancies.

1.4 THE OBJECTIVES OF THE FIRM AND THE DECISION RULES

In section 1.4 of the text we consider the firm's objective function and how the decision rule for obtaining this objective must be modified to reflect the scenario in which the firm operates. Read the following overview of this section.

Overview of the Text, Section 1.4

We assume that the firm wants to **maximize its net worth**, the difference between its assets and its liabilities. Note that revenues add to assets while costs detract from assets (or add to liabilities if they remain unpaid). Profits are equal to revenues minus costs. Profits therefore add to the firm's net worth, while losses detract from net worth. There are four possible scenarios:

* If the firm's time horizon falls within the **present period**, and if the firm has **full information**, neither present-value nor expected-value analysis is required. In this simplest case the firm will maximize net worth by **maximizing its short run profits** in nominal terms.

8

* If the firm's time horizon falls in a **future period** and cash flows are envisioned with **certainty**, the firm must **maximize the present value of profits** to maximize its net worth.

* If the firm's time horizon is in the **present period** but cash flows are **uncertain**, the firm must maximize the **expected value of profits** to maximize its net worth.

* If the firm's time horizon is in the **future** and cash flows are **uncertain**, the firm must use both present-value and expected-value analysis. By maximizing the **expected present value of profits**, the firm will maximize its net worth.

READING: Now read section 1.5 in the text. After you have read it, answer the following questions.

Self-test Questions

18. Explain why the maximization of nominal profits in the case where expected-present-value analysis is not required, is the same as maximizing the firm's net worth.

19. Which is the most likely scenario for a business firm? Which, of the four considered, do you think would be the second most likely?

20. Without looking at table 1.6 in the text, fill in the appropriate decision criteria in the following table:

	TIME HORIZON FALLS IN THE:	
	PRESENT PERIOD	FUTURE PERIOD
CERTAINTY		
UNCERTAINTY		

Check your answers against mine in the Answer Key.

READING: Now read section 1.6, the summary of chapter 1, and then answer the ten "Discussion Questions" at the end of chapter 1 to test your recall of the major principles and concepts encountered throughout the chapter. After completing these answers, check them against mine in the Answer Key, and reconcile any major differences.

Practice Problems

Let's now work on a couple of problems, to make sure we can apply the concepts.

21. Read problem 1-7, a decision problem involving the Swiss Crest Embroidery Company's choice between two different machines.

(a) After you have read through the problem, fill in the gaps in the following tables:

MACHINE A

Year	Cash flow	Type	Discount factor	Present value
0	---------	----	-------	------------
1	---------	----	-------	------------
2	---------	----	-------	------------
3	---------	----	-------	------------
4	---------	----	-------	------------
end of 4	---------	----	-------	------------
			Total	============

MACHINE B

Year	Cash flow	Type	Discount factor	Present value
1	---------	----	-------	------------
end of 1	---------	----	-------	------------
2	---------	----	-------	------------
3	---------	----	-------	------------
4	---------	----	-------	------------
end of 4	---------	----	-------	------------
			TOTAL	============

Note that there are both lump-sum cash flows (arriving at year-end) and daily cash flows, necessitating different discount factors for cash flows received in the same year in three instances.

(b) Advise management which machine they should select, adding your rationalization for your choice.

After completing the calculations and your short report to management, compare your answers with those in the Answer Key. If there are any differences, satisfy yourself that you fully understand the issues involved before proceeding.

22. Read problem 1-10, concerning the Fearless Ambition Racing Team, and then fill in the gaps in the following table:

REBUILD				BUY NEW		
Cost	Prob.	E.V.		Cost	Prob.	E.V.
----	----	----		----	----	----
----	----	----		----	----	----
----	----	----		----	----	----
----	----	----		----	----	----
----	----	----		----	----	----
----	----	----		----	----	----
	TOTAL	====			TOTAL	====

(b) To calculate the expected present value, we must discount the totals found in part (a) by the appropriate discount factors. Do this by yourself, taking care to use the discount factors applicable for year-end or daily cash flows, as appropriate. Note that, in the "Buy new" option, part of the total is discounted under one cash-flow convention and the remainder under the other cash-flow convention.

(c) Advise the manager which option is superior in expected-present-value terms.

Now compare your answers with mine in the Answer Key. There is a Quick Quiz on the next page. If you don't think you're ready for it, read back over the chapter first.

QUICK QUIZ - CHAPTER ONE

Q1. Models should be evaluated according to their _____, which is either _____, _____, or _____ . (4 points)

Q2. To find the economic value of a cashflow, it must be discounted at the _____ rate. (1)

Q3. If cashflows do not occur at year end, but are distributed throughout the year, it is more accurate to discount them using _____ discount factors. (1)

Q4. The firm's time horizon is found at the end of its _____ . (1)

Q5. The expected value of a decision is the weighted average of the possible outcomes of that decision, where the weights are the _____ . (2)

Q6. Certainty means _____ information, while uncertainty means _____ information. (2)

Q7. The present value of a million dollar lottery win that pays $50,000 each year for 20 years, assuming you could earn 10% on the money, is _____ . (3)

Q8. If the firm's time horizon falls in the future, but cashflows are perfectly foreseen, the firm should maximize the _____ value of decisions in order to maximize its _____ . (2)

Q9. What is the present value of the $50 your grandparents say they will give you a year from now, assuming an 8% opportunity interest rate? _____ . (2)

Q10. What is the present value of the money you will spend on junk food in the next year (assuming $250 over the year and 9% interest income foregone)? _____ . (2)

Check your answers against those in the Answer Key. Award yourself a grade on the following basis.

Score:	18 - 20	15 - 17	12 - 14	10 - 11	9 or less
Grade:	A	B	C	D	F

CHAPTER 2:   DECISION MAKING UNDER RISK AND UNCERTAINTY

2.1 INTRODUCTION

Summary

The major elements in chapter 2 can be listed as follows:

1. Expected-value analysis and present-value analysis are brought together in the context of **decision trees** that show the various combinations of possible outcomes that might follow a decision.

2. The **degree of risk** involved in any decision is measured, and the concepts of **risk aversion, risk neutrality,** and **risk preference** are examined.

3. Several new **decision criteria** are introduced that **adjust for risk** and allow the risk-averse decision maker to choose the best decision.

4. Better information makes better decisions, but the **search cost** of obtaining more information may outweigh the **value of information.**

5. Decisions can be evaluated on the basis of several guidelines, but under risk and uncertainty good decisions don't always turn out well.

We shall proceed through these topics, pausing to test your comprehension as we go with a series of self-test questions and problems to work through.

Learning Objectives

In this chapter you can expect to learn the following:

*   How to construct and use decision trees to make decisions.

*   How to measure the risk associated with a decision.

*   How to rank decisions in order of preference for the risk-averse decision maker.

*   How to evaluate decisions that have been made.

2.2   DECISION TREES AND EXPECTED PRESENT VALUE ANALYSIS

Overview of the Text, Section 2.2

A **decision tree** is a schematic device used to array complex decision problems; it is necessary for the solution of problems involving expected-present-value analysis with probability distributions in each of the first and subsequent years. With more than one probability distribution determining the potential outcomes, we must calculate the joint probabilities of each of the potential outcomes. These joint probabilities are then used to calculate the expected present value of the decision.

A **joint probability** is the probability that two or more events will jointly occur. This joint probability is simply the product of the probabilities that the events will occur separately. Thus we multiply the probability of one event by the probability of another to find the joint probability.

For example, if demand in the first year might be high, medium, or low, with probabilities 0.2, 0.5, and 0.3, and in the second year might also be high, medium, or low, with probabilities 0.4, 0.4, and 0.2, what is the joint probability that demand will be high both years? The answer is 0.08, or 8%, being the product of 0.2 and 0.4.

In a decision tree the cashflows are first converted to present-value terms, and then summed to find the net present value of each **terminal** outcome. There will be m^n terminal outcomes, where m is the number of possible outcomes in each period and n is the number of periods considered. (In the above high, medium, low example there would be 9 terminal outcomes, or possible combinations at the end of the firm's planning period.)

To find the **expected present value** of a **multiperiod uncertain decision,** the NPV values of the terminal outcomes are weighted by the joint probabilities to find the EPV of the joint probability distribution. This sounds complicated, but decision trees make it quite easy, as you will see.

READING: Now read sections 2.1 and 2.2 of the textbook, where a decision tree is used to clarify and solve a decision problem concerning the choice between two machines in the face of uncertain demand over two years.

When you finish reading that section, come back here and do the following self-test questions.

Self-test Questions

23. What is the probability of getting two heads in a row when tossing a coin?

24. How many possible outcomes are there if you rolled two (six-sided) dice?

25. What is the expected value of tossing a coin to see who pays for lunch?

Now compare your answers with mine in the Answer Key, just to make sure you are "on track." If so, continue. If not, read the foregoing overview and the section in the text again.

2.3   RISK ANALYSIS OF DECISION ALTERNATIVES

The EPV criteria does not adjust for the degree of risk, nor does it consider the decision maker's attitude toward risk and uncertainty. These issues are now addressed.

Overview of the Text, Section 2.3

This section of the text introduces a **measure of the risk** and uncertainty surrounding a decision. When risk is quantified it can be incorporated into the analysis and allows us to adjust for risk on an objective basis.

The existence of risk and uncertainty means that there is a prior probability distribution of outcomes associated with any decision. We say that a decision is **more risky** if there is **greater dispersion** of the potential outcomes. Dispersion means the range between the lowest expected outcome and the highest expected outcome. But we are not simply concerned with the range of outcomes. In addition, it is important to consider how likely it is that each outcome will occur.

The **standard deviation** of a probability distribution can be used as a measure of risk because the standard deviation incorporates both the range of outcomes and the probability of each outcome occurring. It measures the weighted average absolute deviation of all potential outcomes from the expected value, where the weights are the joint probabilities. The standard deviation is found by first subtracting each outcome from the mean outcome, which in this case is the EPV. The resulting deviations are then squared, weighted by the joint probabilities, and then summed to find the **variance**. The square root of the variance is the standard deviation.

Decision makers may like, dislike, or simply not care about the risk involved in their decisions. **Risk aversion**, or the dislike of risk, is the most likely attitude of business decision makers since they are held accountable for their decisions by more senior management, the board of directors, and ultimately the shareholders. **Risk averters will take risks**, however; they simply need to be compensated for so doing, and will trade-off risk for return, sometimes preferring the decision which promises both higher risk and higher EPV. For a risk averter, the EPV from a decision gives **utility** (psychic satisfaction), whereas the risk gives **disutility** (negative utility). The combination of risk and return is what counts. If the net utility is greater for the more risky alternative the risk-averse decision maker will choose it.

Indifference curves are lines depicting combinations of variables which give equal amounts of utility. Indifference curves for a risk averter will be positively sloped in risk-return space, because in order to stay at the same level of utility as risk is increased, the risk averter will require more expected value as well.

The slopes of the indifference curves will reflect the decision maker's **degree of risk aversion**. Flatter indifference curves indicate a relatively low trade-off of return for risk and hence indicate that the decision maker is only slightly risk averse. Steeper indifference curves indicate a relatively high trade-off of return for risk, and hence indicate that the decision maker is more highly risk averse.

Risk preference means that the individual derives utility from risk, while **risk neutrality** means that the individual is unconcerned with risk. Few business decision makers can afford to have these risk attitudes, but consumers often exhibit these attitudes in gambling, sporting, and recreational activities.

READING: Now read section 2.3 in the text for more detail. Then come back here and answer the following questions.

Self-test Questions

26. Why is the range of possible outcomes a poor measure of risk?

27. Outline the steps involved in calculating the standard deviation of a probability distribution.

28. Under what circumstances, if any, will a risk averter take risks?

29. Would a risk averter ever prefer the higher-risk option? Why?

30. Explain the decision maker's degree of risk aversion in terms of the amount of additional return that person would require to accept additional risk.

Check your answers against mine in the Answer Key. How are you doing?

Practice Problem

31. A firm plans to introduce a new product. If first-year demand is "heavy," the firm expects to earn $10,000 profits; if "medium" it expects to earn $5,000 profits; and if "light" it expects to earn $1,000 profits. The probabilities are 0.30 for heavy, 0.50 for medium, and 0.20 for light. In the second year there may be entry of other firms producing the same product. If no entry occurs, year-two profits will be double the first year's. If entry occurs, year-two profits will be only one-quarter of the first year's. The probability of entry is 0.8 if the first-year demand is heavy, 0.5 if first-year demand is medium, and 0.1 if first-year demand is light. The firm's opportunity discount rate is 15%. Initial costs will be $4,000, payable immediately.

(a) Set this problem up in a decision tree format.

(b) What is the EPV of the new product?

(c) What is the standard deviation of the (joint) probability distribution? (Hint: Express profits in thousands.)

Check your answers with those found in the Answer Key. If they don't agree, reconcile any differences and satisfy yourself that you fully understand the calculation of standard deviation and the construction of decision trees before continuing.

2.4 ADJUSTMENT FOR RISK IN DECISION MAKING

Now that we have a measure of risk, we can use it to adjust for the differing amounts of risk associated with different decision alternatives. Read the following overview of this topic.

Overview of the Text, Section 2.4

Four methods of incorporating the differing riskiness of different decision alternatives are discussed in this section of

17

the text. Each of these has virtues and problems for use in practical business situations.

The **coefficient of variation** (CV) is a statistic that is simply the ratio of the standard deviation to the expected present value. In effect, it shows the amount of risk per dollar of return. The risk-averse decision maker would choose the decision alternative with the least risk per dollar of return and hence chooses the alternative with the smallest CV.

The **expected-value-using-different-discount-rates** criterion adjusts for risk by utilizing a higher opportunity discount rate (ODR) for the more risky alternatives. Rather than discounting all alternatives by the same ODR, as in the earlier discussion of the expected-present-value criterion, the dispersion of outcomes is foreseen and the ODR is adjusted accordingly.

The **certainty-equivalent** (CE) criterion uses utility theory to find a cash sum (which is available with zero risk) that would give the decision maker the same utility as the combination of risk and return represented by a decision alternative. That is, the decision alternative and its "certainty equivalent" are on the same indifference curve. For the utility-maximizing decision maker, the decision alternative on the highest indifference curve is the preferred alternative.

The **maximin** criterion selects the decision alternative which promises the highest (maxi) of the smallest (min) outcomes. The worst outcome for each decision alternative is identified, and the largest of these worst outcomes identifies the preferred strategy under this criterion.

The **choice among decision criteria** depends on three main issues. If the decision is repeated many times, the simple expected-value criterion will suffice. Sometimes the actual outcome will exceed the expected value, other times it will fall short, but over many such decisions the law of averages will ensure that the firm comes out ahead of where it would be if it used any other strategy. In effect the firm can afford to be risk neutral for any particular decision if this type of decision is repeated frequently.

The **magnitude of the potential outcomes** is an important factor influencing the choice among decision criteria. If some of the potential outcomes are losses and, furthermore, some of these losses are very large and impossible to bear without causing bankruptcy or other insufferable problems, the decision maker may decide to avoid that decision alternative altogether. The maximin criterion is then the appropriate criterion.

The decision maker's **attitude towards risk** is the final factor influencing the choice of decision criterion. Risk averters will use the CV, or the EPV-with-different-ODR's, or the CE criterion, in order to factor risk into their decision process. The simple EPV criterion is sufficient for someone who is risk neutral. Risk preferrers would use the CE criterion and choose the alternative which places them on the highest indifference curve.

Note that in some situations the advice given by **the CE criterion may conflict** with that given by both the CV and the EPV-with-different-ODR's criteria. This is because the CE criterion recognizes that the risk-return trade-off is not likely to be constant: rather, it is expected to increase (progressively larger increments in return will be necessary to compensate for given increments of risk) as the total amount of risk is increased.

READING: Now turn to the text and read section 2.4. Underline or highlight all definitions and important concepts. When you are finished, write short answers to the self-test questions below.

<u>Self-test Questions</u>

32. What is the difference between risk-adjusted return and return-adjusted risk? Which one does the coefficient of variation measure?

33. Why would it be more difficult and more expensive to utilize the expected-value-with-differing-discount-rates criterion, rather than the coefficient-of-variation criterion?

34. What is the certainty equivalent of a decision alternative? Restate your answer in terms of an indifference curve.

35. Why is there a potential conflict between the certainty-equivalent criterion and the coefficient-of-variation criterion? When are these criteria unambiguously in agreement?

36. When is the coefficient-of-variation criterion potentially misleading, and how should we phrase our recommendation in such a case?

37. When is the maximin criterion appropriate?

38. When is the expected-present-value criterion appropriate?

When you have completed your short answers to these questions, compare them with mine in the Answer Key.

Practice Problem

39. Turn to problem 2-6 in the text. Answer parts (a) through (e). Note that to convert the sales-volume data shown into profit figures, you need to subtract the per-unit variable costs from the appropriate price and multiply the balance by the volume of sales.

   When you have finished, check with the answer key to see if you were correct. If not, satisfy yourself that you fully understand what went wrong so that the same mistake will not happen again.

2.5 SEARCH COSTS AND THE VALUE OF INFORMATION

This is a short section of the text which considers the cost of information, and whether or not the firm should seek further information before making decisions.

Overview of the Text, Section 2.5

Search costs are the costs of generating additional information for decision making. Search costs include the costs of obtaining data and the processing and conversion of that data into the desired form, such as expected present values.

   The **value of information** is the additional profits the firm can earn due to the additional information secured by research activity. If it had information as to the business environment which would prevail, the firm could increase profits by choosing the strategy which maximizes profits under those conditions. But before it knows what the conditions will be (before it searches), the firm must rely on the prior probability distribution of those conditions, and thus it must calculate a probabilistic value of information.

   The value of information is equal to the difference between the expected present value with full information and the highest EPV the firm could achieve with its existing information.

READING: Now read section 2.5 of the text. Pay special attention to the calculation of the value of information. Note that the profit values in Table 2-9 come from the fully-worked examples in Tables 2-2 and 2-3 earlier in the text.

Self-test Questions

40. What sorts of activities constitute search activity?

41. Describe how the value of information is calculated.

Now check your answers against mine in the Answer Key. Then proceed to the following practice problem.

Practice Problem

42. Turn to problem 2-4, at the end of chapter 2 in the text, which concerns a decision to be made between Hot Dogs and Ice Cream.

(a) Calculate the expected value of each alternative.

(b) Calculate the value of information.

After completing your calculations, check your answers against mine in the Answer Key. If you missed something, go back over it and make sure you understand it.

2.6 EVALUATING DECISIONS, AND SENSITIVITY ANALYSIS

We now consider what makes a decision a good one or a bad one, and how to qualify our advice to decision makers in order to incorporate doubts we might have about the recommended decision.

Overview of the Text, Section 2.6

A decision has to be rated as a good one if the decision maker can answer yes to the following questions:

1. Was sufficient information acquired? (Was information search taken to the point where it was no longer profitable to search?)

2. Was this information properly interpreted? (Were all cashflows converted to EPV terms using the appropriate cashflow convention?)

3. Was the appropriate decision criterion used? (Was the firm's objective best served, taking into account the firm's attitude toward risk?)

4. Was the timing appropriate? (Did the expected benefits of waiting no longer outweigh the expected benefits of going ahead?)

5. Was sensitivity analysis conducted and considered? (Is the decision vulnerable to the accuracy of its

underlying assumptions, and if so, were these assumptions re-examined?)

Note that **good decisions** sometimes turn out badly and that bad decisions sometimes turn out very nicely. We should expect this from the prior probability distribution of outcomes, but we should never count on good luck, or blame bad luck, in business decision making. Thus we should judge a decision not by its actual outcome but rather by its <u>a priori</u> adherence to good decision-making principles.

READING: Now read section 2.6 in the text, noting all new terms and concepts. Then write answers to the following questions.

Self-test Questions

43. What are the three basic considerations when evaluating a decision?

44. What is the appropriate timing of a decision?

45. What is sensitivity analysis, and what would you do if your chosen alternative is sensitive to its underlying assumptions?

Check your answers against those in the Answer Key.

READING: Now read section 2.7, which is the summary to chapter 2, in order to review the main points of the chapter.

Self-test Questions

Write short answers to the Discussion Questions in the text at the end of chapter 2. Attempt all ten questions, and compare your answers with mine in the Answer Key.

Practice Problem

46. Read problem 2-4 at the end of chapter 2 in the text. It concerns the Express Delivery Company. Answer questions (a) through (d) following that problem.

When you have finished, compare your answers with those shown in the Answer Key. After completing all this work you should be ready to tackle the following Quick Quiz. Good Luck!

QUICK QUIZ - CHAPTER TWO

Q1.   The joint probability of two events occurring is the _____ of the probabilities that each will occur separately.   (1)

Q2.   The value of a terminal outcome is _____
      _____   (2)

Q3.   The risk of a decision is measured by the _____
      _____   (2)

Q4.   To calculate the standard deviation of a probability distribution, one would subtract the EPV from each _____ _____ , then multiply these _____ by their _____ . Summing these we find the _____ of the probability distribution, and the _____ of this is the standard deviation. (5)

Q5.   Risk preferrers get _____ from risk, risk averters get _____ from risk, and those who are risk neutral get _____ from risk.   (3)

Q6.   The coefficient of variation is the _____ divided by the _____   (1)

Q7.   The maximin decision is the one with _____
      _____   (1)

Q8.   The certainty equivalent of a decision is _____
      _____   (2)

Q9.   A decision is a good one, a priori, if it _____
      _____
      _____
      _____   (5)

Q10. Sensitivity analysis requires the decision maker to vary the underlying assumptions to see if _____
      _____
      _____   (3)

Check your answers against those in the Answer Key, and grade your effort on the following basis:

Score: 22 - 25   19 - 21   16 - 18   13 - 15   12 or less
Grade: A   B   C   D   F

CHAPTER 3: UTILITY ANALYSIS OF CONSUMER BEHAVIOR

3.1 INTRODUCTION

Summary

Having established the broad framework for decision making, we now go back to basics on the demand side in order to better understand why demand exists for the firm's product and how this demand can be influenced by the firm. This chapter has two main sections:

1. **Indifference curve analysis of consumer behavior.** This section builds and uses the indifference curve model to **predict consumers' responses** to **changes in prices, incomes**, and their **tastes and preferences** patterns.

2. **Attribute analysis of consumer behavior.** This section focuses on the attributes of products (their features or characteristics), and uses indifference curves to explain consumer reactions to economic stimuli. This approach allows the introduction of **new products, repositioning** of existing products, identification of **target markets**, and so on.

Learning Objectives

From the managerial economics perspective, it is important to understand how consumers are likely to act and react in particular circumstances and in response to particular economic stimuli, such as changes in price, incomes, availability of substitute products, and so on. When you have finished this chapter you will be able to:

*   Use the indifference curve model to demonstrate the reactions of consumers to changes in prices, incomes, and their taste and preference patterns.

*   Understand the law of diminishing marginal utility and the theoretical basis for downward sloping demand curves.

*   State the marginal conditions for the maximization of the consumer's total utility.

*   Analyze the demand for a product in terms of its inherent quality attributes.

*   Identify target markets and gaps in the market where a new or repositioned product might be located.

3.2 INDIFFERENCE CURVE ANALYSIS OF CONSUMER BEHAVIOR

The **indifference curve model** is based on the utility theory of consumer behavior, and is concerned with identifying the probable responses of consumers to changes in economic variables.

<u>Overview of the Text, Section 3.2</u>

Indifference-curve analysis is based on the concept of **utility**. Utility is the psychic satisfaction that consumers receive from the purchase and consumption of goods and services. Buying an ice cream or a pair of shoes makes you feel good. This good feeling is utility, and the expectation of deriving utility is what induces us to part with our hard-earned income.

We assume that **consumers attempt to maximize the utility** that can be obtained from their incomes. Thus they will prefer a combination of goods and services which gives more utility, rather than another combination which gives less utility. If two combinations of goods and services give the same amount of utility, we say the consumer is **indifferent** between the two combinations. For example, for your lunch you might be indifferent between a sandwich and a salad. This means you expect the same utility from either product and that, if sandwiches and salads cost the same amount, you would be willing to choose by flipping a coin or by letting someone else order for you.

An **indifference curve** is a line joining all combinations of goods which give the same level of utility. Points on higher indifference curves are preferred to points on lower indifference curves, since they represent more utility and since consumers attempt to maximize utility. Indifference curves slope downward and to the right (when both goods give utility), they do not cross, and they are convex from below. These properties of indifference curves follow from the four assumptions underlying this analysis, which are, briefly, that consumers can **rank** combinations of goods, that their preferences are **transitive**, that consumers are **insatiable**, and that they experience **diminishing marginal utility** from all goods.

Marginal utility (MU) is the utility added (or subtracted) by the consumption of one more (or one less) unit of a particular product. MU will decline as progressively more units of a particular product are consumed. This is the **"law of diminishing marginal utility."** In the simple model we assume nonsatiation, meaning that MU declines but remains positive, such that more is always preferred to less. The **marginal rate of substitution** is shown by the slope of an indifference curve and represents the trade-off between products that keeps the consumer at the same level of total utility.

The consumer's **budget constraint** is the total expenditure he or she can make during the period under consideration. Given a limited income, or budget, some combinations of goods will be affordable, others unaffordable. The consumer must allocate his or her income such that the **utility-maximizing combination** of products is purchased. This occurs on the highest-attainable indifference curve, which will be just **tangent** to the budget-constraint line, given the convexity of indifference curves and the straight-line budget constraint.

The **utility-maximizing rule** is to consume each product up to the point where its ratio of marginal utility to price is the same as for all other products. In effect, the last dollar spent on each product should give the consumer the same amount of utility.

If there is a **price change** for one of the products, the consumer's utility-maximizing response is to buy more of that product if its price falls or, conversely, less of that product if its price increases, ceteris paribus. If the price of one product changes, the budget-constraint line must swing around, since its slope depends on the price ratio of the two products under review. This means that a new set of attainable combinations is defined, and the consumer selects the highest-attainable indifference curve which is just tangent to the new budget line.

Repeating this adjustment by the consumer for further price changes, a series of tangency points would be found, each one a utility-maximizing combination of products given the relative prices prevailing. The line joining these tangency points is known as the **price-consumption curve**, and it demonstrates the typically inverse relationship between the price of a product and the quantity demanded of that product, other things being equal. This inverse relationship is known as the **law of demand**. Thus the demand curve is typically downward sloping to the right.

When the consumer's **income changes**, the budget line shifts outward for income increases or shifts inward for reductions in income. A new tangency point is then found for utility maximization at the new income level. The change in quantity demanded as a result of the change in income is called the **income effect**. If income and the quantity demanded of a product move in the same direction, we say the income effect is positive and the product is a **normal** or **superior good**. If, alternatively, income and consumption of a particular product move in opposite directions, we say the income effect is negative and call this product an **inferior good**.

   Changes in consumer tastes and preferences are reflected by a shift of the indifference curves. This in turn causes a new utility-maximizing tangency point as the consumer reallocates his or her income to maximize utility under the new tastes and preferences structure. Obviously, if tastes change in favor of a particular product the consumer will buy more of that product (and less of others) as a result.

READING: Now turn to the textbook and read sections 3.1 and 3.2. Pay particular attention to the technicalities covered in the text but glossed over in the above overview. Underline or highlight all new terms and important points and concepts.

   After carefully reading the text sections, write out short answers to the following self-test questions.

Self-test questions

47.   Define an indifference curve, and state the four properties of indifference curves.

48.   What are the four assumptions underlying indifference curve analysis?

49.   Why does the marginal rate of substitution decline progressively as we move down to the right along an indifference curve in product space?

50.   Why is the budget-constraint line a straight line?

51.   What is the utility maximizing rule? State this verbally and then in symbols. Generalize this rule to a situation in which there are many products available to the consumer.

52.   Define the price effect.

53.   What is the law of demand? Briefly state the theoretical basis for this phenomenon.

54.   Why would the income effect be negative? What are consumers doing in this case?

55.   Suppose a consumer decides he doesn't like product X as much as he used to. Explain how this would affect his consumption of that product and of all other products.

   After writing short answers to these questions, check them against mine in the Answer Key and reconcile any differences.

3.3 ATTRIBUTE ANALYSIS OF CONSUMER CHOICE

We turn now to an extension of indifference-curve analysis which examines the consumer's demand for products not in terms of the products _per se_, but in terms of the **attributes** of those products. The **attributes** of a product are the benefits or services that the product provides. For example, the attributes of a motel room might be perceived as shelter, comfort, and security. Different motel rooms offer different quantities and combinations of these attributes, usually at different prices, and the consumer considers both the price and the attributes before choosing among the available products which satisfy his or her needs for shelter, comfort, and security.

Attribute analysis allows us to examine in detail consumer **choice between and among substitute products.** Why brand A instead of brand B? This question is very important to the practicing manager who is trying to maintain or increase the market share of brand A (or B). How do we deal with **new products**? Again, a critical issue for the practicing manager attempting to design and introduce new products. Attribute analysis provides the answers, whereas the traditional indifference curve analysis of products cannot.

Overview of the Text, Section 3.3

Consumer demand for products is a derived demand, derived from consumers' demand for the attributes provided by the products. The products are simply the package in which the desired attributes must be purchased. Assuming only two attributes are desired, we can analyze the consumer's decision process in a two-dimensional graph, with one attribute on each axis. **Products can be represented as rays from the origin** in this attribute space, since the rays depict the ratio of one attribute to the other, as perceived in each product. The attainable set of attributes is limited by the consumer's budget constraint, such that there is an outer boundary, known as the **efficiency frontier**, to the combinations of attributes which the consumer can afford.

The consumer will have an **indifference map** in attribute space, being willing to trade off some of one attribute for more of another while staying at the same level of utility. Superimposing these indifference curves on the efficiency frontier we can find the combination of attributes, and hence the combination of products, which allows attainment of the highest indifference curve and which, therefore, maximizes utility for the consumer.

The **price effect** is easily demonstrated using attribute analysis. If the price of a product falls, consumers tend to buy more of that product and less of the substitute products, and the opposite occurs for a price rise. Similarly the **income effect**, for both superior and inferior goods, is easily shown. For increases in income the efficiency frontier shifts outward and the consumer will buy more of goods that are superior and less of goods that are inferior.

The **consumer's perceptions** of the attribute content of each product may change - due to an advertising campaign, for example. This will typically shift the product ray(s) and the efficiency frontier, causing a new tangency point with the highest-attainable indifference curve and thus a new utility-maximizing combination of attributes (and products). A change in consumer tastes, on the other hand, is reflected by a shifting of the indifference curves and again will most likely lead to a new combination of attributes (and products) being chosen.

New products can be designed to exploit gaps in the market using attribute analysis and can be added to the existing graph as a new ray from the origin. **Market segments** are subgroups within the market for a group of substitute products. The people in these subgroups have similar tastes and preferences, and one or more segments may be viewed by the manager as the **target market** for his or her product.

READING: Now turn to Section 3.3 in the text and read carefully through the details of attribute analysis.

After you have finished, write short answers to the following questions.

Self-test questions

56. What is an attribute and how can products be represented in attribute space?

57. What three issues determine the length of the attribute ray from the origin to the efficiency frontier?

58. How can the consumer achieve a position on the efficiency frontier between two rays? When is the efficiency frontier simply a series of points?

59. Explain separately how price reductions, changes of perceptions, and changes of taste are represented in attribute space?

60. How would you design a new product in order to capture a substantial share of an existing market?

61. What are market segments? Explain this in terms of the marginal rates of substitution of consumers.

When you have finished writing your answers, check them against mine in the answer key to ensure that you know all the important points. Then continue with the following short reading assignment.

READING: Read Section 3.4, the summary to chapter 3, to refresh your memory on the entire chapter, and then proceed to the following questions.

Self-test questions

Write short answers to each of the ten "Discussion Questions" at the end of chapter 3. After completing this task compare your answers with mine in the Answer Key. Then proceed to the following practice problems.

Practice problems

62. Do problem 3-1 at the end of the chapter in the text. When you finish, compare your answer with mine in the Answer Key. If you missed any important points, think it through again and satisfy yourself that you understand all the issues.

63. Do problem 3-3 from the text. Check your answer against mine in the Answer Key.

64. Do problem 3-7 from the text. This will test whether you understand and can apply most of the important issues in attribute analysis. When you're finished, look at my answer in the Answer Key and judge whether or not you fully understand all the concepts.

Are you ready for the Quick Quiz? Good luck!

QUICK QUIZ - CHAPTER THREE

Q1. An indifference curve is a locus of _____
    _____ (1)

Q2. The indifference curve model is a(n) _____
    model of consumer behavior.   (1)

Q3. The utility-maximizing rule is to purchase goods until _____
    _____ for each good
    is _____ and the _____ is all _____(3)

Q4. In goods space, _____ indifference curves are
    preferred to _____curves, they are _____
    sloping, they do not _____, and they are _____
    from below.   (4)

Q5. The marginal rate of substitution is the _____
    _____ for _____ such that
    _____ stays constant.   (2)

Q6. A inferior good is one for which the income effect is
    _____ , whereas the quantity demanded of a superior
    good will _____ when income _____.   (2)

Q7. The efficiency frontier will shift outward for three reasons
    which are (i)_____ (ii)_____
    _____ and (iii)_____   (3)

Q8. Advertising can accomplish a change in both consumers'
    perceptions and in their preferences. In attribute analysis
    the first would cause _____
    _____and the second would cause
    _____   (2)

Q9. A firm would consider repositioning its product in attribute
    space if it thought that this would allow it to reach the
    highest _____ of a greater number of
    _____ than it presently does.   (2)

Q10. Market segments are characterized by consumers whose
    marginal _____ between the _____
    contained in the _____ are _____ (4)

Check your answers and see how you scored on the following scale.

Score: 22 - 25   19 - 21   16 - 18   13 - 15   12 or less
Grade: A   B   C   D   F

APPENDIX 3A: INDIFFERENCE CURVE ANALYSIS OF THE INCOME AND
SUBSTITUTION EFFECTS OF A PRICE CHANGE

Summary

In this appendix we use indifference curve analysis to:

1.   Separate the income and substitution effects of a price
      reduction for a superior good.

2.   Separate the income and substitution effects of a price
      increase for a superior good.

3.   Separate the income and substitution effects of a price
      reduction for an inferior good.

4.   Introduce Giffen goods as the extreme (and unlikely)
      case of inferior goods.

Learning Objectives

When you have completed this appendix you will be able to:

*   Separate the income and substitution effects of a price
      change for any case, whether superior or inferior good,
      and whether for a price increase or a price decrease.

*   List the analytical steps required to accomplish this
      task.

*   Explain why the substitution effect is always negative
      and why the income effect is either positive or
      negative.

Overview of Appendix 3A

Whenever the price of a product changes, there is a consequent
income effect, because the purchasing power of the consumer's
monetary or nominal income is changed. That is, the consumer's
real income (monetary income divided by an index of prices) will
have changed. If the price of a product falls, for example the
consumer can buy all that was bought before and still have a
little money left over. The consumer can buy more of any product
with this extra purchasing power. Thus a reduced price causes
the consumer's real income to rise; oppositely, a price increase
causes real income to fall, ceteris paribus.

     Thus the price effect, the negative relationship between
price and quantity demanded which is illustrated by the demand

32

curve, is comprised of an income effect and another effect, which we call the substitution effect. The **substitution effect** is that part of the change in the quantity demanded that is due to the change in relative prices, when other things, <u>including real income</u>, are held constant. We can separate the price effect into the income and substitution effects by hypothetically adjusting the consumer's money income such that real income remains constant after a price change. The amount of income adjustment necessary indicates the income effect and the remainder is the substitution effect.

For normal or **superior goods** the income and substitution effects will **reinforce** each other. For example, if price falls the consumer will buy more because of the income effect and also buy more because of the substitution effect. For **inferior goods** the income and substitution effects **offset** each other to some degree. For example, if price falls the income effect is to buy less while the substitution effect is to buy more. In the extreme case, known as **Giffen goods**, the income effect outweighs the substitution effect and there would be a **perverse price effect**, with price and quantity demanded being positively related.

READING: Now read Appendix 3A in the text. When you have finished, answer the following self-test questions.

Self-test questions

65. Write out the steps involved in separating the income and substitution effects of a price change.

66. How would the indifference maps look different for a consumer who regards X as an inferior good, compared to another consumer who regards X as a superior good?

After you have written your answers to these two questions, check them against mine in the Answer Key. Then write short answers to the five Discussion Questions that are found at the end of Appendix 3A, and then compare your answers with mine in the Answer Key.

Practice Problems

67. Answer problem 3A-2 at the end of Appendix 3A.

68. Answer problem 3A-3 at the end of Appendix 3A.

After finishing your graphs and verbal answers, check the Answer Key before continuing to the Quick Quiz.

QUICK QUIZ - APPENDIX 3A

Q1.   The substitution effect is the change in _____
       due to a change in _____, after compensating for
       the _____, which is the change in quantity
       demanded that is due to a change in _____
       resulting from a change in _____ (5)

Q2.   For a superior good the income effect will be _____
       and the substitution effect will be _____, and
       they will _____ each other.   (3)

Q3.   If the price of an inferior good increases, we expect the
       quantity demanded to _____, this comprising the sum
       of a(n) _____ in quantity demanded due to the
       income effect and a(n) _____ in quantity demanded
       due to the substitution effect.   (3)

Q4.   A Giffen good is characterized by a _____ income
       effect that _____ a _____ substitution
       effect.   (3)

Q5.   If a storekeeper sold 200 boxes of candy in April, when the
       price was $4 per box, and 250 boxes in May, when the price
       was $5 per box, this does not mean that candy is a Giffen
       good, because _____ (1)

Now check your answers and add your score to find your grade.

Score: 14 - 15   12 - 13   10 - 11   8 - 9   0 - 8
Grade: A   B   C   D   F

CHAPTER 4:   MARKET DEMAND ANALYSIS FOR DECISION MAKING

4.1   INTRODUCTION

Summary

In this chapter we examine the determinants of market demand for the firm's product. Market demand is simply the aggregation of the demands of individual consumers. The chapter is divided into four main sections covering the following topics:

1.   The **demand function** and the demand curve. The demand function lists all determinants of demand, while the **demand curve** relates quantity demanded to price alone, with <u>ceteris paribus</u>. Given a demand curve, we can calculate **total revenue** and **marginal revenue**.

2.   **Price elasticity of demand.** This is a measure of the relative responsiveness of quantity demanded to a change in the price level.

3.   **Income elasticity of demand.** This measures the relative responsiveness of quantity demanded to a change in consumers' incomes.

4.   **Cross elasticities** and other elasticities. Cross elasticities measure the responsiveness of quantity demanded of one product to a change in the price, or advertising, of another product.

<u>Learning Objectives</u>

After completing this chapter you will be able to:

*   Distinguish between a movement along the demand curve and a shift of the demand curve, and know what causes the demand curve to shift.

*   Derive the demand, marginal revenue, and total revenue curves, given information about the demand function.

*   Categorize demand as either elastic, unitary, or inelastic, depending on the value of price elasticity.

*   Derive a demand curve, given information concerning the current price, output, and price elasticity.

*   Categorize products as superior or inferior goods, necessities or luxuries, substitutes or complements, depending on their income and cross elasticities.

4.2   THE DEMAND FUNCTION AND THE DEMAND CURVE

Overview of the Text, Section 4.2

The **demand function** is the functional relationship existing between the quantity demanded of a product and the variables which determine that quantity demanded.   Quantity demanded depends on the price of the product, prices of substitute and complementary products, advertising and promotional efforts, product quality and design, the place(s) of sale, consumer incomes, consumer tastes and consumer expectations, as well as other factors in specific cases.

The **demand curve** is simply the functional relationship between price and quantity demanded, holding all other factors constant.   It can be derived from the demand function by aggregating the influence of all factors except price into a single term.   Economists, by convention, express the demand curve as "price is a function of quantity demanded," notwithstanding their recognition that quantity demanded depends on price.

Movements along a demand curve occur when that product's price changes but all other factors remain unchanged.   **Shifts** of the demand curve occur when any one of the other underlying determinants of the demand curve (such as income or advertising efforts) changes.

Total revenue (TR) is calculated as price times quantity sold. Total revenue will increase as price is reduced from relatively high levels at first, but later falls if price is reduced still further. **Marginal revenue** (MR) is the change in total revenue for a one-unit change in quantity. It follows that MR is positive for prices on the upper half of the demand curve, and is negative for prices on the lower half of the demand curve. **Average revenue** is total revenue divided by quantity and is thus the same as the price level in markets where there is a single price.

READING: Now read sections 4.1 and 4.2 in the textbook. Underline or highlight all new terms and concepts to help fix them in your memory and make them easier to find when you are skimming through the book to refresh your memory before the exam.

After reading those pages, write short answers to the self-test questions on the following page.

Self-test Questions

69. Distinguish between the demand function and the demand curve.

70. Name at least six variables you think would be significant determinants of the demand for ice cream.

71. Distinguish between movements along, and shifts of, a demand curve. What causes each one?

72. Define total revenue and marginal revenue, and state the relationship existing between the demand curve and the marginal revenue curve.

Now check your answers against mine in the Answer Key.

Practice Problem

73. Read problem 4-3, concerning Fritz Reinhart beer, at the end of chapter 4. Then answer the questions here, not the questions following problem 4-3.

(a) Find an expression for the demand curve.

To find the demand curve we collapse the demand function into $Q_X = A - 1,931.6P_X$, where A is the sum of all other influences on demand except P_X. Thus, given

$$Q_X = 2,486.5 - 1,931.6P_X + 283.9P_Y + 168.2A_X - 18.8A_Y$$

substitute the values for P_Y, A_X, and A_Y below, and calculate the value of Q_X.

$Q_X = 2,486.5 - 1,931.6P_X + 283.9(\underline{\quad}) + 168.2(\underline{\quad}) - 18.8(\underline{\quad})$

$\quad = 2,468.5 - 1,931.6P_X + \underline{\qquad} + \underline{\qquad} - \underline{\qquad}$

$\quad = \underline{\qquad} - 1.931.6P_X$

Rearranging to find the demand curve in the form $P_X = a + bQ_X$ we have:

$\quad P_X = \underline{\qquad} /1,931.6 - 1/1,931.6 \ Q_X$

or $\quad P_X = \underline{\qquad} - \underline{\qquad} Q_X.$

(b) Now, what price would maximize total revenue? We know TR is maximized when $MR_X = 0$, and that $MR_X = a + 2bQ_X$.

Thus MR_X = _____ - _____ Q_X

Setting MR = 0 = _____ - _____ Q_X, we find

$\quad$ Q_X = _____ units.

Substituting for this Q_X in the demand curve we find:

$\qquad P_X$ = _____ - 1/1,931.6 (_____)

$\qquad$ = _____ .

This is the revenue-maximizing price.

(c) Supposing marginal cost is constant at \$2, what is the profit-maximizing price? To answer this, set MR = MC = 2, and solve for Q_X, then substitute for Q_X in the demand curve.

Thus, $\quad$ 2 = _____ - _____ Q_X

$\quad$ or $\quad$ Q_X = _____ / _____

$\qquad$ = _____ .

and $\qquad$ P_X = _____ - 1/1,931.6 (_____)

$\qquad$ = _____ .

This is the profit-maximizing price. If this price is different from \$4.50, then the firm should adjust its price in order to maximize profits.

$\qquad$ After completing your answers, check them against mine in the Answer Key. If you have any difficulties, read back through the section in the text and clarify your understanding of the terms and concepts involved.

4.3   PRICE ELASTICITY OF DEMAND

In the next three sections of chapter 4 we will be concerned with a concept known as **elasticity**. An elasticity is a number indicating the relative responsiveness of one variable to a change in one of its determining variables. We shall consider price elasticity, income elasticity, and cross-price elasticity.

Overview of the Text, Section 4.3

Price elasticity measures the relative responsiveness of quantity demanded to a change in the price level. Price elasticity is negative for all (except Giffen) goods, although as a convention we view its numerical value in absolute terms, saying, for example, that elasticity of -2 is more elastic than elasticity of -1. Price elasticity is the percentage change in Q_X divided by the percentage change in P_X. It is typically negative because one of the above-mentioned changes is negative as we move up or down a negatively-sloping demand curve.

The value of **price elasticity varies from zero to infinity** as we move up along a straight-line demand curve. At the midpoint of such a demand curve, the value of elasticity is one (in absolute terms, remember). Above the midpoint, elasticity is greater than one and below the midpoint it is less than one.

Price elasticity indicates whether **total revenue will rise or fall,** and hence whether marginal revenue is positive or negative, for a change in price from any particular level to another. When price elasticity is greater than one, we must be looking at the upper part of the demand curve, where MR is positive and TR rises if price is reduced. Oppositely, if price elasticity is less than one, we must be looking at the lower part of the demand curve, where MR is negative and TR declines if price is reduced.

Point elasticity is the elasticity concept to use when the change in price is very small, whereas **arc elasticity** should be used when the price change is larger.

If we know the price elasticity, and the current price and output level, we can construct an expression for the demand curve, and hence for the marginal and total revenue curves as well.

If we had to guess the approximate value of price elasticity of demand we would expect demand to be more elastic the greater the number of substitutes a product has and the larger the proportion of income its purchase represents.

READING: Now read section 4.3 in the text, underlining all new terms and concepts. Then write answers to the following questions.

Self-test Questions

74. Define price elasticity of demand once in words, once in percentage terms and once in terms of the slope of the demand curve.

75. What is the relationship between total revenue, marginal revenue, and price elasticity?

76. When is the point elasticity measure appropriate, and when is the arc elasticity measure appropriate?

Check your answers against those in the Answer Key.

Practice Problem

77. (a) Given P = $10.00, Q = 5,000 units, MC = $4.00, and price elasticity of -1.25, what is the profit-maximizing price?

To answer this, recall that price elasticity,

$$e = dQ/dP \times P/Q$$

Thus $-1.25 = dQ/dP \times 10/5,000$

and dP/dQ = _____.

Note that dP/dQ = b, as in the demand curve P = a + bQ. Since we know values for P, Q, and b, we can solve for a.

$$a = P - bQ$$

Thus a = 10 - _____(5,000)

    = _____.

and P = _____ - _____ Q

Hence MR = _____ - _____ Q

Now, set MR = MC = 4, solve for Q, then substitute for Q in the demand curve to find the profit-maximizing price, the same way you did earlier. Write your answer down and check it later.

(b) Now find the revenue-maximizing price.

Now check your answers against mine in the Answer Key.

78. For the Fritz Reinhart problem, calculate the price elasticity of demand at the current price.

Since price elasticity equals dQ_X/dP_X x P_X/Q_X, we need the dQ_X/dP_X value and the current price and quantity levels in order to make the calculation. Note that the dQ_X/dP_X term is shown in the demand function as -1,931.6. We were given P_X, and we calculated Q_X. So, calculate the price elasticity using these figures.

Now check your answers against mine in the Answer Key. If you understand everything, proceed. If not, go back and make sure you completely understand the material.

4.4   INCOME ELASTICITY OF DEMAND

Overview of the Text, Section 4.4

Income elasticity measures the relative responsiveness of quantity demanded to a change in the incomes of consumers. Expressed differently, income elasticity is the percentage change in quantity demanded divided by the percentage change in incomes. It may be measured either as a point elasticity or as an arc elasticity, depending on the magnitude of the income change.

Income elasticity may have either a positive or a negative sign. **Positive income elasticity** indicates a normal or superior good. We now subdivide superior goods into two categories: the product is a **necessity good** if the income elasticity is positive but less than one, whereas it is a **luxury good** if the value is positive and greater than one. **Inferior goods** are identified by their **negative income elasticities**.

Firms should be expected to have in their **product line** examples of all three types of product. The demand for luxury goods is relatively volatile with respect to income changes. In a recession, for example, when consumer incomes fall, the demand for luxury goods will fall by a greater percentage. To balance this, the firm might produce some inferior goods, whose demand actually increases in a recession. Necessity goods move in the same direction as consumer incomes, but to a lesser degree.

READING: Now read section 4.4 in the text. When you are finished, answer the following questions.

Self-test Questions

79. Define the income elasticity of demand, verbally and symbolically.

80. What does the positive or negative sign to the income elasticity value indicate?

Practice Problem

81. Suppose the demand function for radar detectors is Q = 500 - 15P + 2Y, where the current price (P) is $200 and the income level (Y) is $18,000.

(a) What is the income elasticity of demand?

(b) Categorize the product as either a luxury, necessity, or inferior good.

Check your answers against those in the Answer Key, and continue.

4.5 CROSS ELASTICITIES AND OTHER ELASTICITIES

Overview of the Text, Section 4.5

Cross elasticity measures the relative responsiveness of the quantity demanded of product X to a change in the price of another product, Y. For example, it shows the percentage change in the quantity demanded of coffee when there is a change in the price of tea. Known also as cross-price elasticity, it may be calculated either as a point elasticity or an arc elasticity depending on the size of the change in the price P_y.

Cross elasticity may be either positive or negative. Positive cross elasticities indicate **substitutes** because, for example, the increased price of product Y causes an increased demand for product X as consumers substitute from Y to X. Negative cross elasticities indicate **complements** because, for example, the increased price of product Y causes a reduced demand for X, as consumers reduce their purchases of both X and Y which are consumed jointly in some way. Examples of complements are coffee and cream, or automobiles and gasoline.

Elasticities can also be calculated for each of the other independent variables in the demand function. **Elasticities summarize the impact** of each determining variable on the quantity demanded in a simple number which is easily interpreted.

READING: Now read section 4.5 and the summary section 4.6 in the text. Underline all new terms and concepts. Then write short answers to the following questions.

Self-test Questions

82. Define the cross-price elasticity of demand, and then define the cross-advertising elasticity of demand.

83. Would you expect the cross-price and the cross-advertising elasticities (between two products) to have the same sign? Why?

    Check your answers against mine in the Answer Key. Then write short answers to each of the ten Discussion Questions at the end of chapter 4 to test your recall and understanding of the entire chapter.

    When you have finished this task, check your answers against mine in the Answer Key. Are you keeping up a high standard?

Practice Problems

84. Turn to problem 4-2 in the text, which concerns Billabong Boomerangs Inc. Then answer the three parts to the problem, and, finally, check your answers against mine in the Answer Key.

85. Now read problem 4-4 in the text, which concerns the Gutowski Grocery Company. This is a more difficult problem requiring several analytical steps to derive the information you need. Try to do it by yourself. If you run into problems come back and read the following hints, one at a time, in case you don't need all of them to get you going.

Hint 1: Profits = Total Revenue - Total Costs, and Total Costs = Total Variable Costs + Total Fixed (i.e, all other) Costs.

Hint 2: Your elasticity calculation will be an arc elasticity because there is a discrete change in price from $4.45 to $3.99.

Hint 3: Find the two values of quantity demanded that you need for the arc-elasticity calculation by solving for Q in the profit equation given in hint 1.

Hint 4: The profit maximizing price requires that MC = MR. Note that MC = AVC when the latter remains constant.

Hint 5:   The qualifications refer to the data, the predictions,
     and all other underlying assumptions on which the
     predictions are based.

     When you've finished, check your answer against mine in the
Answer Key.   No doubt you have noticed that these problems are
starting to be more of a challenge, but I'm sure that you're
developing the "mental muscle" to handle it.

     In case you want some extra practice before attempting the
Quick Quiz on the next page, I suggest you do another one of the
problems at the end of chapter 4. These are similar to the
problems you have just completed and will serve to reinforce the
concepts and methodologies in your memory banks. Brief answers
to all problems are found in Appendix C at the back of the text.

QUICK QUIZ - CHAPTER FOUR

Q1. The controllable (or strategic) variables in the demand function are _____ , _____ , _____ , and _____ . (4)

Q2. Through advertising and promotion, the firm can exert some influence on consumer _____ and also on their _____ . (2)

Q3. The coefficient to price in the demand function is equal to the slope of the demand curve. True or false? _____ (2)

Q4. If Q = 2,000 - 4P + 2A + 3Y, and A = 18,000 and Y = 14,000, then the demand curve can be expressed as P = _____ - _____ Q. (2)

Q5. A price decrease for a substitute good will shift the demand curve for X _____ward and the cross elasticity will be _____ . (2)

Q6. The two main determinants of the price elasticity of demand are _____ and _____ (2)

Q7. A superior good with income elasticity greater than one is known as a _____ . (1)

Q8. If price is $10, quantity demanded is 100, and price elasticity of demand is -1.5, then the demand curve can be expressed as P = _____ - _____ Q. (4)

Q9. An arc elasticity measure is used when the change in the independent variable is _____ , and it (arc elasticity) can be viewed as the _____ elasticity over the _____ of values. (3)

Q10. When demand is inelastic, the marginal revenue is _____ , total revenue is _____ related to price, and profits _____ maximized. (3)

Check your answers in the Answer Key, and see what your grade is.

Score: 22 - 25   19 - 21   16 - 18   13 - 15   12 or less
Grade: A   B   C   D   F

CHAPTER 5:   ESTIMATION OF THE DEMAND FUNCTION

5.1   INTRODUCTION

Summary

In this chapter we are concerned with the estimation of the demand function facing the firm. The task of demand estimation is to ascertain the values of the coefficients to each of the determining variables in the demand function. We can discuss demand estimation under two broad headings:

1. **Marketing research techniques** for estimating the slope and location of the demand curve and the impact of things that shift the demand curve. These techniques include **interviews** and **surveys, simulated market situations,** and **direct market experiments.**

2. **Statistical techniques** for assigning precise values to all coefficients in the demand function. **Regression analysis** is used to determine the impact of all determining variables on the quantity demanded.

Learning Objectives

By the time you finish this chapter you will be able to:

* List the types of marketing research techniques that can be utilized to generate information for the estimation of demand curves.

* List the problem areas that one must avoid when conducting interviews, consumer experiments, and market tests.

* Use the data generated from marketing research to establish an estimate of the demand curve.

* Describe how regression analysis works to assign values to the coefficients in the demand function.

* List the six major pitfalls of regression analysis and explain what each one means.

* Interpret the output of a computer regression program.

* Establish a confidence interval for your prediction of quantity demanded at any given price.

5.1 INTERVIEWS, SURVEYS, AND EXPERIMENTS

Overview of the Text, Section 5.2

Interviews and **surveys** involve a questionnaire that is administered personally, by mail, or by telephone. After responses are tabulated, the predicted reactions of the market to hypothetical changes in prices, promotional strategies, and so on, are estimated. These predictions form the basis for our estimates of the coefficients in the demand function. To be effective, interviews and surveys must avoid several problems which may be encountered; these problems include non-random samples, buyers' intentions not being carried out, interviewer bias, and other problems of questionnaire formulation.

Simulated market situations, also known as **consumer clinics,** are an artificial shopping environment in which all variables are held constant except the one under observation. Participants use play money to "buy" products (which they keep) and the researcher observes the differences in quantity demanded for different groups of participants and attributes this to the change in the variable under observation. These simulated markets can be expensive to set up and organize and are worthless unless the participants are randomly selected from the general market for the product in question.

Direct market experiments involve a change in a controllable variable in a regional market while that variable is held constant in other regional markets. In the real world it is unlikely that <u>ceteris paribus</u> will prevail for very long, and the results will be distorted unless all other variables influencing the quantity demanded are controlled for. The markets chosen for the test and control markets must be socioeconomically representative of the broader market in which the product is sold. Direct marketing of goods, via television, radio, space advertisements, and direct mail, provides a special opportunity to conduct market experiments, since different groups of consumers can be offered different prices, for example, and their different responses are easily recorded. But direct market experiments also have their share of problems and are typically not inexpensive to undertake.

READING: Now read sections 5.1 and 5.2 in the text. Underline all new terms and important concepts. When you're finished, write short answers to the following questions.

Self-test Questions

86. Distinguish between demand estimation and demand forecasting.

87. List at least four problems that might arise and cause interviews and surveys to give unreliable estimates of the coefficients in the demand function.

88. What are consumer clinics and how would you organize one to judge the impact of changes in the price of a particular product?

89. Why is direct marketing an ideal vehicle for direct market experiments?

    After you have finished your answers check them against mine in the Answer Key.

Practice Problems

90. Turn to problem 5-1, concerning Jose Hermanos Tequila, at the end of chapter 5. Read this problem, then work through and write out your answers to the four parts of the question. If you have trouble, you may need one or more of the following hints. Don't look at them unless you need to!

Hint 1: Use graph paper, or carefully measured scales on your price and quantity axis, so that you can more easily and accurately estimate the intercept and slope of the demand curve.

Hint 2: The sample size was only 100 persons in each case, whereas the total market is 10,000 times larger. At each price level we should expect 10,000 times more demand in total. Alternatively, for every change in price there will be 10,000 times the sample change in quantity demanded.

Hint 3: Find the MR curve from your estimated demand curve, and set MR = 0.

Hint 4: Use the reciprocal of the slope term from part (b) for the price elasticity calculation.

91. Now do problem 5-2 in the text, concerning the Direct Deal Marketing Company. Note that the actual market will be 200 times the sample size. And, in case you've forgotten, the profit-maximizing rule is MC = MR. Hint: Don't use the

quantity values that are provided when you calculate the price elasticity at each price level, since this would introduce the random deviations into your calculations. The line of best fit should be used to find predicted quantity values at each price level.

After you've finished writing up your answers, compare them with mine in the answer key. If you have any residual doubts, check back through sections 5.1 and 5.2 and clarify these before proceeding.

5.3   REGRESSION ANALYSIS OF CONSUMER DEMAND

Regression analysis is a statistical technique which determines the values of the intercept and slope of the line of best fit. We can thus use this technique to estimate demand curves as well as the impact of any other variables on the quantity demanded of a particular product or service.

Overview of the Text, Section 5.3

Regression analysis can be used to find our best estimate of the relationship between any variable and its determining variables. It can be applied to either **time-series** or **cross-section** observations of the dependent and independent variables. For **linear regression,** the form of the relationship must be linear, or, if curvilinear, the form must be linearized by logarithmic or other transformation.

The **"method of least squares"** is used to find the line of best fit to the data. This **line of best fit** minimizes the sum of the squares of the **deviations** of the actual values of the dependent variable from the predicted value of the variable. The line of best fit will have an intercept term and a slope term, which are easily calculated by substituting values into the two formulas provided in the text.

Given the line of best fit we can also calculate several statistics which allow us to judge the reliability of our estimated line of best fit. The **coefficient of determination** indicates the proportion of the variation in quantity demanded which is explained by variation in the independent variable(s). The **standard error of estimate** indicates the size of the **confidence interval,** or band to either side of the predicted value, within which future observations are expected to fall. The **standard error of the coefficient** allows a similar confidence interval to be calculated for the slope term associated with each independent variable.

The **predictive power** of the regression equation can be measured by the ratio of the standard error of estimate to the mean value of the dependent variable. One rule of thumb is that this ratio should be less than five percent.

When using regression analysis one must be aware of six major **problem areas.** Some of these are difficult to pronounce but not too hard to understand. They can be listed as follows: **specification errors, measurement errors, the identification problem, multicollinearity, heteroscedasticity,** and **auto-correlation.** Understanding the nature of these potential problems allows the researcher to obtain better results and to better appreciate the information content of those results.

READING: Now read section 5.3 in the text. Proceed slowly and methodically, underlining all new terms and concepts. "Read" the algebraic expressions, to make sure you understand what they are saying. Remember, they are simply a convenient shorthand means of expressing the underlying concepts.

When you've finished reading that section, write short answers to the following questions.

<u>Self-test Questions</u>

92. Distinguish between time-series and cross-section data.

93. What is the line of best fit? What is it an estimate of?

94. What is the coefficient of determination and what does it tell us?

95. Explain the notion of the confidence interval surrounding the predicted value for the dependent variable.

96. What does the standard error of the coefficient tell us?

97. What are the three potential specification errors?

98. What is the simultaneous relationships, or identification, problem?

99. What is multicollinearity, and when can it be tolerated?

100. What is heteroscedasticity and how would you discover you had it ?

101. What is autocorrelation, and why should you only expect to find it in time-series data?

After completing this short quiz on the concepts and terms involved in regression analysis compare your answers with mine in the Answer Key. Make sure you understand these issues before proceeding.

READING: Now read the summary to chapter 5 to review the entire chapter before attempting the ten Discussion Questions.

Self-test Questions

Write short answers to each of the ten "Discussion Questions" at the end of chapter 5. After completing this task, compare your answers with mine in the Answer Key and proceed.

Practice Problems

102. Read problem 5-4, concerning the Red Baron Flying School.

(a) Carefully plot the prices against quantities demanded on a piece of paper, and estimate the intercept and slope values of the line of best fit. These estimates will serve as a reference point to check your calculations against those in part (b).

(b) Calculate the regression statistics by filling in the gaps in the following table.

X	Y	XY	X^2	Y^2

TOTALS

Mean X = _____ / 6   Mean Y = _____ / 6

= _____ .   = _____ .

Slope term (beta)   =   _____

                     =   _____

                     =   _____ .

Intercept (alpha)   =   _____ - (_____)(_____)

                     =   _____

Thus,   Y =   _____ .

Therefore P =   _____ .

(c) Using either one of these expressions, estimate the flying
     hours per day if the price is set at $23 per hour.

     Answer: _____ hours per day.

(d) Set MC = MR, given MC = 10, and an expression for MR derived
     from the estimated demand curve, and solve for the profit-
     maximizing Q value.

     Answer: Q = _____ .

Now substitute this Q value in the demand curve to find the
profit-maximizing price.

     Answer: P = _____ .

Now, should Mr. Heck change his price? Why or why not?

     Answer: _____

     _____ .

Finally, as a good habit to get into, re-think your methodology
and re-check your calculations before being satisfied with your
answers. Then check them against mine in the Answer Key.

103. Now do the Lifestyle Leisure Company problem, which is
problem 5-5 in the text. This problem will allow you to review
both chapters 4 and 5 since many of the concepts were first
introduced in chapter 4.

When you are finished compare your answers with mine in the Answer Key. If you have made mistakes, go back and set them straight, and make sure you understand all the material.

Are you ready for the Quick Quiz?

QUICK QUIZ - CHAPTER FIVE

Q1. Demand estimation involves estimating _____
_____, whereas
demand forecasting involves estimating _____
_____(2)

Q2. Name three problems that may arise with a questionnaire
survey: _____, _____
_____and_____(3)

Q3. The line of best fit is chosen such that the sum of _____
_____
_____(1)

Q4. Interviewer bias is a bias that may enter survey results due
to _____
_____(2)

Q5. With market experiments it is important to have a control
market because _____
_____(2)

Q6. Cross-section data is collected from _____
_____, whereas time
series data collected from_____
_____(2)

Q7. The regression equation explains the variation in _____
_____ in terms of the _____
_____(2)

Q8. The coefficient of determination indicates the _____
_____
_____(2)

Q9. The rule-of-thumb test for the significance of the beta
coefficients in regression analysis is that _____
_____(2)

Q10. Heteroscedasticity is present if _____
_____
while multicollinearity is present if_____
_____(2)

Check your answers against those in the Answer Key. How did you
do?

Score: 17 - 20   14 - 16   12 - 13   10 - 11   9 or less
Grade: A   B   C   D   F

APPENDIX 5A: DEMAND FORECASTING

Summary

In this appendix we examine the following types of demand forecasting techniques:

1. **Regression models** that take causal relationships already determined and use these to predict future values of the dependent variable.

2. **Time series models** that take the past relationships and extend these into the future. These include trend projection, moving averages, and exponential smoothing.

3. **Time series decomposition.** This technique decomposes past data into its trend, cyclical, seasonal, and irregular components, and uses these to build a forecast for the future period.

4. The use of **macroeconomic forecasts** to predict the course of the firm's sales in future periods. These include intention surveys, barometric indicators, and expert opinions expressed in the business press.

Learning Objectives

When you finish this Appendix you will be able to:

*   Use regression equations to forecast a value of demand in a future period, and attach a confidence interval to this forecast.

*   Calculate trend lines and moving averages in order to make simple projections concerning demand in future periods.

*   Use the exponential smoothing model to forecast future levels of quantity demanded.

*   Decompose a time series into its components and then build a forecast of future demand using the trend value and the cyclical and seasonal indices.

*   List the sources of information on macroeconomic variables that may be important determinants of the firm's future demand.

Overview of Appendix 5A

Demand forecasting is concerned with ascertaining the level of demand in future periods. It is important for long range business planning and investment considerations, as well as for day-to-day decisions that have future demand consequences.

Regression models that explain the determinants of demand in the present period can be used to predict the level of demand in future periods, by using the estimated coefficients and applying these to estimated future values of the independent variables. The latter may be estimated by simply projecting their most recent values, or as the expected value of a probability distribution of possible outcomes. For some variables, such as the interest rate for consumer borrowing, the general price level, and income levels, forecasts by a variety of experts are published periodically in the business press.

Time series forecasting models generate predictions for future values of demand based on the past values of demand. Simple **trend projections** extend the rate of change of demand into the future, but fail to take into account recent events that are not part of the data base. **Moving averages** are useful when past data exhibits unpredictable fluctuations, but they weight all items equally and tend to underestimate recent trends in the data. **Exponential smoothing models** attach exponentially declining weights to the past observations, giving the most weight to the most recent observation. These models also adjust for previous forecast error, and have minimal data requirements.

Time series decomposition takes past observations of the firm's demand and decomposes these into their **trend, cyclical, seasonal,** and **irregular** components. The data is first de-seasonalized using a moving average, then a trend line is fitted. Regular fluctuations around the trend line allow identification of the cyclical factor due to business cycles. The remaining deviations from the trend line represent the irregular component and are assumed to be due to random events. To forecast next period's demand, the trend value is projected into the next period and is weighted by both a cyclical and a seasonal index. The irregular component has an expected value of zero, but past deviations allow us to establish confidence intervals around the forecast value of demand.

Macroeconomic forecasting of variables like GNP, the general price level, interest rates, foreign exchange rates, and so on, provide information on variables that will typically influence the firm's future demand situation. A great deal of this is available to the firm in the business press at minimal cost.

Intention surveys are useful, since they reveal the plans of investors, of purchasing agents, and of consumers who are contemplating purchases of a wide range of assets, raw materials, components, and consumer durables. **Barometric indicators** predict changes in variables that are probably important to the·firm's future demand. **Leading series indicators, composite leading indices, and** diffusion indices are used as barometric indicators.

READING: Now read Appendix 5A in the text. Underline all new terms and concepts to help fix them in your mind. Then answer the self-test questions.

Self-test Questions

Write short answers to each of the eight Discussion Questions that are found at the end of Appendix 5A.

When you have finished, compare your answers with mine in the Answer Key. If you are satisfied with your understanding of the material, proceed to the practice problems.

Practice Problems

104. Read problem 5A-4 at the end of Appendix 5A. Then work through the questions asked.

(a) To answer this, we simply "plug in" the most recent estimates of the independent variables.

S = 34,586.29 + 108.79 (_____) - 28.73 (_____) - 15.43 (_____)

   = 34,586.29 + _____ - _____ - _____

   = _____ .

(b) The 95% confidence interval is found by adding and subtracting twice the standard error of estimate to and from the predicted value of S.

Upper confidence limit = _____ + 2 (_____)

                     = _____ .

Lower confidence limit = _____ - 2 (_____)

                     = _____ .

(c) Predictive power can be evaluated by reference to the coefficient of determination, and the ratio of the standard error to the prediction. Note that if the standard error of any coefficient does not pass the "two times" test of significance at the 95% confidence level, this is not a great problem in a predictive model. Inclusion of that variable probably serves to raise the R^2 and the predictive power of the equation. Write your answer down for later comparison with mine.

(d) What other influences on demand can you think of that are not mentioned?

Check your answers against mine in the Answer Key, and proceed to the next problem.

105. Read problem 5A-6, concerning Hubert Hockey Equipment, and answer the questions following it.

(a) To find the trend value in the 73rd period we simply substitute 73 for t in the trend equation. Thus,

$$Q = 12,564.89 + 128.47 (73)$$

$$= \underline{\hspace{2cm}} .$$

We need to weight this value by both the cyclical and seasonal indices to find the predicted value of Q.

Predicted Q = _____ (0.956)(1.122)

= _____ .

(b) Upper confidence bound = _____ + 2 (_____)

= _____ .

Lower confidence bound = _____ - 2 (_____)

= _____ .

(c) If 90% of the standard error is due to cyclical variation, then only 10%, or 88.694, is due to random events. Thus the 95% confidence interval around the predicted value of Q will be plus or minus twice 88.694. Write your answers here:

Upper confidence bound: _____ ; Lower confidence bound: _____ .

(d) On the next page give details about your underlying assumptions and qualifications.

Concerning the implicit assumption of data accuracy and completeness, _____
_____
_____
_____ .

Concerning the assumption of <u>ceteris paribus</u>, _____
_____
_____
_____
_____ .

Concerning the pitfalls of regression analysis specifically, ____
_____
_____
_____
_____
_____ .

Check your answers against mine in the Answer Key.

Are you ready for the Quick Quiz?

QUICK QUIZ - APPENDIX 5A

Q1. Naive methods of demand forecasting simply _____
     _____ without
     _____(2)

Q2. For a regression forecasting model it is more important to
     have a high value for the_____
     than it is to have all independent variables _____
     _____(2)

Q3. Recursive forecasting involves_____
     _____(2)

Q4. For an exponential smoothing model one would choose the
     weight that _____
     _____(3)

Q5. The seasonal index for a time series can be calculated as
     the _____
     _____(2)

Q6. To calculate a four-period centered moving average would
     require that_____ separate averages be calculated.   (1)

Q7. The standard error of estimate of the trend line includes
     the influence of _____ and _____influences
     on demand.   (2)

Q8. Consensus forecasts of macroeconomic variables can be
     obtained by _____ the predictions of _____,
     and these predictions appear periodically in _____
     _____, such as _____(4)

Q9. A leading indicator is called that because _____
     _____(1)

Q10. A diffusion index indicates the proportion _____
     _____(1)

Check your answers and see what grade you earned.

Score: 17 - 20   14 - 16   12 - 13   10 - 11   9 or less
Grade: A   B   C   D   F

CHAPTER 6:   PRODUCTION FUNCTIONS AND COST CURVES

6.1   INTRODUCTION

Summary

This chapter introduces and develops the following concepts and topics:

1.   The **production function** relationship between the inputs of resources and the output of goods and services in both the **short run** and the **long run** production periods.

2.   The concept of **diminishing returns in production** when some inputs are in fixed supply.

3.   The shape of the **cost curves** depends on the efficiency of the production process.

4.   In the long run the firm may experience **economies of plant size, constant returns to plant size,** or **diseconomies of plant size.**

5.   Other influences on the cost of production include **learning curve** effects and **pecuniary economies.**

Learning Objectives

By the end of this chapter you will be able to:

*   Distinguish between the short and the long run in terms of the variability of inputs to the production process.

*   Define the law of diminishing returns and discuss its impact on the marginal and average costs of production.

*   Determine the cost-minimizing reaction of the firm to changes in the prices of resources.

*   Demonstrate that the shape of the cost curves are related to the marginal productivity of the inputs in the production process.

*   Differentiate between economies of plant size, economies of scale, multiplant economies, and pecuniary economies.

*   Explain the impact of changes in input productivity, including the learning effect.

6.2 PRODUCTION IN THE SHORT RUN

Overview of the Text, Section 6.2

Production is a process in which inputs become outputs. These inputs are referred to as **resources,** or factors of production. The outputs are known as products, or **goods and services.**

Inputs are dichotomized as either fixed or variable in the short run, and the **short run** is a period of time in which at least some inputs are fixed, such that the output level is constrained to some maximum amount. The **long run** is a situation in which fixed inputs can be adjusted to any level (either larger or smaller) and hence the output level is unconstrained. **Variable inputs** are those which can be varied directly with the desired output level, while **fixed inputs** remain fixed regardless of fluctuations in the output level.

"**Labor**" is the term given to all the inputs which are variable in the short run. These variable inputs may include laborers, raw materials, **component parts, and energy.** "Capital" is the term given to the fixed inputs, which are also known as "the plant." Fixed inputs would usually include most administrative and professional personnel, all land, buildings, equipment, vehicles, and machinery. The **state of technology** determines the **productivity** of labor and capital and hence determines the level of output associated with each combination of labor and capital.

The **law of diminishing returns** says that, as progressively more labor is added to the fixed capital in the short run, the increments to output will, after some point, become progressively smaller and may eventually become negative. Thus the marginal productivity of labor may increase at first, and then might stay constant, but beyond some point diminishing returns will be evidenced by the marginal product of labor declining. In terms of total product, total product may rise at an increasing rate at first, but, after the point where diminishing returns set in, total product will increase at a decreasing rate and will eventually reach a peak and decline.

READING: Now read sections 6.1 and 6.2 in the text. Read slowly and carefully, highlighting all new terms and concepts, in order to better absorb these new ideas.

After completing the reading, write a short answer to each of the following questions.

Self-test Questions

106. Distinguish between the short run and the long run.

107. Which of the following inputs would qualify as labor and which as capital?
    a. Raw materials
    b. Casual labor
    c. Highly-skilled labor
    d. Management personnel
    e. Electric energy
    f. Buildings and machinery

108. What is the relationship between the state of technology and the productivity of the inputs?

109. What is the law of variable proportions? How is it different from the law of diminishing returns?

110. What is a point of inflection, and what does that point on the total product curve signify?

    Now check your answers against mine in the answer key. Make sure that you fully understand the above-mentioned terms and concepts before continuing.

Practice Problems

111. Read problem 6-1 in the text, concerning Donald K. Brown and Company, and answer the questions pertaining to that case.

    When you have finished, check your answers against those in the Answer Key, and continue.

6.3 SHORT AND LONG RUN COST CURVES

Overview of the Text, Section 6.3

The production functions for the short and long run are cast in **physical terms.** But since both labor and capital have a cost attached, we can easily "monetize" the production function to obtain a cost function. For example, suppose 10 units of labor and 4 units of capital can produce 40 units of output per hour, and that labor costs $8 per unit and capital costs $20 per unit. The 40 units of output will therefore cost $80 for the variable inputs and another $80 for the fixed inputs, giving a total cost of $160, or an average cost of $4 per unit.

We first consider the **total variable cost** (TVC) curve and the associated **average variable cost** (AVC) and **marginal cost** (MC) curves. Then we consider total fixed cost (TFC), and the average fixed cost (AFC). Adding the AFC to the AVC we find the short-run average cost (SAC) curves. We note that the shape of these cost curves depends upon the underlying production relationships. For example, if there are **increasing returns to the variable** factors in production, **marginal cost will be falling**, and this in turn will be pulling down the AVC and SAC values. Conversely, if there are **diminishing returns in production, marginal cost will be rising**, and this in turn will be pulling up the AVC and SAC values. It follows that the MC curve must cut the minimum point on each of the AVC and SAC curves.

The **shape of the cost curves** thus depends upon whether labor is experiencing increasing, or constant, or diminishing returns in the production process. In some production processes there will be a wide range of outputs over which labor enjoys constant returns, and thus marginal costs will be constant over that same range. In other production processes we might see diminishing returns set in almost immediately, such that marginal costs are rising throughout the relevant range of outputs.

Firms will find it desirable to keep per unit costs relatively stable if possible. **Constant marginal costs** can be achieved if the fixed inputs are divisible, since the optimal capital labor ratio can be maintained over a range of output levels. If demand fluctuates, the firm can produce at a constant rate, building up **inventories** when demand is relatively low and selling from inventory when demand exceeds production. Firms also **subcontract** out to other firms, and establish **back-order lists**, rather than be forced to produce at high output rates where marginal cost would be rising steeply.

In the short run the firm will operate as long as the **price exceeds average variable costs** of production, since fixed costs cannot be varied and it is better to make some contribution to them than none at all. In the long run the firm will go out of business if it cannot cover its total costs incurred.

Long run average costs (LAC) are the average costs when the firm is **free to vary all inputs**. In the long run the firm can move from one SAC curve to another to find the least cost of producing any particular output level. The LAC curve shows the minimum average cost for each output level and is actually an **envelope curve** of all the SAC curves.

The **choice of plant** size is a long run decision problem. Note that the long run is a menu of short run situations. Faced with a number of alternative short-run situations the firm must select one of these, build the plant, and begin (or continue) production. When demand is stable, the firm would choose the plant size that has the **lowest SAC** at that output level. When **demand is uncertain**, the firm should choose the plant size that minimizes the **expected value** of SAC.

The **long run marginal cost** (LMC) curve is a hypothetical construct showing the marginal cost of producing each extra unit of output when the firm can vary the inputs of all resources. It lies below the LAC when that curve is falling, cuts LAC at its minimum point, and lies above LAC when LAC is rising.

Economies of plant size are evident when the LAC is falling to the right - that is, when progressively larger plants allow progressively lower average costs of production at their minimum point. If the LAC is horizontal, this means **constant returns to plant size**, and if LAC rises on the right-hand size we have evidence of **diseconomies of plant size**.

Multiplant operation can benefit the firm's cost structure by spreading some fixed costs over more than one plant. Thus the SAC curves for the first plant sink downward as some of the fixed costs are transferred to another plant's SAC curve. Similarly, the purchase in bulk of raw materials should allow larger multiplant firms to achieve **pecuniary economies** which are reflected in a lowering of their SAC curves.

The **learning curve** relates cost per unit to cumulative output levels, and indicates that as the firm's experience in producing the product grows, management and workers find ways to increase production per period and thus reduce the per unit costs. This **increased labor productivity** is often seen when production processes are first established.

READING: Now read section 6.2 in the text. Make sure that you understand the shape and the location of all the cost curves and how these relate to the underlying production process.

When you are finished reading, write a short answer to each of the following questions.

Self-test Questions

112. Why is the value of the slope of a ray from the origin to a point on the total variable cost curve equal to the value of the average variable cost?

113. Why is the marginal cost equal to the average variable cost when the latter is at its minimum?

114. What is the relationship between the marginal product of the variable factors and the marginal cost of output?

115. Explain why the SAC curve converges towards the AVC curve as the output level increases.

116. Why does the SAC curve continue to fall for a short range of output beyond the point where AVC has reached its minimum and started to rise?

117. Explain why the divisibility of some items of fixed inputs can allow the firm to maintain AVC at its minimum level over an extended range of output levels.

118. What is the short-run supply decision rule? If the reduction in price is temporary, should the firm liquidate its plant?

119. When is the LAC curve a smooth curve without any kinks in it?

120. Define economies of plant size, constant returns to plant size, and diseconomies of plant size.

When finished, check your answers against mine in the answer key.

Practice Problem

121. Draw a a total product curve to represent a production process in which there are initially increasing returns to the variable factors, then a prolonged range of constant returns to the variable factors, and finally diminishing returns to the variable factors. Now construct the AVC, MC, and SAC curves associated with that production process.

When you have finished, compare your answers with mine in the Answer Key. How are you doing? If not so well, simply go back and read that part of the text again, before continuing.

READING: Read section 6.4, the summary to chapter 6 in the text, in order to review the contents of the entire chapter.

Self-test Questions

Write a short answer to each one of the ten Discussion Questions at the end of chapter 6.

After completing that task, compare your answers with mine in the Answer Key. I hope you did well.

Practice Problems

122. Read problem 6-5 in the text, concerning Gewerz Fabricators, and then work through the calculations and answer the questions asked.

    If you need help, refer to the following hints.

Hint 1:   An SAC curve can be derived from the production information in each row of the table given.

Hint 2:   You can monetize the input data since the cost per unit of the labor and capital inputs are given.

Hint 3:   There will be economies of plant size if the minimum point of successive SAC curves is lower as we move to the right.

Hint 4:   The probability distribution of demand over the range 200 to 300 units (which we do not know) is important. Since we are not given any information on the probabilities, use the "equiprobability of the unknown" rule, and treat all outcomes between 200 and 300 as equally likely to occur.

Hint 5:   Divide that 200 - 300 output range into, say, ten ranges of 10 units each, and estimate from your graph the SAC at the midpoint of each of these smaller ranges. Weight each one by the 10% probability and find the expected value of SAC in each plant that looks feasible.

123. Now do the Beaudry Automobile Corporation problem, which is problem 6-6. In this problem there is a probability distribution of demand that you can use to find the plant offering the highest expected value of profit.

When you have finished, compare your answers with mine in the Answer Key. If all has gone well, then you're ready for the Quick Quiz. If not, then a few extra minutes repair work at this time will save you extra trouble later on.

QUICK QUIZ - CHAPTER 6

Q1.   The short run is defined as _____
      _____ (1)

Q2.   The long run can be considered as a menu of _____
      _____ (2)

Q3.   The law of diminishing returns states that _____
      _____
      _____ (3)

Q4.   When total product is rising at an increasing rate, marginal
      cost will be _____ and average variable cost will be
      _____.   (2)

Q5.   When marginal cost is equal to average variable cost, short
      run average cost will be _____, because average fixed
      cost is _____ (2)

Q6.   A linear total variable cost curve will be experienced over
      the relevant range if _____
      _____ or if plant is _____ (2)

Q7.   Three ways to stabilize production rates, and hence output
      cost levels, are _____ , _____
      _____, and _____ (3)

Q8.   Economies of plant size are evident when _____
      _____
      _____ (2)

Q9.   Full capacity output is commonly meant to refer to the point
      where _____ (1)

Q10. The rate of learning in a production process can be measured
      as _____
      _____ (2)

Check your answers against those in the Answer Key, and award
yourself a grade.

Score: 17 - 20   14 - 16   12 - 13   10 - 11   9 or less
Grade: A   B   C   D   F

APPENDIX 6A: ISOQUANT-ISOCOST ANALYSIS OF PRODUCTION AND COSTS

Summary

In this appendix we introduce isoquant and isocost curves, and use these to examine the firm's production problem, which is to produce any given output level at minimum cost. Isoquants and isocosts are conceptually similar to indifference curves and budget lines in the theory of consumer behavior. Using isoquant-isocost analysis we:

1. Distinguish between **technical efficiency** and **economic efficiency** in production.

2. Show the **least-cost expansion path** in both the short run and long run contexts.

3. Demonstrate that the firm will **substitute away from a resource** when its price increases relative to other resources.

4. Explain why it is economically efficient for production to be more **labor intensive in low-wage** economies.

Learning Objectives

By the time you finish this appendix you will be able to:

* Use isoquant-isocost analysis to demonstrate the basic substitutability of resources in the production process.

* Show the least-cost combination of inputs for any output level, in both the short and the long run.

* Predict the cost-minimizing response of the firm to a change in relative input prices.

* Explain why production from low-wage economies will be more labor-intensive, and why this will not necessarily be less expensive than more capital-intensive production in a high-wage economy.

* Use isoquant-isocost analysis to explain substitution between variable inputs in the short run.

Overview of Appendix 6A

Isoquants are lines depicting input combinations that produce the same output level. An **isoquant map** is a family of isoquant curves in input space. Each isoquant curve is convex to the origin due to the assumption of diminishing marginal productivity. Unlike indifference curves, isoquants may bend back because we allow marginal productivity to become negative. That is, at relatively high capital-labor ratios the marginal product of capital will become negative, and oppositely, at relatively high labor-capital ratios the marginal product of labor will become negative. If either marginal product (MP) is negative, the isoquant curve will bend back and exhibit a positive slope.

Technical efficiency means that there are no wasted inputs. Thus, any reduction in either labor or capital would cause output to fall. This means that the MP of all inputs must be positive. Hence technical efficiency is exhibited on the negatively-sloping section of an isoquant curve. The **marginal rate of technical substitution** (MRTS) is the rate at which one input can be substituted for another, such that output remains constant. It is thus equal to the slope of the isoquant curve at any input combination. We can show that the MRTS is equal to the ratio of the marginal products.

An **isocost curve** shows combinations of inputs that cost the same amount. Given constant prices of the labor and capital inputs, the isocost curve is a straight line, since there is a constant trade-off between labor and capital: as more of one is added, less of the other is affordable. Suppose labor costs $10 per unit and capital costs $20 per unit. If another unit of labor is added, costs would increase by $10 unless capital input was reduced by half a unit. Thus the slope of the isocost curve is −1/2, the negative of the labor price to capital price ratio.

Economic efficiency means the least-cost combination of capital and labor to produce any given output level; economic efficiency is found where the isoquant curve is tangent to the isocost curve. Given the budget constraint represented by the isocost curve, **tangency** with the highest-attainable isoquant curve indicates the highest-attainable output level and the cost-minimizing input combination. This tangency solution means that the optimal condition can be expressed in terms of the equality between the MRTS and the input price ratio.

In the long run, the **expansion path** shows the least-cost combinations of inputs for all output levels when the firm is free to vary all inputs. It thus shows the same information as the LAC curve, albeit in a different form. The short-run expansion path, showing the least-cost input combinations for different output levels when capital is constrained to a particular level, is in fact the total product (TP) curve, viewed from a different angle.

Changes in the relative prices of inputs will lead, given sufficient time for adjustment, to a different optimal combination of inputs to produce any given output level. **Factor substitution** will take place as the manager substitutes away from the input whose cost increase and substitutes in favor of other inputs which are now relatively less expensive. In the short run the firm will substitute between variable inputs if their relative prices change.

Different economies usually have different input price ratios. This means that the optimal input combination for a given output level will also be different, <u>ceteris paribus</u>, because the slope of the isocost curve will be different. Similarly, if labor and capital productivities differ between regions or nations, the slope of the isoquant curves will be different (for any given input combination) and the optimal input combination will differ, other things being equal.

READING: Now read Appendix 6A. Underline all new terms and concepts in order to help fix them in your memory. Then come back here and answer the following questions.

<u>Self-test Questions</u>

124. From memory define the following terms:
    a. An isoquant curve
    b. Technical efficiency
    c. The marginal rate of technical substitution
    d. Economic efficiency
    e. An isocost line
    f. The (long run) expansion path

125. Why are isoquants allowed to bend back and have sections with positive slope, whereas indifference curves in consumer behavior theory were not allowed to bend back?

<u>Practice Problems</u>

129. Suppose a firm has adjusted to the economically efficient combination of capital and labor in order to produce its desired output level. (Its market share is 2,000 units per period and its inventories are at the desired level; it therefore wishes to produce 2,000 units per period.) Now

suppose that the cost of labor increases, with <u>ceteris paribus</u>. Using isoquant-isocost curves, show how the firm would react (a) first in the short run, and (b) then in the long run.

130. Using isoquant-isocost curves, show (a) why you would expect the manufacturing industry of say, Taiwan, to be more labor intensive than the manufacturing industry in this country, and (b) why Taiwan may also be able to produce the same output level at a smaller total cost.

131. Using isoquant-isocost analysis, explain why the production of silk shirts would be expected to use more labor but fewer yards of cloth (for each shirt) than would the production of cotton shirts.

This question might be a little tough for you at this point. If you need to, use the following hints.

Hint 1:   Put labor on the horizontal axis and materials on the vertical axis.   Materials will represent silk in one case and cotton in another.

Hint 2:   Think about wasted material, and how more labor time spent carefully cutting the material will reduce this waste.

Hint 3:   Silk costs more per yard than cotton does, whereas labor for cutting and sewing shirts would cost the same regardless of what material the shirts are made from.

When you are finished, check your answers against mine in the Answer Key. Then proceed to the following questions.

Self-test Questions

Write short answers to each of the five Discussion Questions at the end of Appendix 6A.

Practice Problem

132. Read problem 6A-1, concerning the Himam Foods Corporation, at the end of Appendix 6A, and answer the questions following it.

When you have finished, check your answers against mine in the Answer Key. Are you ready for the Quick Quiz?

QUICK QUIZ - APPENDIX 6A

Q1. The marginal rate of substitution is negative for technically efficient input combinations, because the marginal product of labor is _____ and the marginal product of capital is _____. (3)

Q2. The slope of an isocost curve is _____
_____ (1)

Q3. The long run expansion path shows _____
_____
_____ (2)

Q4. If the price of labor increases, and the firm's output level must be maintained, we expect the firm to hire _____ labor in the short run, and in the long run it would _____
_____, given ceteris paribus.(2)

Q5. Textiles from China might cost consumers in this country less than domestically-produced textiles, because _____
_____
_____ (2)

     Check your answers against those in the Answer Key, and give yourself a grade according to the following scale.

Score:	10	8 - 9	6 - 7	5	4 or less
Grade:	A	B	C	D	F

APPENDIX 6B: LINEAR PROGRAMMING ANALYSIS

Summary

Linear programming is a solution technique that is applicable to the firm's production problem if both cost per unit of production and the market price per unit of the product do not vary with the output levels. In this appendix we:

1.   Show the **graphical solution** of a multiproduct production problem where the firm must combine several inputs to **maximize profit from two or more products.**

2.   Describe the solution procedure in terms of **corner solutions** and **isoprofit curves.**

3.   Demonstrate the **algebraic method** of solving the linear programming problem, following the introduction of **slack variables.**

4.   Introduce and solve the **dual problem,** which is a restatement of the primal problem. Solving the dual problem allows the **shadow prices of the inputs** to be derived.

Learning Objectives

After reading this appendix and working through the overview, self-test questions, and practice problems in this study guide, you will be able to:

*   Depict graphically any two-product linear programming problem, and show the optimal combination of products that should be produced.

*   Convert any constraint, and the objective function, into an expression that is linear in the two product variables.

*   Introduce slack variables and solve a linear programming problem algebraically.

*   Solve the dual problem of any linear programming problem and thereby generate values for the shadow prices of the inputs to the production process.

Overview of Appendix 6B

Linear programming is a mathematical solution procedure that can be used to solve production and other types of decision problems. It requires that the objective function and each of the constraints be linear relationships. In the production context this means that the **prices and the average variable costs** of the two or more outputs **must be constant.**

The **constraints** are the availability of inputs that are fixed: this may relate to machine time available or labor time available when labor is effectively a fixed input. If a machine takes two hours to produce a unit of output X and three hours to produce a unit of output Y, and has 40 hours total availability per week, we say the constraint is 2X + 3Y is less than or equal to 40. That is, the values of X and Y must be such that their total machine time does not exceed the machine-time constraint.

Given simple linear equations for all constraints and the profit function it is easy to **depict the problem graphically in product space.** The area that lies below all constraint lines encompasses the **feasible region** of output values.

The **profit equation** is also a linear equation in the two outputs variables, given the constancy of price and AVC. (Strictly, it is the "contribution" to overheads and profit that is linear and that we wish to maximize.) Suppose the P - AVC difference (the contribution margin) was $5 for product X and $8 for product Y. This will result in a family of **isoprofit** lines that have linear slopes, since the trade-off between producing (and selling) another unit of X in place of another unit of Y will be constant at -8/5.

The highest isoprofit curve that touches the feasible region will indicate the optimal output combination. It will occur at a **corner solution,** or the intersection of two or more constraints. Knowledge of this allows **algebraic solution** of the linear programming problem, since we simply solve for X and Y at the intersection of each pair of constraint lines and evaluate the solution values in terms of profitability, choosing the corner solution with the greatest profitability.

Since two constraints are binding at the corner solution, we could increase output and profit if we could relax one of the constraints. The increase in profit that would result from the relaxation of a constraint is known as the **shadow price** of that constraint.

For every (primal) maximization problem there is a (dual) minimization problem. In this case the **dual problem** is to minimize the remaining value of the firm's fixed resources, measured in terms of the shadow prices of the resources times the amount of each resource remaining unutilized. Solving the dual problem yields shadow prices for each resource and thus indicates which resource is most profitably expanded.

READING: Now read Appendix 6B, underlining all new terms and concepts. Then answer the following questions.

Self-test Questions

Write answers to each of the ten Discussion Questions at the end of Appendix 6B. When you have finished, check your answers against those found in the Answer Key.

Practice Problems

133. Read problem 6B-1, concerning Frank's Fish Packing Company, following Appendix 6B, and answer the questions asked.

Hint: Recall that you need to express each constraint as a linear equation in terms of two variables, the outputs X and Y. Start with the equation that states that the separating process requirements of X and Y will be equal to 205 when the constraint is binding. Then restate this in terms of the Y variable to find the intercept and slope terms of this constraint line in product space.

When you have finished, check your answers against those in the Answer Key.

134. Read problem 6B-3, concerning the Grimes Gravel Company, at the end of Appendix 6B, and answer the questions asked.

Hint: Remember to insert slack variables in each constraint equation, then set up the variables in a table and systematically set three variables to zero, solve for the remaining three, and evaluate the profits at each of these corner solutions.

When you have finished, check your answers against those in the Answer Key. How did you do? Are you ready for the Quick Quiz?

QUICK QUIZ - APPENDIX 6B

Q1. For the linear programming technique to be applicable, the
     _____ must consume the resources at a _____
     _____, and the _____ must be constant
     for successive units of each variable.   (3)

Q2. The constraint equation for any input to the production
     process represents a locus of the _____
     _____ (2)

Q3. A slack variable represents _____
     _____ (1)

Q4. A shadow price indicates _____
     _____ (2)

Q5. The procedure for solving a linear programming problem
     algebraically is to introduce _____ to the
     constraints, set _____ variables to zero (where there
     are n variables and m constraints), solve for _____
     _____, and evaluate the _____
     at each of _____ solutions.   (5)

Q6. The dual problem of a maximization problem is to _____
     _____
     _____
     _____ (2)

Check your answers against those in the Answer Key and award
yourself a grade on the following basis.

Score: 14 - 15   12 - 13   10 - 11   8 - 9   7 or less
Grade: A   B   C   D   F

CHAPTER 7:   COST CONCEPTS FOR DECISION MAKING

7.1   INTRODUCTION

Summary

In this chapter we examine a variety of cost concepts which are important for managerial decision making. We consider:

1.   The differences, and the agreement, between **economic and accounting cost and profit concepts.**

2.   A variety of cost concepts, including **direct costs, indirect costs, explicit costs, implicit costs, opportunity costs,** and **sunk costs.**

3.   **Incremental costs,** which may be present period explicit costs, opportunity costs, or future costs, and which are the **relevant cost** concept for decision making.

4.   **Contribution analysis,** which considers the difference between incremental revenues and incremental costs. Under this heading we examine the choice between investment alternatives, make or buy decisions, and take it or leave it decisions.

Learning Objectives

By the end of this chapter you will be able to:

*   Distinguish between economic and accounting views of costs and profits, and understand why they differ.

*   Determine which costs are incremental, and which are not, with regard to any decision that is to be made.

*   Classify costs into categories for decision making purposes.

*   Calculate the incremental revenues which might be expected to flow from a decision.

*   Decide which decision alternative offers the greatest contribution to overheads and profits.

7.2 ECONOMIC VS. ACCOUNTING CONCEPTS OF COSTS AND PROFITS

Overview of the Text, Section 7.2

Accountants and economists may differ in their views when it comes to costs, because their purposes may differ. **Financial accountants** have as their main purpose the calculation of costs which they feel "should" be charged against revenues in order to "properly" compute profits. Profits are seen as the residual income to the owners of the firm, and constitute the owners' reward for having invested in the firm. Financial accountants report, essentially, to the shareholders, the Stock exchanges, and the tax authorities. They are subject to certain rules, or conventions, concerning how they may treat particular costs. These conventions are necessary to avoid distortions of reported income which could confuse or mislead the investing public and the tax collector.

But these conventions and rules are not always completely appropriate for decision making. Hence **managerial accountants** and **managerial economists** often use different cost and profit concepts in order to ensure that the firm best pursues its objective of net worth maximization. If profits are expected to be augmented as a result of a decision, this means that the firm's net worth will increase. If the firm has a choice among several different decisions which could be taken to solve a particular problem, it will choose the one which promises the greatest additional profit, subject to risk considerations, as we saw in chapter 2.

In **business situations**, particularly where the firm produces more than one type of product, it is not always easy to dichotomize costs as either fixed or variable. Some costs are clearly variable and others are clearly fixed, but others have both a fixed and variable component - e.g., electric energy costs which are incurred partly to heat and light the workplace and partly to run the electric motors on the production line. Of course, if one spent enough money on search costs, one probably could carefully divide up such costs into a fixed component and a variable component. But would it be worth it ? Typically not, and accountants don't waste money trying to calculate the exact level of variable and fixed costs. Instead they speak of **direct costs**, that can be separated and identified directly with the production of a particular unit of output, and **indirect costs**, which are joint, or overhead costs, for all units of output. Indirect costs are not easily separable and allocable to each separate unit of output. Direct costs are certainly variable costs, but some parts of indirect costs are also variable in the economists' sense, since they will vary with the level of output.

Explicit costs refer to those costs for which there is a present-period outlay for goods or services received, such as the payments for raw materials, energy, and wages. Implicit costs refer to those costs which do not have a present-period outlay involved, but which should nevertheless be imputed against revenues in order to properly calculate the profits of a decision. Resources which are owned by the firm, such as plant and equipment, buildings, and the labor of the owner-manager in small business enterprises, have an opportunity cost of being employed in the business. Their opportunity cost is the foregone income they could earn in alternative employment. For example, suppose the building could be rented to another business and earn $800 per month. Alternatively, if the firm did not own the building it would have to pay $800 per month to rent it. This opportunity cost of the building must be included as an implicit charge against revenues in order to be sure that the firm's capital is best invested in this particular business, rather than in some alternative investment.

Sunk costs are those incurred in the past, prior to the decision to be made. These will be valued at their historic cost, or the nominal price paid at the time of acquisition of the building, equipment, inventory, or other asset. Suppose the firm considers selling an item from inventory which cost $8 when purchased in 1985. The current cost of this item is $10. The cost to be charged against revenues is not the historic, sunk cost of $8, but the opportunity cost of $10. After all, the market price of this item is now $10, and it would cost $10 to replace it in inventory.

In managerial economics we wish to value all costs at their opportunity cost. That is, all inputs to the production process should be valued at their opportunity costs. Explicit costs of wages, materials, and energy, purchased in the present period, will be valued at their market price and so will already be in opportunity cost terms. Implicit costs of owned resources, such as inventories, the services of assets, and the services of owner-managers, must be imputed against revenues at their opportunity costs. The total opportunity costs of all resources utilized in the production process are the economic costs of production. If total revenues exceed total costs in this sense we have economic profits, also known as pure profits. These are pure profits because they are revenues over and above the opportunity cost of all inputs, and thus represent the excess returns the firm is earning by investing in this business rather than putting each resource in its next-best-alternative employment.

Normal profits are earned when TR = TC, and the latter is calculated to include the opportunity costs of all inputs. Firms will be content with normal profits because that represents as much as they could earn elsewhere with their resources. In accounting profit terms, normal profit means an accounting profit sufficient to keep the firm in that line of business rather than liquidating and investing its resources elsewhere. Normal profits include considerations for risk since the opportunity cost of all resources is calculated with the <u>ceteris paribus</u> caveat - that is, what is the value of this or that resource in its next best use, <u>at equal risk</u>? Thus the opportunity cost of more risky ventures would be higher than for less risky ventures.

READING: Now read sections 7.1 and 7.2 in the text. Underline or highlight all new terms and concepts.

When you are finished, write a short answer to each of the following questions.

Self-test Questions

135. Define, and give an example of each of the following:
    (a) direct costs
    (b) indirect costs
    (c) explicit costs
    (d) opportunity costs
    (e) historic costs

136. How would you calculate the economic costs of production?

137. Define normal profits. How does the normal profit concept incorporate the degree of risk involved in the business?

After finishing your answers, check them against mine in the Answer Key. All these terms should be clear in your mind before you continue.

Practice Problems

138. William Winstell owns and operates a small trucking business. He has two Mack trucks and operates the business from a large building which he owns and which provides office space, a workshop and repair facility, and storage space. William runs the business himself but hires two drivers and a secretary. His financial statement last year was as shown on the next page:

Revenues		$122,500
Costs		
Drivers' wages	$32,000	
Secretary's wages	12,500	
Office expenses	2,800	
City taxes	4,200	
Fuel and repairs	28,600	
Depreciation on trucks	10,000	
Depreciation on plant and buildings	6,000	
Miscellaneous expenses	1,400	97,500
Profits		$ 25,000

Lately, William has been wondering if he should be in this business at all. He has been offered a similar job with a competitor paying $20,000 per annum, and he could sell the trucks for $80,000 in total and the plant and buildings for $100,000 and invest the proceeds to earn a 10% rate of return with comparable risk. If he expects his explicit costs and revenues, and the depreciation charges, to be the same next year, what do you advise him to do? Explain your recommendation in full and make explicit all assumptions and qualifications involved.

When you have finished, check your answer against mine in the Answer Key. If all is well, proceed to the next section.

7.3   INCREMENTAL COST ANALYSIS

Overview of the Text, Section 7.3

For decision making purposes we must distinguish between those costs which are relevant to the decision and those which are irrelevant. The **relevant costs** are those which are **incremental to the decision**. That is, the relevant costs are those that will be incurred subsequent to the decision. These relevant costs may be comprised of both explicit and implicit costs, and both fixed and variable costs - they will include all costs that are incurred as a result of the decision. **Irrelevant costs** include sunk costs and committed costs - that is, costs which have been incurred prior to the decision and those which must be paid in the future regardless of this decision.

Incremental costs fall easily into three categories. **Present period explicit costs** are usually easily identifiable, and include wages, materials, and energy costs resulting from the decision. These costs may also include the cost of new equipment required, the purchase of other assets, or the salaries of new personnel who will be hired as a result of this decision.

Opportunity costs are the foregone income the owned resources could have earned in an alternative use. This alternative income is evaluated as the highest income it could earn elsewhere, at equal risk and under similar work conditions. In the case of owned assets, the opportunity costs are either the interest income foregone on the money tied up in the assets, or the contribution to overheads and profit the assets could make in the production of some other product, or the decline in the asset's market value over the production period. We choose the highest of these alternative income sources and call this the asset's opportunity cost.

Future costs include any explicit costs which can be deferred until a future period, any expected future costs such as lawsuits, loss of business, and the like. These future costs must be valued in expected present value terms, of course.

READING: Now read section 7.3 in the text, noting all new concepts and terms. When you have finished, come back and answer the following questions.

Self-test Questions

139. Define incremental costs.

140. What are the three categories of incremental costs?

141. How would you calculate future incremental costs?

Check your answers against those in the Answer Key, and continue.

7.4   CONTRIBUTION ANALYSIS

Overview of the Text, Section 7.4

The **contribution** of a decision is the difference between incremental revenues and incremental costs. Decisions should be made if their contribution is positive. If more than one decision is possible for a particular problem such that the two or more decision alternatives are mutually exclusive, the decision maker will choose the decision alternative with the greatest contribution. This contribution represents the contribution to overheads and profits of the decision. If enough decisions are taken (with positive contribution) then the firm will cover its overheads and actually make a profit.

The **incremental revenues** from a decision fall into the same three categories as do incremental costs. There may be present period explicit revenues, such as sales revenue, refunds, cash prizes, and so on. There may be **opportunity revenues**, which are costs avoided. An example of an opportunity revenue is the layoff costs avoided if you do win a contract as a result of a decision to tender a low bid. Winning the contract means the firm does not need to lay off its workers, thus the money that would have been spent laying off workers stays in the bank, and the firm is that much better off than it would have been had it not won the contract. Finally, there are **future revenues**, which include the expected present value of new business which may be generated as a result of the current decision.

In **contribution analysis** of decision problems, the main task is to identify the incremental costs and revenues. If the decision involves increased production, the change in total variable cost will be an incremental cost, as will any incremental fixed costs, like the cost of additional machines required. Most often opportunity costs and future costs are unstated – it is the decision maker's responsibility to consider the possibility of their existence and, if possible, calculate the expected present value of these costs. If insufficient information is given, but you think such costs are likely, you would incorporate your reservations into your final recommendation, in the form of sensitivity analysis. For example, if decision A offers $1,000 more contribution than decision B, yet decision A would involve the loss of quality control and potential future lawsuits, you might recommend that decision B be adopted because the probable expected present value of those costs could exceed the $1,000 difference in contribution as calculated.

Contribution analysis is used in a variety of decision types. In the text we consider three main types. The **Project A vs. project B** type of decision is for the comparison of alternatives that are mutually exclusive ways of solving the same decision problem. They are presumed to be the best two alternatives, although this presumption should always be questioned. **Make or buy** decisions consider the contribution consequences of making a product in-house rather than contracting for its production from an external source. Again, there is a presumption that the best external source has been located. **Take it or leave it** decisions are those where someone offers to purchase the firm's product at a price somewhat below its normal price, and the firm must decide whether the firm's objectives are best served by accepting this offer or by rejecting it.

READING: Now read section 7.4 in the text. Proceed slowly and methodically in order to fully understand the application of contribution analysis.

Next, write short answers to the following review questions.

Self-test Questions

142. What types of revenues and costs would you look for when calculating the contribution of a decision? Give an example of each type.

143. In arriving at your estimate of incremental costs you will have to make assumptions about the variability or fixity of some cost categories. How should you incorporate these assumptions into your final recommendation?

144. In a make-or-buy decision, the buy alternative will have several risks or disadvantages that the "make" alternative will not have, or at least, these issues will differ in degree. What are these issues?

145. In a take-it-or-leave-it decision, what issues must be considered in addition to the easily quantifiable costs associated with the "take it" alternative?

Check your answers against mine in the Answer Key to see if you have established a sufficient understanding of the issues involved.

READING: Now read section 7.5, the summary to chapter 7 in the text, to review the contents of the entire chapter.

Self-test Questions

Write short answers to each of the ten Discussion Questions at the end of the chapter.

When you have finished, compare your answers with mine in the Answer Key. Then do the following practice problems.

Practice Problems

146. Read problem 7-2 at the end of chapter 7, concerning the Crombie Castings Company, and answer the questions asked. There are some hints on the next page, if you need them.

You shouldn't be looking here unless you have already read the problem and don't know where to begin!

Hint 1: This is a make-or-buy problem and we must calculate the incremental costs and revenues of each alternative. The buy alternative is fairly simple, except for the unmentioned problems which may follow a buy decision. The make alternative requires calculation of incremental costs. Fortunately we are told that average variable costs are constant, so marginal costs are constant too.

Hint 2: Direct labor is not a present-period explicit cost, since it is in the plant now, but working on another product. It does enter into the incremental costs, but via opportunity costs. Materials costs are present-period explicit costs, however.

Hint 3: The opportunity costs of not producing 80,000 units of B will be the contribution made by those units not only to overheads but also to the labor cost previously covered by those 80,000 units.

Hint 4: You should qualify your decision by reference to, and with sensitivity analysis of, the assumptions on which your recommendation is based.

    When you finish writing your answer, check it against mine in the Answer Key.

147. Read problem 7-4, concerning the XYZ company problem, then answer the questions asked. If you need to, refer to the following hints.

Hint 1: Whether you treat indirect factory labor as a fixed cost or a variable cost is a matter of taste, since we don't know from the information given whether it varies with output, and if so, by how much. In either case, the opposite case should be mentioned as a qualification to your recommendation. That is, if you exclude it as a variable cost, your incremental costs might be as much as $6,437 too low, if in fact it is totally variable.

Hint 2: Weigh all other considerations, which you are unable to measure given the information provided, and consider these against the potential contribution of the "take it" alternative. If the contribution is relatively small, these other issues might outweigh that contribution and suggest that it is better to leave it.

When you are finished, compare your answer with mine in the Answer Key.

148. Read the Corcoran Calculator problem (number 7-6) at the end of chapter 7. Do the calculations and write up your recommendation (with appropriate qualifications). Note that this make-or-buy problem involves calculation and comparison of net present values and that some cash flows are lump sum while others occur throughout years one and two.

    When you are finished, compare your answer with mine in the Answer Key. Are you willing to try one more? This next problem has a quite complex opportunity cost situation. If you can figure it out you can be assured that you really understand the opportunity cost concept.

149. Read problem 7-5, concerning the Clark Rent-a-Truck Company, and answer the question asked. Note that you have to calculate the expected value of the opportunity costs, and that there is a joint probability involved.

    Check your answer against mine in the Answer Key.

    Are you ready for the Quick Quiz?

QUICK QUIZ - CHAPTER 7

Q1. Financial accountants view profits as the _____
     _____ , whereas
     managerial economists view (economic) profits as _____
     _____ (2)

Q2. To find total variable costs from accounting data, one would
     seek all those costs that _____
     _____ and would _____ office supplies
     and management salaries. (2)

Q3. Depreciation expense, as reported by accountants, will be a
     correct assessment of the economic cost of an asset only if
     _____
     _____ (2)

Q4. The opportunity cost of an item to be taken from inventory
     would be its sunk cost if _____
     _____ (1)

Q5. Normal profits exist when _____ just equals
     _____ , and the latter is calculated to include
     _____ (3)

Q6. Pure or economic profits indicate that the firm's owned
     resources are earning _____
     _____ , at equal _____ (2)

Q7. Maximizing contribution and maximizing profits amount to the
     same thing because _____
     _____
     _____ (2)

Q8. In the "buy" alternative of the make or buy decision, the
     firm may give up control over two important issues: these
     are _____ and _____ (2)

Q9. Some future costs are not incremental costs, since they are
     _____ (1)

Q10. If resources are to be diverted from the production of
     product A in order to produce product B, the opportunity
     cost is _____
     _____ (3)

Check your answers against those in the Answer Key.

Score: 18 - 20   15 - 17   12 - 14   10 - 11   9 or less
Grade: A   B   C   D   F

APPENDIX 7A: BREAKEVEN ANALYSIS: APPLICATIONS AND LIMITATIONS

Summary

In this appendix we examine the use of breakeven analysis as a decision-making tool. Main points include:

1.   The **breakeven volume** is the output level where total revenue equals and thereafter exceeds total costs.

2.   **Linear total revenue and total cost curves** are often used in breakeven analysis, and this may be a tolerable approximation over the relevant range in many cases.

3.   Breakeven analysis may be used in the **planning phase** to select the price and quality of a product to be marketed.

4.   Breakeven analysis should be used as an **extension of contribution analysis** for results in keeping with the firm's objective to maximize its net worth.

Learning Objectives

After studying this appendix you will be able to:

*   Utilize the graphical or algebraic approach to determine the breakeven volume for any production process.

*   Use breakeven analysis as a basis for selecting the firm's plant size under conditions of demand uncertainty.

*   Understand the concept of operating leverage and its relationship with breakeven analysis.

*   Note the limitations of breakeven analysis as a decision-making tool.

Overview of Appendix 7A

Breakeven analysis is a simple graphical or algebraic tool used in decision making. It shows the output or sales volume where total revenue first exceeds total costs. Under conditions of demand uncertainty the firm will want to know where the breakeven point is before embarking on risky ventures. It should then investigate whether the chances are high enough that actual demand will exceed that level.

Breakeven analysis can be conducted using the **curvilinear TR and TC** curves, or may be simplified to the case of **linear** TR and TC curves, if linearity of total revenues and costs are a sufficient approximation of the actual cost and revenue relationships within the relevant range.

In the **planning phase** the decision maker can consider different price-quality combinations and estimate the breakeven volume for each one before testing whether these output levels are feasible under market conditions. The **simple formula Q = TFC/CM** shows the breakeven volume is determined by the level of the firm's total fixed costs divided by the contribution margin (which is P - AVC).

The level of location and shape of the TC curve has implications for the **quality of the product**, since higher quality typically costs more to produce. Thus the firm can consider different price and quality combinations and establish the breakeven volumes for each combination. It must then consider the probability that demand will meet or exceed the breakeven volume for each price-quality combination, and will choose the one with the highest expected value of contribution.

Operating leverage is the sensitivity of total profits to changes in volume, and is affected by the choice of price and quality values. The higher the price per unit and the lower the unit cost, the more will profits increase once the breakeven point is surpassed.

READING: Now read Appendix 7A, noting all new terms and concepts. Then answer the following questions.

Self-test Questions

Answer the five Discussion Questions at the end of Appendix 7A and then check your answers against mine in the Answer Key.

Practice Problems

150. Read problem 7A-1 and answer the questions asked.

When you are finished, check your answers against mine in the Answer Key.

151. Read problem 7A-3 and answer the questions asked.

Compare your answers with those in the Answer Key. Are you ready for the Quick Quiz?

QUICK QUIZ - APPENDIX 7A

Q1. Linear breakeven analysis is applicable if linearity is a sufficient approximation of the _____ and the _____ within the _____ (3)

Q2. Having established the breakeven volume, the next thing the decision maker needs to know is _____ _____ (2)

Q3. In linear breakeven analysis, _____ changes will shift the total revenue curve, whereas quality changes will shift the _____ (2)

Q4. The breakeven volume can be calculated by dividing _____ _____ by _____ (2)

Q5. Operating leverage may be thought of as the elasticity of _____ with respect to _____ (2)

Q6. Breakeven analysis should consider only _____ costs if it is to help the firm maximize its net worth. (1)

Check your answers against those in the Answer Key, and give yourself a grade on the following basis.

Score: 11 - 12   9 - 10   7 - 8   6   5 or less
Grade: A   B   C   D   F

CHAPTER 8:   COST ESTIMATION AND FORECASTING

8.1   INTRODUCTION

Summary

In this chapter we are concerned with the estimation of the short and long run cost curves, as applicable in the present period and as applicable in future periods. We cover the following topics:

1.   Short run cost curves can be estimated using simple **extrapolation**, **gradient** analysis, **regression analysis**, or the **engineering technique**.

2.   Studies of short run cost curves typically show **constant marginal costs** within the **relevant range**.

3.   **Long run cost curves**, or the family of short run cost curves that are available at any point of time, can be estimated using regression analysis or the engineering technique.

4.   **Forecasting costs** in future periods can proceed on the basis of the projected changes in factor prices and productivities, as well as by estimating the **learning curve**.

Learning Objectives

By the time you finish this chapter you will be able to:

*   Use simple extrapolation and gradient analysis to obtain a crude estimate of the firm's cost curves, on the basis of very little data.

*   Use regression analysis of time-series data to derive an expression for the total variable cost curve, and from this derive expressions for the AVC and MC curves.

*   Apply regression analysis to cross-section data to estimate the long run average cost curve facing the firm.

*   Use the engineering technique to estimate both short and long run cost curves.

*   Estimate the learning curve in production given several initial cost-output observations.

8.2   SHORT RUN COST ESTIMATION

Overview of the Text, Section 8.2

What is the **shape and location of the firm's TVC and TC curves,**
and what, consequently, will be the level of the average and
marginal costs at various levels of output?   To answer these
questions, we consider several methods of cost estimation which
proceed, on the basis of known data, to estimate points on the
cost curves such that we are able to picture the various cost
curves pertaining to a particular production process.

Often the firm only knows one cost-output combination for
sure - its **present** levels of cost and output.   From these levels
the firm may **extrapolate** forward and backwards to sketch in its
TC and other cost curves.   If the firm has no information to
suggest otherwise, it may assume that marginal costs will be
constant at the current level.   Later observations will support
or refute that assumption.   If a decision must be made on the
basis of such an extrapolation, the decision maker should examine
the sensitivity of the decision to the assumption of constant
marginal costs.   If a slight increase in MC would reverse the
decision, for example, the firm is better advised to delay the
decision until search procedure can be conducted to ascertain the
actual behavior of marginal costs.

Given two or more cost-output observations we can conduct
gradient analysis. The gradient we are interested in is the slope
of the total cost curve, and this, as you know, will be a measure
of marginal costs.   But since the cost-output observations are
typically at discrete intervals from each other, the gradient
will actually be the mean of the marginal cost values over each
interval.   The gradient is calculated as the change in total
costs divided by the change in output. If we have several
cost-output observations we can calculate several gradients and
sketch in our best estimate of the firm's SAC, AVC, and MC
curves, by interpolating between these gradient points.

Regression analysis can be applied to find the line of best fit
for the cost-output observations when there are several
observations.   For short-run cost curves these observations must
be time-series data - observations from a particular plant over a
sequence of time periods (e.g., weekly cost and output levels
from March to July).   The first pitfall to avoid is specification
error, since the assumed form of the TC or TVC function dictates
the shape of the MC, AVC, and SAC curves as well.   Thus we must
be careful to observe a scatter plot of the data, or choose the
functional form allowing the highest R^2 value, in order to avoid
pre-judging the shape of the cost curves. Regression analysis
also gives us the standard error of estimate and the standard

error of the coefficient, which allow us to construct confidence intervals around the estimated TC, or any other cost level, at a given output level. These may be thought of as best-case, worst-case scenarios for management's consideration.

The **engineering technique** of cost estimation, unlike the above methods which start from observations of cost-output levels, starts from the physical production function relationship between the output and the various inputs. We begin with a matrix showing the amount of each resource required to produce each of several output levels. We then **monetize the input data** (by multiplying by the input cost per unit), in order to calculate the total variable cost of producing each of those output levels. It is then a simple matter to calculate and plot AVC and gradient values and then interpolate between these points to show the estimated cost curves.

Studies of cost-curve estimation typically show constant marginal costs over the range of cost-output observations. The range of outputs is often quite narrow, and this result reflects the desire of firms to operate in the range of outputs to the left of the full capacity level (where MC = SAC) such that they have some excess capacity to utilize in case they need it. Draw a graph of SAC, AVC, and MC and you will see that the MC curve could easily be relatively flat in this area near its minimum point. Thus the empirical evidence does not refute the law of diminishing returns. It seems that firms prefer to operate in the range before diminishing returns (rising MC) become significant. Occasional uses of full capacity (to catch up after a labor strike or a breakdown, or to satisfy a growing market while a larger plant is being constructed, for example) could be expected to show diminishing returns and rising MC.

READING: Now read sections 8.1 and 8.2 in the text. Underline or highlight all new concepts and terms to fix them more clearly in your memory.

When you are finished reading, write short answers to the following questions.

Self-test Questions

152. What are the risks involved in the extrapolation of present cost levels to higher or lower output levels?

153. How is the gradient of total costs calculated, and when is the gradient of total costs equal to marginal costs?

154. Explain what would be the consequences of measurement error and specification error in regression analysis of the cost functions.

155. Given a regression equation showing total cost as a function of output, what does the standard error of estimate tell us?

156. What is the engineering technique of cost estimation? Outline the steps involved.

157. If studies consistently indicate constant marginal costs, explain why this does not necessarily refute the law of diminishing returns.

    After you have written down your answers, check them against mine in the Answer Key, and proceed if your answers are correct.

Practice Problems

158. Read problem 8-1, concerning the Rakita Racquets Company, at the end of chapter 8, and then answer the questions here in the study guide, rather than the questions in the text.

(a) Suppose that at the end of July, Mr. Rakita wants an estimate of his marginal cost of restringing racquets. Use gradient analysis to derive an estimate of MC.

(b) Arrange the observations into ascending order by volume (racquets restrung), calculate the AVC at each output level and estimate the MC over each output range.

(c) Plot the AVC and MC values calculated on a graph.

(d) Plot the TVC data against output, and draw in a freehand line of best fit. From this line, estimate the incremental costs of increasing output from 7,000 to 10,000 units.

159. Read problem 8-3, concerning the Patches Printing Company, and answer the questions following it.

    In this problem you have to draw a graph of the MC and AVC curves, superimpose the demand and marginal revenue curves, and estimate the profit-maximizing output and price levels from your graph. So draw it carefully!

    After you have finished, check your answers against mine in the Answer Key, and proceed.

8.3 LONG RUN COST ESTIMATION

<u>Overview of the Text, Section 8.3</u>

Long-run cost estimation can be viewed as the estimation of all the short-run cost situations available to the firm at any point of time. The long run is when the firm chooses among the possible plant sizes available to it. Thus we need to repeat the short-run cost estimation procedures for every possible plant size, or at least for those plant sizes which appear to offer the most efficient production of the firm's desired output level. We could do this with gradient or regression analysis for each plant, or by using the engineering technique for each plant, following the same procedures discussed above, and repeating these for each plant size considered.

Alternatively, we could conduct **regression analysis** on **cross-section data** obtained from several different firms during a particular production period. The line of best fit to this data would represent our estimate of the long-run total cost curve, and we could easily calculate LAC and LMC from the regression equation. There are problems with this method, however, since a cross section of existing firms will exhibit differing vintages of capital, and perhaps face different input prices and productivities. What we are seeking is the LAC curve assuming that all plant sizes represent the current technology and the same input prices and productivities.

The **engineering technique** is probably the best technique for estimating long run cost curves, since the production functions can be based on the most-recent technology. Also, input prices can be adjusted to reflect any recent changes before the production function is monetized to find the TVC curve.

Studies of the long-run cost curve have shown the existence of economies of plant size, initially, followed by a range of constant returns to plant size. Diseconomies of plant size are rarely observed, indicating that decision makers foresee the onset of diseconomies and perhaps build two smaller plants rather than one larger plant.

READING: Now read section 8.3 in the text, underlining or highlighting all new terms and concepts.

When you have finished reading, write a short answer to each of the following questions.

Self-test Questions

160. If regression analysis of cross-section data indicates that
a quadratic function best fits the cost-output observations,
what does this indicate about the existence of economies or
diseconomies of plant size?

161. What problems might be encountered in the use of regression
analysis using cross-section data to estimate the long-run
average cost curve?

162. Why is the engineering technique likely to be the best
technique for long-run cost estimation? When would it be
difficult to use?

After writing down your answers, check them against mine in
the Answer Key, and proceed.

Practice Problem

163. Read problem 8-7, concerning the Done Brown Cookie Company.

(a) Use the engineering technique to derive a schedule of TC,
TVC, SAC, AVC, and MC values for each plant.

(b) Use the probability distribution of demand to establish a
probability distribution of profits, and select the plant
size that maximizes the expected value of profits.

(c) What assumptions and qualifications underlie your analysis?

Check your answers against those in the Answer Key, and proceed.

8.4   COST FORECASTING

Overview of the Text, Section 8.4

Cost forecasting is distinguished from cost estimation on the
basis of time. **Cost estimation** is concerned with the shape and
location of the cost curves in the **present period**, whereas **cost
forecasting** is concerned with the shape and location of those
cost curves in a **future period**.

Costs will be different in the future, as compared to the
present levels, if either the prices of inputs differ or the
productivity of the inputs differs in the future as compared to
the present. Concerning the future prices of inputs, we should
distinguish between an inflation-caused increase in all input

prices and a change in the real prices of inputs. If all input prices rise by the same proportion as the rate of inflation, then the real prices may not have changed. More important, the price ratio will not have changed, and the combination that was economically efficient in the past will remain so. If one input becomes more expensive than another in real terms, we should expect firms to substitute away from that input and toward other inputs.

Changes in factor productivities should be expected as time passes. Both labor and capital tend to become more productive as a result of more education, better training and better equipment (for labor) and higher technology, greater reliability and better operators (for capital). If the productivity of one input increases at a faster rate than others, firms will tend to substitute in favor of that input, other things being equal. But increasing productivity will attract better remuneration for that resource, and the input's increased price will tend to reduce demand for that input.

Thus **future cost levels** must be based on predictions as to the rate of change of factor prices and productivities. These predictions might be simple extrapolations of past increases (trend projections), or might be formed with the aid of complex models. One fairly simple model for cost forecasting is the **learning curve,** which shows cost per unit as a decreasing function of cumulative output. As the firm's experience in production accumulates, the cost per unit tends to decline, due to workers' greater familiarity with the production process, as well as to improvements made to the production process to save time, materials, and reduce wastage, breakage, or spoilage. Empirical tests indicate that unit costs tend to decline by a rather steady percentage each time output is doubled. Typically, when the firm's cumulative output doubles, the firm can expect its unit costs to decline by about 20%.

The **learning curve is a power function** with a negative exponent; that is, $SAC = aQ^b$, where the exponent, b, will typically show a negative sign. This expression can be linearized using logarithms, and then we can use linear regression to estimate the parameters a and b. This is demonstrated in the text. Given a regression equation for the learning curve, it is a simple matter to forecast unit cost levels at future cumulative output totals by substituting for Q in the above expression, and solving for SAC.

READING: Now read section 8.4 in the text. You may need to refer back to section 5.3 in chapter 5 if you have forgotten some of the details involved in calculating the regression equation.

When you have finished reading, write short answers to the following questions.

Self-test Questions

164. What will happen, and why, to the least-cost combination of capital and labor in future periods, if labor prices (wages) rise at a faster rate than the cost of capital, with _ceteris paribus?_

165. What will happen to the least-cost combination of inputs if the productivity of capital grows more quickly than that of labor, given _ceteris paribus?_

166. What is the learning curve and what does it show?

167. What is the implication of the learning curve for the firm's SAC, AVC, and MC curves?

168. If I say the "percentage of learning" is 21.5%, what do I mean?

After writing your answers, check them against mine in the Answer Key to see if you understood all the issues.

READING: Now read section 8.5, the summary to chapter 8, to refresh your memory on the content of that chapter, before doing the following questions.

Self-test Questions

Write a short answer to each of the ten Discussion Questions at the end of chapter 8.

When you have finished, compare them with my answers in the Answer Key. If any of your answers lack important detail, turn back to the relevant section in the chapter and read it through again.

Practice Problems

169. Read problem 8-2, concerning the Minical Electronics Company, in the text, and answer the questions asked.

170. Read problem 8-6, concerning the Argus Boat Company, in the text, do the calculations and write out your answers to the three parts of the question. There are some hints overleaf.

Hint 1:   Marginal and average-variable-cost curves are derived by monetizing the production data provided to find TVC, and then calculating AVC and MC (using gradients) from the TVC data.

Hint 2:   Total fixed cost for next month are the overhead costs of $24,000 which presumably include the salesman's expense account.   The set-up, packing, and shipping costs for this deal are not part of next month's fixed costs unless the deal is accepted.   Ignore them for the first part of the question.

Hint 3:   The appropriate decision will be the alternative (take it or leave it) with the highest expected value of contribution. Do not simply use the expected value of demand and the cost and revenue levels at this point, because that would mean you have reduced the probability distribution to a single point estimate, with   an   effective   probability   of   one.   The   probability distribution given allows you to calculate the contribution at each output level, and then find the expected value of these contributions.   (If both the probability distribution and the cost structure were _symmetric_ about the expected value of demand, the simple approach would give the same answer, but neither is symmetric.)

When you have finished, compare your answers with mine in the Answer Key.

171. Read problem 8-10, concerning the Fairway Golf Cart Company, and answer the questions asked. The following tables might be helpful.

PER UNIT COST	CUMULATIVE Q	LOG. OF COST	LOG. OF OUTPUT
1,582	1,000	_____	_____
1,215	2,000	_____	_____
1,095	3,000	_____	_____
975	4,000	_____	_____
900	5,000	_____	_____

Y	X	XY	X^2	Y^2
___	___	___	___	___
___	___	___	___	___
___	___	___	___	___
___	___	___	___	___
___	___	___	___	___
=========	==========	============	===========	==========

Mean Y = _____ / 5 = _____.

Mean X = _____ / 5 = _____.

Slope term   = _____

              = _____

              = _____.

Intercept term = _____

              = _____

              = _____.

Antilog of intercept term = _____.

Thus, learning curve expression is SAC = _____

For Q = 10,000 units, SAC = _____

              = _____

              = _____.

For Q = 20,000 units, SAC = _____

              = _____

              = _____.

R^2 = _____

     = _____

     = _____

     = _____

     = _____.

S_e = _____

     = _____

     = _____

     = _____.

Now write your answers to the questions asked and compare them
with mine in the Answer Key. Then proceed to the Quick Quiz.

QUICK QUIZ - CHAPTER 8

Q1.   The gradient of total costs indicates the _____

       _____ (2)

Q2.   When using regression analysis to estimate short run cost
       curves, we use _____ data and make sure that the
       _____ of the regression equation is
       appropriate by choosing the functional form having the
       _____ (3)

Q3.   A best-case, worst-case, estimate of total variable costs
       can be estimated by adding _____

       _____ (2)

Q4.   The engineering technique of cost estimation first attempts
       to estimate the _____
       and then _____

       _____ (2)

Q5.   Cross-section data is unreliable for estimating the long run
       cost curve because _____

       _____ (3)

Q6.   If a power function best fits the cost-output data, and the
       intercept term is positive and the exponent is greater than
       one, this indicates _____ of plant size.   (1)

Q7.   Of the six regression pitfalls, the most likely one to be an
       insurmountable problem in long run cost estimation using
       cross-section data is _____ (1)

Q8.   Studies of long run cost curves indicate that _____

       _____ (2)

Q9.   To forecast future values of costs for any particular output
       level one needs to first forecast changes in _____

       _____ (2)

Q10.   The learning curve reflects the _____ productivity
       of _____ as the cumulative
       output level grows.   (2)

Check your answers against those in the Answer Key and award
yourself a grade on the following basis.

Score: 18 - 20   15 - 17   12 - 14   10 - 11   9 or less
Grade: A   B   C   D   F

CHAPTER 9:   MODELS OF THE FIRM'S PRICING DECISION

9.1   INTRODUCTION

Summary

In this chapter we bring together the demand and cost analyses of earlier chapters and apply these to the development of models of the firm's pricing and output decision. Topics include:

1.   There are **seven assumptions** underlying any model of the firm's pricing and output decision.

2.   There are four basic market forms, namely **pure competition, monopolistic competition, oligopoly,** and **monopoly.**

3.   A distinguishing feature of oligopolies is the **mutual dependence** of the firms, since one's actions will have significant impact on the sales and profits of the others.

4.   There are **many models of oligopoly,** each based on seven underlying assumptions, that seek to explain and predict the behavior of business firms.

Learning Objectives

When you have finished this chapter you will be able to:

*   Identify the seven assumptions that form the basis for any theory of the firm's pricing and output decision.

*   Demonstrate how price is determined, and how the firms set their output levels, in purely competitive markets.

*   Show how monopolists and monopolistic competitors set their price and output levels.

*   Explain why profit-maximizing firms facing a kinked demand curve may not change their price despite shifts of the cost and demand curves.

*   Explain the role of conscious parallelism and price leadership in coordinating price adjustments in oligopolies.

*   Discuss the strategies that a firm would follow in order to pursue longer term objectives.

9.2   PRICE DETERMINATION WHERE NO REACTIONS ARE EXPECTED

Overview of the Text, Section 9.2

In this section we examine a series of models of the firm's pricing behavior in which the firm faces a ceteris paribus demand curve, since it **expects no reactions from rivals** when it adjusts its price or output levels. Understanding these graphical models will serve to sharpen your conceptual and analytical skills, and will allow you to appreciate how these models and concepts can be used in business situations to make better decisions.

There are many models of the firm which purport to explain pricing behavior in different structural and behavioral situations. What these models have in common is **seven basic assumptions.** The models, and their pricing implications, differ only because one or more of the seven underlying assumptions differ. The seven assumptions are four structural assumptions (**number of sellers, cost conditions, number of buyers,** and extent of **product differentiation**) and three behavioral assumptions (the firm's **objective function,** the **strategic variables,** and the firm's **expectation of rivals' reactions**).

There are **four basic market forms** in traditional microeconomic theory. These are pure competition, monopolistic competition, oligopoly, and monopoly. The essential differences between these market forms come down to two of the seven assumptions - the number of sellers and the degree of product differentiation.

Pure competition has many sellers and zero product differentiation (identical products). Price is determined by the aggregate forces of supply and demand in such markets because no single buyer or seller can directly influence the market price. Thus the intersection of the market demand curve with the market supply curve determines the equilibrium price. Each seller then produces to the point where MC = MR in order to maximize profits. The firm's MR curve will be coextensive with the demand curve, both being horizontal at the market price, since the firm can sell all it wants to at the market price.

The profit-maximizing rule (MC = MR) is the same for the firm regardless of the market form in which it finds itself. For the **monopolist,** a single seller facing a market-demand curve, the marginal-revenue curve will have the same intercept and twice the slope of the demand curve. The monopolist will produce at the output level where MC cuts MR. By extending a line vertically to the demand curve, we find the price at which the firm can sell this profit-maximizing quantity. Monopolies exist and persist over time because of barriers to the entry of other firms, which usually take the form of substantial cost disadvantages faced by potential entrants to the market.

Monopolistic competition has many sellers and slightly differentiated products. Thus, these firms face a downward sloping demand curve which is nevertheless quite elastic due to the availability of many close substitutes. Output is extended to the point where MC rises to meet the falling MR, and the profit-maximizing price is found by extension of a line up to the demand curve.

READING: Now read sections 9.1 and 9.2 in the text, noting all new terms and concepts and paying particular attention to the graphs. Then come back here and answer the following questions.

Self-test Questions

172. What is the critical difference between "few" and "many" firms?

173. Product differentiation can be measured by the cross-price elasticity of demand, as you will remember from chapter 4. What is the value of cross elasticity in pure competition? In monopoly? In oligopoly? In monopolistic competition?

174. Define the term conjectural variation in words. Now define it algebraically. (Hint: The numerator will be the change in the instigating firm's price.)

175. List the seven assumptions of pure competition. Why is "full information" part of the cost and demand assumptions?

176. Monopolistic competition differs from pure competition in just one respect. What is it? Name one or more markets which you think fulfil the conditions for monopolistic competition.

177. How would a firm become a monopoly? Why would it remain a monopoly?

Check your answers against those in the Answer Key, and continue.

Practice Problems

178. Show, using graphs, how the firm in pure competition would react to a shift outward of the market demand curve in the short run.

179. Suppose a monopolist benefits from the learning curve such that its cost curves shift downward. How would a profit-maximizing monopolist react to this? (Use a graph to support your answer.)

Check your answers and continue to the next section.

9.3   PRICE DETERMINATION IN OLIGOPOLIES

Overview of the Text, Section 9.3

   Oligopoly is the term given to a market in which there are only a few sellers, and their products are typically differentiated to some degree. Most real-world markets are oligopolies, and there are dozens of models of oligopolies to reflect the differences encountered in the real world. For some oligopolists the **demand curve is kinked** because the firm has two different expectations of rivals' reactions: it expects that price increases will be ignored by rivals, whereas price reductions will be matched by rivals. Thus the firm faces a ceteris paribus demand curve for price increases and a mutatis mutandis demand curve for price decreases. (Mutatis mutandis means "taking into account the changes which do occur.")

   With a kinked demand curve (KDC) there is necessarily a kinked marginal-revenue curve which also has a **vertical discontinuity** (or gap) in it. This gap in the MR allows prices to remain at the same level in a KDC oligopoly despite shifts in the cost and demand curves (within limits). This **rigidity of prices** is a special feature of the KDC model and explains what is often observed in real-world situations where prices change only infrequently rather than in response to every little shift or fluctuation in the cost and demand curves.

   Nevertheless, oligopolists are frequently observed changing prices, and it is clear that the KDC model is too simple to be a general model of oligopoly. The model of **conscious parallelism** is essentially the KDC model with one further modification to the conjectural variation assumption. Conscious parallelism is a phenomenon whereby firms independently undertake price changes, but each is conscious that the other firms are simultaneously undertaking similar price changes. Thus, the firms consciously act in a parallel manner. If all firms suffer increased labor costs at the same time, due to an industry-wide wage agreement, for example, all firms will most likely want to increase their prices. Especially if there has been a practice of passing on these wage increase in the past, the firm might expect all firms to be ready and willing to raise prices at this time. Thus all firms independently, yet jointly, raise their prices in conscious parallelism. This can be shown as a simple modification to the KDC model and allows that model to explain why firms sometimes hold prices rigid despite cost increases but at other times readily pass on to consumers cost increases that are common to all firms.

Price leadership occurs when one firm raises or lowers its price and then the other firms follow suit, adjusting their prices to the same extent. Price leaders are willing to take the risk that the other firms will not follow suit and are typically firms which have gained the respect, or fear, of the other firms.

Barometric price leaders act like a barometer and sense when all other firms are ready for a price adjustment. **Low-cost price leaders** change price when it suits them; they expect the others to follow rather than provoke a price war with the low-cost firm. **Dominant-firm price leaders** similarly choose the price which maximizes their own profits, and the other firms follow in their own best interests.

Price differentials across firms may be observed in oligopolies, due to different quality (and cost) situations. The price leader in this case leads the range of prices up or down to its new level. For example, if the price leader raises price by 10% and all others do likewise, the relative prices will be unchanged at the new higher level.

READING: Now read section 9.3 in the text, underlining or highlighting all new terms, concepts, and definitions.

When you have finished reading, write short answers to the following questions.

Self-test Questions

180. Outline the assumptions required for a kinked demand curve in oligopoly.

181. Define the _mutatis mutandis_ demand curve faced by an oligopolist that recognizes its mutual dependence.

182. Explain the construction of the MR curve which accompanies a kinked demand curve. Under what circumstances will the lower part of the MR curve (below the gap) lie completely below the horizontal axis?

183. Why is the KDC model of oligopoly not a complete model of price determination? What _does_ it explain or predict?

184. In the conscious parallelism model, what would happen if the firm raised prices more than the other firms raised theirs?

185. What is the conjectural variation for the price leader, and what is it for the price followers?

186. What are the characteristics of a barometric price leader?

187. Explain, in words only, how the low-cost-firm price leader chooses the price level.

188. When product differentiation is asymmetric, we expect price differentials. How does price leadership work in this situation?

189. Explain, in words only, how the dominant-firm price leader chooses the price level.

After you have written down your answers to these questions, compare them with mine in the Answer Key and note any shortcomings (in either yours or mine!)

Practice Problem

190. Suppose that manufacturers of hockey sticks constitute an oligopoly which faces a market-demand situation which varies seasonally. Show, using a graph and a hypothetical initial KDC situation, how far the demand curves could shift to the right before one of these firms would want to raise its price.

After completing this problem, check the Answer Key and continue.

9.4   PRICING FOR LONGER-TERM OBJECTIVES

Overview of the Text, Section 9.4

Short-run profit maximization is not likely to be an appropriate objective function for many oligopolistic firms, since their time horizon would most likely extend beyond the short run. We now turn to the context of firms facing uncertainty, with **time horizons falling in future periods.** As we saw in chapter 1 of the text, maximization of the firm's net worth under those circumstances will be achieved by maximizing the expected present value of the firm's profit stream from the present to the time horizon.

Maximization of the firm's expected present value of profits can alternatively be called **long-term profit maximization**. To maximize its long-term profits under uncertainty, the firm must form expectations of demand at various prices in each period, as well as expectations of shifts in cost curves between the present period and the time horizon. If the search costs are expected to outweigh the value of the information derived, the firm will forego search and adopt an alternative objective function which is expected to give similar results without the search costs.

One such "proxy" policy is the **maximization of sales** in the short run, **subject to a minimum profit constraint**. The greater are sales in the present period the greater will be repeat sales in future periods, the greater will be sales of complementary and accessary products and services in future periods, and the less likely will be new firms to enter the market (since price will be lower and this market will look less profitable to potential entrants.) All these things work in the direction of greater long-term profits. This policy may not give the same revenue stream as would be possible given full search and EPV analysis, but neither does it incur the search costs. At the bottom line the firm could even show greater profits as a result of using this proxy policy.

Limit pricing to deter entry is another policy applicable in the short run which has long term profit-maximizing implications. By setting current prices low enough to deter the entry of new firms, the oligopolist ensures that future-period demand will not have to be shared with more firms. Also, the lower price in the present period expands present and future sales, as discussed above. Potential entrants may be higher-cost entrants, in which case the firm can make a profit and still make it impossible for the potential entrant to survive. On the other hand, a potential entrant may have equal or even lower costs, in which case its entry can be forestalled by bluffing tactics.

Contestable markets are markets which have minimal barriers to entry or exit. Thus purely competitive and monopolistically competitive markets are contestable, but so too are some oligopoly and monopoly markets. In the latter two cases we should expect the firms to practice limit pricing.

Growth maximization, maximizing the **utility of management**, and **satisficing**, may also be proxy policies for long run profit maximization. Satisficing means achieving satisfactory target levels in several variables which include profits, sales volume, inventory/sales ratios, and so forth. Consistent pursuit of targets, and periodic upgrading of these targets, ensures that the end result will be a bottom-line profit figure sufficiently close to (or above) the EPV profit figure.

READING: Now read section 9.4 in the text, underlining or highlighting all new terms and concepts.

When you have finished reading section 9.4, write short answers to each of the following questions.

<u>Self-test Questions</u>

191. In order to reach the same "bottom line" (a similar profit stream over the firm's planning period) how close does the revenue stream of proxy policy have to be to that of the EPV approach?

192. Why is short-run sales maximization a proxy for long-term profit maximization, and why is the minimum profit target desirable?

193. Outline in words how an oligopolist could deter the entry of a high-cost firm.

194. When the potential entrant is a low-cost firm, how can entry be deterred?

195. What is a contestable market, and what impact is this likely to have on a price leader's price?

196. Explain briefly why growth maximization, maximization of managerial utility, and satisficing can each be regarded as proxy policies for long-term profit maximization.

When you have finished writing out your answers, check them against mine in the Answer Key, and then proceed.

READING: Now read section 9.5, the summary to chapter 9, to review the contents of the entire chapter before answering the following questions.

<u>Self-test Questions</u>

Write short answers to each of the ten Discussion Questions at the end of chapter 9.

When you have finished, compare your answers with mine in the Answer Key.

Practice Problems

197. Read problem 9-5, concerning the low-cost price leader called Struktatuff, and answer the questions asked.

198. Read problem 9-6, concerning the dominant firm oligopoly, at the end of chapter 9, and proceed to answer the questions asked. You can either answer this question from a graph, carefully drawn, or you may prefer to solve it using algebra. If you need help, consult the hints below.

Hint 1: To find the residual-demand curve we must first find the sum of the marginal costs curves for the smaller firms. This curve will have the same intercept value but its slope will be twenty times flatter, compared to a single small firm.

Hint 2: The residual-demand curve must meet the market-demand curve when P = $15, since the small firms supply nothing below that. You can calculate the slope of the residual-demand curve, between its intercept on the price axis and its intercept with the demand curve, using a dP/dQ formula.

199. Read problem 9-8 in the text and write out your answers to the questions asked. Don't bother to calculate the EPV's of the two alternative profit streams. Simply discuss the issues involved and arrive at an approximate limit price. The following hints may be necessary, but first have a good solid try at the problem by yourself.

Hint 1: Calculate the potential entrant's average costs for the first year and for the later year when its share of the market finally equals one sixth of the market.

Hint 2: Find the market demand curve from the price, quantity, and elasticity figures given. Each firm's mutatis mutandis demand curve will have six times the slope.

Hint 3: Assume that the post-entry price would be determined by a low-cost price leader, one of the original five firms.

When you have finished, check your analysis against mine in the Answer Key.

Are you ready for the Quick Quiz?

QUICK QUIZ - CHAPTER 9

Q1.   The traditional market forms can be distinguished from each other on the basis of two underlying assumptions, namely _____ and _____ (2)

Q2.   In pure competition the price is determined by _____ _____ and firms select their output levels by equating _____ (2)

Q3.   A natural monopoly is one for whom _____ _____ (2)

Q4.   A monopolistic competitor thinks it faces a <u>ceteris paribus</u> demand curve because _____ _____ (2)

Q5.   A <u>mutatis mutandis</u> demand curve is faced by an oligopolist in several models, including _____, _____, and _____ (3)

Q6.   In the long run a dominant firm price leader may lose market share because _____ _____ (1)

Q7.   Sales maximization subject to a profit constraint tends to augment long term profits for three main reasons, which are _____, _____ _____, and _____ (3)

Q8.   The limit price is the highest price that will _____ _____ (2)

Q9.   A contestable market is characterized by _____ _____ (1)

Q10. Satisficing means to _____ _____ (2)

Check your answers against those in the Answer Key, and give yourself a grade on the following basis.

Score: 18 - 20   15 - 17   12 - 14   10 - 11   9 or less
Grade: A   B   C   D   F

APPENDIX 9A: FURTHER MODELS OF PRICING BEHAVIOR

Summary

This appendix considers several more complex pricing models, including the following situations:

1.   Multiplant firms and Cartels. In these situations there is a single entity controlling the production decisions in two or more plants.

2.   Price Discrimination. Different prices may be charged to different consumers, based on their differing price elasticities of demand.

3.   Transfer pricing. When an item is transferred between divisions of a firm, the price of that item must be carefully chosen if the firm's profit is to be maximized.

4.   Delivered pricing. In markets where the seller delivers the product to the place of consumption or use in another production process, the price must reflect the cost of delivery if the firm is to maximize profits.

Learning Objectives

When you finish this appendix you will be able to:

*   Use the technique of horizontal addition to find the combined marginal cost curves for a multiplant firm, or to find the combined marginal revenue curve for the price discriminator.

*   Show how the profit-maximizing price is selected in the multiplant firm and cartel situation.

*   Demonstrate that a firm can maximize profits by charging different prices to different customers, discriminating on the basis of their price elasticities.

*   Find the profit-maximizing transfer price in the cases where there is no external market for the transferred product, where the external market is purely competitive, and where the external market is imperfectly competitive.

*   Demonstrate the impact of transportation costs on the delivered price in a spatial market.

113

Overview of Appendix 9A

The models of pricing behavior examined in this appendix use the basic **profit-maximizing rule (MC = MR)**, but the interpretation of either MC or MR is typically a little different. With multiplant firms and cartels we need to construct a composite MC curve, since there is more than one plant from which the firm (or cartel) could draw its production. When a firm can segregate its markets we need to construct a composite MR curve, since the firm can sell its output in two or more separate markets.

A **multiplant firm** has two or more plants or production facilities. If these plants have different cost structures it will pay the firm to not operate them all at the same output level. Profits will be maximized by producing more in the lower-cost plants and less in the higher-cost plants. To find the profit-maximizing total output the firm must add horizontally the MC curves of its different plants to find the composite MC curve for the firm as a whole. Where this combined curve cuts the MR curve, total output will be profit maximizing, and the price is found vertically above that on the demand curve.

To allocate the total production between or among the plants, the firm ensures that the level to which MR has fallen in the market is not surpassed in any plant; that is, each plant will produce up to the point where its MC has risen to the level to which MR has fallen. (This is easily seen diagrammatically.)

A **cartel** is a group of firms acting like a multiplant firm. The cartel makes the price and output decisions and instructs each firm on how much to produce in its plant. The analysis is the same as for the multiplant firm - equate MR with the composite MC curve, which is the horizontal sum of the firms' MC curves, and then ensure that each firm produces only up to the point where MC equals the level to which market marginal revenue has fallen.

There is a **profit incentive to cheat on the cartel**, as long as the price reduction can be kept secret from other members of the cartel. Recognizing this, low-cost members of the cartel may find it worthwhile to make "side payments" to higher-cost members to induce them to stay within the cartel pricing agreement.

A **market-sharing cartel** is a group of oligopolies which agree to divide the market up geographically or to maintain their current shares of the market. Cartel agreements are not legal in most modern economies as they tend to restrain competition and impose higher prices on consumers. International cartels exist from time to time, since there are no international laws preventing them.

Price discrimination is possible when the firm can separate the buyers on some basis. **First-degree price discrimination** means that each buyer is asked to pay the maximum he or she would be willing to pay for each unit. Thus the units are sold one at a time, and the price moves slowly down the demand curve from the intercept point on the vertical axis. **Second-degree price discrimination** is done on the basis of time or urgency. Those who want the product sooner will pay more. **Third-degree price discrimination** is done between markets which can be separated, such as the business and household markets for telephone service. The more inelastic is demand, the higher will be the price charged.

For third degree price discrimination the profit-maximizing total output is found by the **horizontal addition** of the MR curves from each market, and then equating this composite MR curve with the firm's MC curve. Allocation of this output between markets is made optimal by ensuring that MR in each market be allowed to fall no further than the level to which MC has risen. Given the optimal total production and its optimal allocation to each market, the price in each market is determined by the demand curve in each market.

Transfer pricing is concerned with the price at which an item is transferred between two separate profit centers within the same firm. To maximize profit of the firm as a whole the transfer price must be chosen to cause the producing division to produce exactly the amount the selling division can sell to maximize the firm's profits. When there is a competitive external market for the transfer good, the transfer price will equal the market price. If the external market is imperfectly competitive, the transfer price will be somewhat less than the external price as the producing division practices price discrimination between its sister division and the external market.

Delivered pricing occurs when there is **spatial competition**, meaning buyers are spread around geographically and the seller must deliver the product to the purchaser. Transportation cost means that the delivered price increases with the distance from the factory door. **Basing-point pricing** is a form of delivered pricing and may be used by oligopolists as a means to collude.

READING: Now read Appendix 9A, noting all new terms and concepts. Work slowly through the more complex graphs, making sure you understand them.

When you are finished reading, write short answers to the following questions.

Self-test Questions

Write answers to each of the ten Discussion Questions at the end of Appendix 9A. When you have finished, check your answers against those in the Answer Key.

Practice Problems

200. Read problem 9A-3, concerning the Bartram Bitumen Company, found at the end of Appendix 9A in the text. Find an approximate answer from your graph rather than attempt an algebraic answer, unless the algebraic method is easier for you.

201. Read problem 9A-5, concerning General Statics Corporation, and answer the questions following. Again, answers obtained from a careful graphing of the demand and cost curves will suffice, although you are encouraged to confirm your answers algebraically.

When you are finished, check your answers against mine in the Answer Key.

Proceed to the Quick Quiz if you are satisfied that you have a good grasp of the preceding material.

QUICK QUIZ - APPENDIX 9A

Q1. The multiplant firm will maximize profits if output in each plant is taken to the point where _____
_____ (1)

Q2. _____ from one cartel member to another may be necessary to prevent a cartel member from undercutting the cartel price.   (1)

Q3. Second-degree price discrimination involves charging a higher price to those who _____
_____ (1)

Q4. The three necessary conditions for price discrimination are _____, _____
_____, and _____ (3)

Q5. In third-degree price discrimination, the market in which _____ will be charged the higher price (1)

Q6. The profit-maximizing transfer price, when there is no external market, is found by equating _____
and _____ to find the optimal output level, and then setting the transfer price equal to _____ (3)

Q7. When there is an imperfectly competitive external market for the transfer good, the transferring division will set an external price which is _____ the transfer price.
(1)

Q8. Delivered pricing is a form of price discrimination, since buyers are discriminated against on the basis of _____
_____ (2)

Q9. Firms can increase their market share in spatial competition by _____, or by _____
_____ (2)

Q10. Cross-hauling may occur in spatial competition for several reasons, including _____
_____
_____
_____ (5)

Check your answers against those in the Answer Key, and calculate your grade according to the following scale.

Score:	18 - 20	15 - 17	12 - 14	10 - 11	9 or less
Grade:	A	B	C	D	F

CHAPTER 10:   PRICING DECISIONS IN PRACTICE

10.1 INTRODUCTION

Summary

This chapter is concerned with the firm's pricing problem in practical situations. We will cover the following topics:

1. **Marginalist pricing** under conditions of **risk and uncertainty.**

2. **Markup pricing** and its reconcilation with the marginalist approach.

3. **Search costs** and their influence on the efficacy of the markup approach.

4. Other pricing topics including **price positioning, product-line pricing, pricing to infer quality, pricing product bundles,** and **promotional pricing.**

Learning Objectives

When you have finished this chapter you will be able to:

*   Identify the profit-maximizing level of the markup.

*   Explain why the markup rate could be "wrong" yet still allow the firm to make more profit than it could if it conducted information search and subsequently set the "right" price.

*   Show that markup pricing allows the firm to practice conscious parallelism and to maintain its real profitability under inflationary conditions.

*   Explain how a product should be positioned in terms of its price, given the quality of that product.

*   Discuss the issues underlying product-line pricing, pricing to infer quality, pricing product bundles, quantity discounts, and promotional pricing.

10.2   MARKUP PRICING

Overview of the Text, Sections 10.1 and 10.2

Marginalist pricing using the MC = MR rule can be practiced if the firm incurs search costs and ascertains the shape and location of its cost and demand curves. Marginalist pricing under uncertainty has essentially been covered in earlier chapters, and is briefly reiterated here. Given estimates of the MC and MR curves, which can be derived using the methods discussed in chapters 4, 5, and 8, the firm can find the output and price level that best serve its objective function. Contribution analysis can also be regarded as a marginalist approach since it is concerned only with changes in total costs and total revenues.

   Markup pricing is a common practice followed by firms in the real world. Rules of thumb like this are appropriate when the expected value of information generated by search activity is less than the costs of search. Markup pricing is a proxy pricing policy which may allow the firm to best pursue its objective function without incurring search costs. To determine price, a percentage markup is added to average variable, or prime, costs. The size of the percentage markup depends on the demand for the product, and, in particular, on the price elasticity of demand. The profit-maximizing markup percentage can be calculated as a function of the price elasticity of demand. The higher the elasticity, the smaller the markup percentage which is profit maximizing.

   In practice the markup rate could be "wrong" to some degree yet still allow the firm to make more profit than it would if it first incurred search costs and then set the "right" price. There is a **range of acceptable markups** which allow at least as much profit without search, as compared to the optimal price after search costs have been incurred. The firm might periodically test whether or not its markup rate lies within the acceptable range either by undertaking search activity or by critically examining the inferred price elasticity which is suggested by the current markup rate.

   Once the firm has found the optimal markup rate it can continue to apply this rate to maximize profit despite shifts in the demand and cost curves, as long as these shifts conform to certain restrictions. That is, the current markup rate will remain profit maximizing if a shift of the demand curve is an **iso-elastic shift** or if both costs and prices shift up or down by the same proportion. (An iso-elastic shift means that the price elasticity at any given price level remains the same after the curve shifts.) Costs and prices may shift up by the same proportion when there is inflation, and in this situation the optimal markup remains optimal despite shifts of the curves.

Markup pricing as a decision-making procedure acts as a coordinating device and is the means by which firms act in **conscious parallelism** in many situations. When labor, raw materials, or energy costs go up, each firm simply marks up the new direct cost level by the old markup rate. Thus all firms tend to raise their prices concurrently, each expecting that the others will do likewise.

READING: Now read sections 10.1 and 10.2 in the text, underlining or highlighting all new terms and concepts.

When you have finished reading, write short answers to the following questions.

Self-test Questions

202. What is the relationship between price, average variable cost, and price elasticity, which must exist if the markup rate is to be the profit-maximizing rate?

203. How can the markup rate be "wrong" yet still give more profits than the "right" price?

204. What factors determine the range of acceptable markup rates?

205. Should the sales-maximizing (subject to a profit target) firm ever spend money on search activity? Explain.

206. Given your current price and AVC, how would you infer the "required" price elasticity if your current markup rate is to be profit maximizing?

207. Under what conditions will the optimal markup remain optimal despite a shift of the demand curve?

208. Under what conditions will the markup rate remain optimal when there is inflation?

209. How does markup pricing policy facilitate conscious parallelism and the avoidance of lost market share?

When you are finished, check your answers against mine in the Answer Key.

Practice Problems

210. Do problem 10-4 (The Laura Ann Boutique) from the text. You may need one or more of the following hints.

Hint 1: Use the formula supplied in the text, equation 10-2, to find the price elasticity implied by the current markup rate.

Hint 2: Use the information given to derive the firm's estimated demand curve, and then construct a table showing TR, TVC, and contribution at each of several output levels. Since fixed costs are constant, maximum profits will be where the firm's contribution is maximized.

Hint 3: The search-cost expense shifts the contribution curve downward and indicates the range of acceptable markups, as in Figure 10-2 in the text.

When you have finished, compare your answers with mine in the Answer Key.

211. Now do problem 10-5 (The Archibald Truck Service) in the text.

When you have written out your answers, compare them with mine in the Answer Key. If there are any problems, sort them out before continuing to the next part of this unit.

10.3 PRICING IN ESTABLISHED MARKETS

Overview of the Text, Section 10.3

We turn now to the examination of some pricing strategies which are applications of the pricing theory we have been considering. We note that there is both an **art and a science of pricing**, and at this point we are leaving the scientific part and entering the artistic part. Pricing in practice is not something that can be learned entirely from books - the basic principles and models can be learned and elements of these can be applied, but it takes experience and a solid appreciation of the market in which you are operating to be a successful price strategist.

In established markets a general price structure will exist already and the question is where to **position the firm's price**. Should it be relatively high, among the more expensive, or among the medium-priced, or one of the lower-priced items in the market?   This issue is resolved by examination of the quality attributes of the firm's product vis-a-vis the attributes of the other products, as perceived by consumers.   In essence the product will be priced at what the consumers think it is worth, in comparison with the other products available.

When a firm has a **product line** of related products, it will price each product such that the contribution from the entire product line is maximized.   This will involve choosing a price for the basic item and then pricing the other goods accordingly. Once the consumer has purchased the basic item (e.g., film), demand for complementary items (e.g., flashcubes) will tend to be less elastic, and we would thus expect higher markups on the complementary items.   Where the product line is comprised of substitutes (e.g., different models of Ford automobiles) the firm must establish the price on its **loss leader** and also its **flagship** and then choose price differentials for the products in between these bottom-of-the-line and top-of-the-line products.   The firm will be constrained by the prices being charged by other firms, of course.

Sometimes the firm will attempt to **convey a message about the quality** of its product by setting a relatively high price. Consumers will interpret the higher price as indicating higher quality if they have no other means of measuring quality or if the search cost of doing so is greater then the price difference between that product and some other product of known quality.   In some cases, consumers will pay much more for products of only slightly greater quality in order to practice **conspicuous consumption.**

Product bundling is the practice of grouping products together into a **package deal,** such as including the software with a computer purchase, or adding a luxury package to an automobile. Pricing product bundles to increase profit involves raising the prices of the goods bought separately and giving a discount on the goods bought jointly. **Quantity discounts** are simply examples of product bundling, since the bundles are simply multiples of the base unit.

Promotional pricing means to reduce the price of the product temporarily by announcing a **sale price.** This may be done to clear excess inventories, to act as a **loss leader,** or as an introductory special. This works best with products that have relatively **high price elasticity of demand,** and works best on consumers with relatively low transport and opportunity costs and with plenty of storage space. **Search goods,** whose quality can be verified easily and at minimal cost prior to purchase, tend to have relatively high price elasticities, and are favorites for promotional pricing.

READING: Now read section 10.3 in the text, noting all new terms and concepts.

When you have finished reading, write short answers to the following review questions.

Self-test Questions

212. What issues would you consider before choosing the price position for your product in an established market?

213. In product line pricing, how would you determine the prices of your various products if these products are (i) complements, and (ii) substitutes, for each other?

214. Under what circumstances would you set a higher price in an attempt to convey information about the quality of your product?

215. Explain why product bundling may induce a person to spend more than they otherwise would have on the firm's products.

216. Why are discounts for larger quantities the same as bundle prices?

217. List the reasons why a firm might use promotional pricing.

218. What are the possible disadvantages of promotional pricing?

219. Why are search goods most often used for promotional pricing?

After you have finished answering these questions, check your answers against mine in the Answer Key before proceeding.

READING: Now read the summary to chapter 10 to refresh your memory of the entire chapter. When that's done, do the following review questions.

Self-test Questions

Write short answers to each of the ten Discussion Questions at the end of chapter 10 in the text.

When you have finished, compare your answers with mine in the Answer Key.

Practice Problems

220. Read problem 10-3 (Pittsburgh Plastics Company) in the text, and answer the questions asked. There are some hints below, if you need them.

Hint 1: The firm's demand curve has been shifting outward at a constant rate for two months, and will presumably do so again in April.

Hint 2: The firm's March demand curve can be estimated using the known price, quantity, and elasticity data provided.

Hint 3: Assume that the demand curve shifts in a parallel fashion, such that the calculated slope term for March also applies to the April demand curve.

When you are finished, check your answers against mine in the Answer Key.

221. Read problem 10-7, concerning Valhalla refrigerators, in the text, and answer the questions asked. There are some hints below, if you need them.

Hint 1: Compare the attributes of the refrigerators, including the implicit quality attributes involved in the brand names, and estimate what each attribute is worth to the consumer.

Hint 2: We are not looking for an exact answer. Use the quality comparison to identify the price ballpark for Valhalla's product.

When you are finished, check your answers against mine in the Answer Key.

222. Read problem 10-9 (Emerson Electric Corporation) in the text, and answer the questions asked.

When you are finished, compare your answers with mine in the Answer Key. If all is well, you are ready for the Quick Quiz.

QUICK QUIZ - CHAPTER 10

Q1. A rule-of-thumb pricing policy is profit-maximizing if _____ (2)

Q2. If the price elasticity of demand is -3, the profit-maximizing markup rate is equal to _____ percent. (2)

Q3. The formula for the hypothetical price elasticity, given price and direct cost per unit, is _____ _____ (2)

Q4. The range of acceptable markups will be greater if_____ _____, _____, and _____ (3)

Q5. The profit-maximizing markup rate will remain profit-maximizing when the demand curve shifts if this shift is an _____ one, or if it shifts only in _____, not _____, terms. (3)

Q6. Price positioning would proceed on the basis of a comparison of _____ _____ (1)

Q7. In a product line, each product should be priced such that it maximizes its _____ (1)

Q8. Price may be used as a proxy for product quality when the search costs of ascertaining quality are _____ (1)

Q9. Product bundling can enhance the firm's profit by extracting more of the _____ from some buyers. (1)

Q10. Promotional pricing will work better for firms if the price elasticity is relatively _____; if the product is a _____ good; if the firm's customers have relatively low _____ costs; and if consumers can build private _____ of the good. (4)

Check your answers against those in the Answer Key, and grade yourself accordingly.

Score:	18 - 20	15 - 17	12 - 14	10 - 11	9 or less
Grade:	A	B	C	D	F

APPENDIX 10A: ILLEGAL PRICING PRACTICES

Summary

Firms must be aware of the law when they set their prices, since certain pricing practices are illegal.   These include:

1. **Price fixing.** The **Sherman Act** of 1890 prohibits collusive agreements among firms to set prices jointly.

2. **Price discrimination.** The **Robinson-Patman Act** of 1936 outlaws price discrimination (legal definition).

3. **Predatory pricing.** The Robinson-Patman Act also outlaws pricing to eliminate a competitor.

4. **Resale price maintenance.** Since the repeal of the "fair trade" laws in 1975, resale prices may be suggested but not enforced in any way.

Learning Objectives

After reading this appendix you will be able to:

*   Outline the legislation that exists regarding illegal pricing and other business practices. These include the Sherman, Clayton, Federal Trade Commission, Robinson-Patman, Wheeler-Lea, and Celler-Kefauver Acts.

*   Distinguish between horizontal and vertical price agreements, and explain why a quantity agreement may be regarded as a price agreement.

*   Explain why price leadership and conscious parallelism are not illegal, as long as there are no signs of an explicit agreement.

*   Explain why some manufacturers would prefer to enforce resale price maintenance.

*   Distinguish between price discrimination that is illegal and that which is allowable.

*   Identify predatory pricing, as distinct from vigorous price competition.

Overview of Appendix 10A

Business firms in the U.S. are subject to laws intended to promote competition between firms such that the public interest is best served. The **Sherman Act** of 1890 first outlawed "conspiracies in restraint of trade," and this was followed by the **Clayton Act** and the establishment of the **Federal Trade Commission** in 1914. The **Robinson-Patman Act** (1936), the **Wheeler-Lea** amendment (1938) and the **Celler-Kefauver** Act (1950) followed.

Price fixing is illegal per se, meaning there is no avenue of appeal. Any agreement to jointly set or adjust prices can draw substantial fines for the firms and prison terms for the managers involved. **Market-sharing agreements** may constitute conspiracies to fix prices, as well, since if outputs are restricted prices tend to rise. Independent action that results in parallel pricing is not in itself illegal; evidence of a conspiracy must be found.

Price discrimination, where the effect is to substantially lessen competition or injure a competitor, is unlawful. A firm can give better prices to some customers if the discounts reflect cost savings for larger orders, if no rivals would be injured, if it is necessary to match competition, or if it is to get rid of obsolete or deteriorating merchandise.

Predatory pricing is involved if a firm reduces price only in some regional markets with the intent of impoverishing one or more of its rivals. It could use its profits in other markets, where its price remains relatively high, to fund a price war against a particular competitor. The line between predatory pricing and vigorous price competition is a fine one that should be well understood by managers.

Resale price maintenance, meaning that manufacturers could effectively set the retail price for their goods, was legal for a long time, ostensibly to protect small firms from the "cut-throat" competition of larger firms. Since 1975, when these so-called "fair trade" laws were repealed, manufacturers may only suggest list prices, allowing retailers to adjust prices at the retail level as they see fit.

READING: Now read Appendix 10A, noting all new terms and concepts and the names of the pieces of legislation that impact upon the firm's pricing decision. Then answer the following questions.

Self-test Questions

Answer the eight Discussion Questions at the end of Appendix 10A, and then compare your answers with mine in the Answer Key. Then attempt the Quick Quiz on the next page.

QUICK QUIZ - APPENDIX 10A

Q1. Price leaders and followers are not guilty of price fixing
unless _____
_____ (2)

Q2. Evidence of a conspiracy to fix prices would include _____
_____
_____
_____ (3)

Q3. There are four defenses against a charge of price
discrimination, and these are _____,
_____, _____
_____, or _____ (4)

Q4. A firm could price aggressively and actually cause one or
more competitors to go out of business, without this being
called predatory pricing, if it _____
_____ (2)

Q5. Resale price maintenance could eliminate price competition
at the retail level if _____
_____ (2)

Q6. Some manufacturers feel that resale price maintenance is
important to protect the quality image of their product
because _____
_____ (2)

Check your answers against those in the Answer Key, and see what
grade you have earned.

Score:	14 - 15	12 - 13	10 - 11	8 - 9	7 or less
Grade:	A	B	C	D	F

CHAPTER 11:   NEW PRODUCT PRICING

Summary

This chapter is concerned with the firm's pricing strategy for new products, both when they are first introduced to the market, and later when there are subsequent shifts of the cost and demand curves. Topics include:

1. **Price skimming.** A high price is set initially to recoup the substantial development cost the firm has typically incurred.

2. **Penetration pricing.** A relatively low price is chosen for greater market penetration, with subsequent impacts on repeat business, sales of complementary goods, and the inhibition of potential entrants.

3. The impact of the **learning effect** on prices. Prices will decline over time as cumulative output grows and costs decline due to the learning effect in production.

4. Prices will also decline if the firm is able to take advantage of **economies of plant size** as demand for the product grows.

5. **New firms will enter** the market, and the initiating firm must share a market that grows at first and later declines.

Learning Objectives

After reading this chapter, and working through the questions and problems, you will be able to:

*   Outline the circumstances in which the skimming price strategy appears superior to the penetration pricing strategy, or vice-versa.

*   Show how the price and the quality of a new product should be considered jointly, prior to the launch of the new product.

*   Separate the impact on prices of the learning effect in production, economies of plant size, entry of new firms, and shifts of the market demand curve due to the product life cycle.

*   Outline the first-mover advantages that are reaped by the firm that introduces a successful new product.

11.2   SETTING THE INITIAL PRICE FOR A NEW PRODUCT

<u>Overview of the Text, Section 11.2</u>

With a new product, the firm will be a **monopolist** initially, if the product is really new. If it is simply a new model or an improved version being touted as new, then it really fits into the established market at a price position reflecting its new quality attributes in comparison with those of other products. With a totally new product the firm can initially practice either price skimming or penetration pricing, depending on the specific circumstances.

Price skimming means to set the price at a relatively high level in order to make large profits initially. We shall see that this may imply a price level equal to, or above, or below the short-run profit-maximizing price level, depending on the specific circumstances. **Penetration pricing** means to set a relatively low price in order to sell more units in the first period and hopefully gain more repeat business and complementary sales in future periods. Moreover, this lower price allows quicker progress down the learning curve and tends to inhibit the entry of new firms.

The skimming price will be the **short-run profit-maximizing** (SRPM) price if the firm's time horizon falls in the present period, or if barriers to entry are absolute, and the firm wishes to maximize the EPV of net worth. Similarly if the product is a fad item, or an emergency service, such that demand will not continue beyond the present period, the skimming price is the SRPM price.

The skimming price will be less than the SRPM price if barriers to entry are high but not insurmountable, and the firm chooses to set a **limit price which is relatively high** because the potential entrant's costs would be relatively high.

The skimming price could be higher than the SRPM price if consumers are expected to draw positive **price-quality inferences** from the high price. The greater perception of quality that results will cause the demand curve to be shifted outward in future periods. Price could be raised above the SRPM level up to the point where the present period profits foregone (by having price higher than the SRPM level) would be almost outweighed by the EPV of additional future profits generated as a result.

Penetration pricing is indicated for firms with time horizons falling in future periods. If **barriers to entry** are relatively high, such that the limit price is relatively high, the firm might achieve the maximization of the EPV of its profit stream by attempting to maximize sales in the short run, subject to a minimum profit constraint. If barriers are somewhat lower, the limit price will be lower, and this will be chosen as the penetration price.

The type of product also influences the initial pricing strategy. **Search goods,** which can be evaluated and emulated relatively easily, lend themselves more to price skimming. The firm should make hay while the sun shines, since entry is inevitable (assuming no patent protection) and post-entry shares of the market will depend on the number of firms in the market at that time. Post-entry profits will tend to be low, since search elasticities have higher elasticities and lower markup rates. Thus the EPV of the firm's profit stream for a search good is likely to be maximized following a skimming strategy, ceteris paribus.

Experience and credence goods, on the other hand, are better candidates for penetration pricing, other things being equal. The price-quality association can perhaps be exploited, these products are more difficult to emulate, and post-entry price elasticity will tend to be lower, and profits higher, than for search goods. Thus the EPV of the firm's profit stream for experience and credence goods is likely to be maximized by a penetration pricing strategy, ceteris paribus.

Thus the choice between price skimming and penetration pricing depends on the **EPV of the profit stream** under each strategy. This in turn depends on the length of the firm's planning period, the opportunity discount rate, as well as the height of the barriers to entry and the type of product.

Joint price and quality determination, prior to the product's manufacture, would proceed on the basis of comparison of several different alternatives, where each price-quality variant is treated as a separate, mutually-exclusive, project. The firm would choose the variant that promises the greatest EPV of profits over its planning period.

READING: Now read sections 11.1 and 11.2 in the text, noting all new terms and concepts. When you are finished, come back and answer the following questions.

Self-test Questions

223. List the conditions under which you would expect the firm to set the short-run profit-maximizing price as the skimming price.

224. Explain why a price higher than the short-run profit-maximizing price might be the EPV-maximizing skimming price.

225. Why would a firm ever set the penetration price at a level that is lower than the limit price?

226. Explain why search goods may be more suitable for skimming strategies while experience and credence goods may be better suited for penetration pricing, other things being equal.

227. When is the limit price a skimming price and when is it a penetration price?

Check your answers against mine in the Answer Key, then proceed.

Practice Problem

228. Suppose that a firm was about to introduce a new product, and had estimated demand for the product, its own costs, the probable costs of entrants, and thus the limit price, such that it was able to calculate the following profit streams. Strategy A is to set the profit-maximizing price in the first year, and somewhat lower prices in later years set in conjunction with the new firms. Strategy B is to set the limit price and deter the entry of new firms throughout the period shown.

	Strategy A profits	Strategy B profits
Year 1	$130,000	$60,000
Year 2	40,000	60,000
Year 3	40,000	60,000
Year 4	40,000	60,000
Year 5	40,000	60,000
Year 6	40,000	60,000

(a) Supposing the opportunity discount rate to be 10%, the funds to arrive at year end, and the time horizon to be six years, which strategy maximizes the firm's EPV of profits?

(b) Now suppose that the opportunity discount rate rises to 14% and other considerations remain the same. Does this change your decision?

(c) Now suppose that the time horizon shrinks to four years. Does this make a difference under the 14% discount rate scenario? How about under the 10% scenario?

Check your answers against mine in the Answer Key, and continue.

11.3 ADJUSTING PRICE OVER TIME

Overview of the Text, Section 11.3

New products are almost inevitably **followed by imitators**, such that the initial monopoly becomes an oligopoly, often in spite of the initial firm's efforts to set a limit price. The new firms struggle for market share, both through price and quality competition. **Prices fall** as a result of both demand and cost changes. As the oligopoly matures, some form of coordinated pricing usually emerges, such as conscious parallelism or price leadership. In this section we look at four demand and cost changes that cause price to fall over time.

First, the **learning effect** in production causes the cost per unit to decline as cumulative production grows. This causes the firm's SAC, AVC, and MC curves to sink downward over time, thus causing the profit-maximizing price, or its sales-maximizing price (with profit target) to decline as well, other things being equal. One of the benefits of penetration pricing is that it allows faster progress along the learning curve.

Second, **economies of plant size** may be realized by the firm as it experiences a strong response to its new product and builds a larger plant to serve the demand that has become evident. When launching a new product, firms tend to be cautious, and their bankers even more so, such that the initial production facilities are often insufficient to handle the demand that eventuates. By enlarging their production facilities to meet demand, firms often benefit from economies of plant size, which means lower cost curves and lower prices tend to follow in order to best serve the firm's objectives.

Third, **entry of new firms** means that the initiating firm will have to share the market demand with one or more firms. Suppose the firms then practice conscious parallelism or price leadership. Each will face a _mutatis mutandis_ demand curve that represents some share of the market, if they coordinate their price changes in some way. Each firm's demand curve will shift downward as another firm enters the market, and this will tend to reduce the prices which best serve the firms' objective functions.

Fourth, there will be **shifts of the market demand curve**, due to the **product life cycle**. The product life cycle hypothesis says that market demand for a new product will grow rapidly at first, then grow more slowly, and eventually decline as newer products emerge to make the product obsolete or inferior. In the early stages of the product life cycle, the relative rates of growth of the market demand and of new entrants is critical. If firms are entering faster than the market is growing, then prices will tend to fall, as each firm's _mutatis mutandis_ demand curve continues to shift to the left. On the other hand, if barriers to entry are relatively difficult to overcome, the market may grow faster than the number of new firms, and this would exert an upward influence on prices.

These four influences on the price level have been considered separately up to this point. In reality, of course, they interact to cause prices of new products to fall as time passes. This is probably a good point to remind you that we mean **real prices**, not the nominal prices we observe in the market. The price of the Escort radar detector (the first to use super-heterodyne circuitry, which effectively put it in a class by itself) has been $245 since the mid-1970's. In real terms, however, this represents a continuing decline in the price level as other firms entered the market with their own versions of the product.

The firm that introduces a new product successfully benefits from **first-mover advantages** that can be summarized **as potential monopoly profits initially** and **higher profit margins later.** The higher profit margins occur because the initiating firm has benefited from learning effects in production before the entrants even begin to slide down their learning curves. Unless the entrants can learn faster than the initiating firm, the latter will always have a cost advantage. The rate of learning may be higher for the entrants, however, since they can follow the leader rather than discover everything for themselves, but it still takes time for them to catch up. These first-mover advantages motivate firms to continually invent and market new products because of the profitability which they expect to derive if the product is successful.

READING: Now read section 11.3 in the text, noting all new terms and concepts. Then answer the following questions.

Self-test Questions

229. If a firm is charging the limit price, will it reduce its price as its costs decline due to the learning effect in production? Why or why not?

230. Explain why economies of plant size would cause the firm that is maximizing sales (subject to a profit constraint) to lower its price.

231. Under what demand and cost circumstances would entry of new firms <u>not</u> cause the price level to change, presuming a smooth transition from a profit-maximizing monopolist to a profit-maximizing price leader?

232. What are the implications of the product life cycle for the market demand curve?

233. What happens to the individual firm's demand curve as the product life cycle continues and entry of new firms occurs?

234. Explain the first-mover advantages which accrue to the firm which successfully introduces a new product.

Check your answers against those in the Answer Key, and proceed.

Practice Problems

235. Show graphically the case of the profit-maximizing price leader's adjustment of the price level when its <u>mutatis mutandis</u> demand curve shifts back in a non-isoelastic fashion, and it is subject to diminishing returns in production.

READING: Now read section 11.4, the summary to chapter 11, to refresh your memory of the entire chapter. Then answer the following questions.

Self-test Questions

Write short answers to each of the ten Discussion Questions at the end of chapter 11. When you have finished, check your answers against mine in the Answer Key.

Practice Problems

236. Read problem 11-1, concerning the Eastman Paint Company, at the end of chapter 11, and answer the questions asked. Prices derived from your graphs will be sufficient. Following are a couple of hints, which you may read if you can't get started on the problem.

Hint 1:   Use the inverse demand curves provided to find conventional demand curves and marginal revenue curves.

Hint 2:   Use the AVC figures provided to find TVC figures, then use gradient analysis to find estimates of the marginal costs over each output range.

Check your answers against mine in the Answer Key.

237. Read problem 11-4 (Boxem-Buddies Inc.) and answer the questions asked. Here are some hints if you need them.

Hint 1:   The limit price will be slightly below the minimum point on the entrant's SAC curve. Calculate TC for several Q values, then find SAC at each level, and interpolate between them on a graph to find the minimum SAC value.

Hint 2:   In the second year, increase the intercept term of the market demand curve by ten percent, and multiply its slope by 3/2 to find the intercept and slope term for the price leader's <u>mutatis mutandis</u> demand curve.

Hint 3:   Although you would normally calculate the EPV of the two profit streams, this will be unnecessary here, as will become obvious.

Check your answers against those in the Answer Key, and proceed to the last problem.

238. Read problem 11-7, concerning Hi-Techniks Incorporated, and answer the questions asked. In this problem you have both the demand curve and the cost curves shifting. Answers derived from a careful graphical analysis will suffice when it comes to finding the limit price, but be careful, since this is not as simple as the preceding problem.

When you have finished, check your answers against those in the Answer Key. Problem 11-7 was quite complex, and if you handled it well, you can certainly handle the Quick Quiz on the next page!

QUICK QUIZ - CHAPTER 11

Q1.   Price skimming involves the short-run profit-maximizing price, except when the firm's time horizon falls in _____, and entry barriers are _____, or consumers make _____ (3)

Q2.   For new products that have a very short product life cycle, the appropriate initial price strategy is probably _____ _____, because _____ _____ (2)

Q3.   If entry of new firms is inevitable and differentiation possibilities are limited, _____ is probably the best strategy. (2)

Q4.   The penetration price will be the price that _____ _____ or the price that _____ whichever is _____ (3)

Q5.   Other things being equal, search goods are likely to maximize EPV if a _____ strategy is used, while experience and credence goods will probably do better if a _____ strategy is used. (2)

Q6.   Cost reductions due to _____ in production or _____ will cause the price of a new product to be _____, unless the firm is following a _____ strategy. (4)

Q7.   The _____ and _____ phases of the product life cycle will exert upward pressure on the price level, unless _____ _____ (4)

Q8.   The first-mover advantages are _____ and _____ (2)

Q9.   The rate of learning in production may be higher for the later entrants as compared to those of the initiating firm and early entrants, because _____ _____ (2)

Q10.   The optimal pricing strategy for a new product is the one that _____ (1)

Check your answers against those in the Answer Key.

Score: 23 - 25   19 - 22   16 - 18   13 - 15   12 or less
Grade: A   B   C   D   F

CHAPTER 12:   COMPETITIVE BIDS AND PRICE QUOTES

12.1 INTRODUCTION

Summary

This chapter is concerned with pricing in a special type of
market where for each sale there is a single buyer who calls for
bids or price quotes from several potential suppliers. Topics
include:

1.   The supplier must ascertain the **incremental costs and
     revenues** associated with winning the contract.

2.   The **optimal bid price** is the one that maximizes the
     firm's expected present value of its net worth.

3.   In practice firms use a **markup pricing** policy to arrive
     at their bid price, and this is reconciled with the EPV
     approach.

4.   Bid pricing for **satisficing firms** involves a series of
     decisions that relate to the targets it seeks to meet.

5.   **Optimal purchasing**, from the buyer's viewpoint, gives
     insights about what it takes to win contracts.

Learning Objectives

When you have completed this chapter and the associated questions
and problems, you will be able to:

*   Advise the firm concerning the minimum bid price it
     should ever consider quoting for any job.

*   Calculate the optimal bid price given information
     concerning the expected present value of the bid at
     several possible price levels.

*   Reconcile the EPV approach and the markup approach to
     bid pricing, and explain how the markup rate needs to
     be adjusted to serve EPV maximization.

*   Explain the sequence of decisions involved in the
     satisficing approach to the bid pricing problem.

*   Utilize value analysis to select the optimal bid from
     the purchaser's viewpoint.

12.2   INCREMENTAL COSTS, REVENUES, AND THE OPTIMAL BID PRICE

Overview of the Text, Sections 12.1 and 12.2

In competitive bid markets there is **only one buyer** but **potentially several sellers.** Uncertainty abounds on both the supply side and the demand side of the market - costs are often uncertain due to the nature of the product, and demand is uncertain because the bids of the other suppliers will not be known in advance. Each supplying firm faces a dilemma: if it sets the price too high, it will not win the contract, while if it sets the price too low, it might win the contract but not cover costs.

Competitive bid markets are ubiquitous, although many people just think of defense contracts when they think of competitive bidding. When you ask for a quote to fix your car, or unplug your sink, or to mend your shoe, you are the buyer in a bid market. Virtually any kind of repair business is a competitive bid market. So too are many professional services markets, such as legal services, in which a single buyer seeks a custom-designed service and asks the supplier how much will it cost.

There are **three main types of bids. Fixed price bids** are those where the bid price is contractual and the risk of cost variation from the anticipated level is borne by the supplier. **Cost-plus-fee bids** are those where the buyer agrees to pay whatever it costs to complete the job, such as in repair jobs generally. Here the cost is typically highly uncertain, _a priori_, and the buyer bears the risk of cost variation. **Incentive bids,** or risk-sharing bids, are those where the buyer and seller agree beforehand to share the difference between expected costs and actual costs in a particular proportion.

We first establish the **minimum bid price,** given that the firm would not bid at a price which would cause it to incur a loss. The minimum bid price will be equal to the **incremental costs** of the contract, less any opportunity revenues or future revenues (such as goodwill) which are expected to accrue as a result of winning the contract. These incremental cost and revenue concepts are familiar to you by now, and their application in this context will serve to reinforce your understanding of them. If these costs and revenues are uncertain and/or occur in future periods, we must reduce all cash flows to their expected present value in order to ascertain the minimum bid price in current period dollars.

Having ascertained the minimum-bid price, the firm then considers prices above this level which would allow positive contribution to overheads and profits. At each of these prices, there will be a **success probability** indicating the probability that the firm will be the lowest bidder. The expected value of each bid price will be the contribution at that price multiplied by the success probability. As the bid price is raised, the success probability will fall. As a result of this, the expected value of contribution will rise at first and then fall as the bid price is raised progressively. The firm will choose the bid price which maximizes the expected value of the bid in order to maximize its expected present net worth.

The main consideration underlying the probability of success is the **potential bids of rival firms.** If we have information on the past bidding patterns of rivals, we may be able to form a probability distribution of the rivals' bids. If we have current information indicating, for example, that a particular rival has undesired excess capacity, we should expect that rival to be more likely to submit a lower bid than the historical data would indicate. Thus, on the basis of past bidding successes at various price-cost ratios, and modifying these for extraordinary circumstances which are perceived to exist at the current time, the firm can derive success probabilities for each of several bid price levels.

Risk aversion may induce the firm to trade off some expected value in favor of a greater likelihood of winning the contract. Similarly, if it is self-serving to do so, the decision maker may bid below the bid price which maximizes the EPV of contribution, in order to increase the probability of winning the contract and serve his or her own objective function rather than the firm's. This is the principal-agent problem, noted in chapter 1.

The **risk of cost variation** will be greater in some types of bid markets than in others. Firms often call for tenders for office supplies, for example. The suppliers of these products know what their costs will be with a high degree of certainty, and thus will be willing to tender fixed price bids. Repair services and new construction, on the other hand, involve a high risk of cost variation from the expected level. As the job gets under way, unexpected expenses may crop up, or the job might turn out to be much easier, and hence less expensive, than expected.

When the risk of cost variation is high, firms may wish to **trade off some of the expected contribution** for **reduced risk of cost variation.** Thus they might tender in the cost-plus-fee mode at a considerably lower bid price, and avoid all the risk of cost variation, or tender a risk-sharing bid at a price somewhat below the fixed-price bid which would maximize their EPV of contribution.

READING: Now read sections 12.1 and 12.2 in the text, noting all new terms and concepts. When you are ready, proceed to the following questions.

Self-test Questions

239. Characterize competitive bid markets in terms of the number of buyers and sellers and the degree of uncertainty regarding the firm's cost and demand curves.

240. Outline the types of bids in terms of who bears the risk of uncertainty on the cost side.

241. What is the minimum level below which the firm would ever consider bidding? Why?

242. How do we determine the optimal bid price? Outline the steps involved.

243. What factors might cause a firm to tender a fixed-price bid above or below the bid price which maximizes the expected present value of contribution?

244. Explain the notion that there is a fixed-price bid, a cost-plus-fee bid, and a series of risk-sharing bids among which the risk-averse supplier will be indifferent.

245. If the buyer is also averse to the risk of cost variation, which type of bid will he or she prefer?

After you finish writing out your answers, check them against mine in the Answer Key.

Practice Problem

246. Read problem 12-1, concerning the Billings Printing Company, at the end of chapter 12, and answer the questions asked.

Check your answers against mine in the Answer Key, and proceed.

12.3   COMPETITIVE BIDDING IN PRACTICE

Overview of the Text, Section 12.3

In practice the **search costs** (of ascertaining the probabilities of success, and the various probability distributions of the various cash flows) tend to be high, and in many cases the search costs are expected to outweigh the value of that information to the firm. As in oligopoly markets, we see the firms forego the EPVC approach and adopt a **markup pricing policy.**

For every bid price determined by the EPVC approach, there is an implicit markup over costs which would give the same price. Over time, and given experience in bidding markets, the firm will select a "standard markup" which it applies to its "standard cost base" in order to arrive at its "standard bid price." We should expect the firm to be willing to adjust this standard price up or down to reflect certain factors, such as low capacity utilization of rivals or extraordinary potential for future sales.

The **markup approach and the EPVC approach can be reconciled** and should lead to similar outcomes in terms of maximizing the firm's net worth. As in the oligopoly context of chapter 11, the markup bid price can be "wrong" to the extent of the search costs avoided. Practicing managers who have had considerable experience in bidding markets will know when they should raise or lower their markup rate to reflect unusual circumstances. They may not always win the contract that they are bidding on, of course, but that is the name of the game - you win some and you lose some!

The **satisficing firm** may follow a somewhat more simple bidding decision process by pursuing the attainment of two main targets. These **targets** relate to the firm's **capacity utilization** and its **profitability,** both of which should surpass a minimum-acceptable level. The satisficing firm will be content to attain these two targets because they will be chosen to allow the firm its desired share of the market, a sufficient cash flow, and satisfactory profits.

The **decision sequence** for a satisficing firm considers first whether the firm has the necessary technology and the capacity to do the job, and whether the success probability seems high enough. If the answer to any of these questions is negative, the decision maker considers whether diversification into this area is desirable, and whether it is important to bid to remain on the buyer's "short list" of potential suppliers. If the answers are still negative, the decision maker considers whether the capacity utilization and profitability targets are being achieved. If not, the firm will bid in an effort to meet these targets.

The satisficing firm's capacity-utilization target might be chosen to be 80% of its full capacity, for example. Its usual markup rate would then be chosen to allow its profitability target to be met if the capacity target is met and there were no unexpected variations in cost. If this markup rate is too high, resulting in too few jobs, the firm must consider reducing its profitability target or reducing its costs in one way or another.

READING: Now read section 12.3 in the text, highlighting all new terms and concepts. When you are finished, write short answers to the following questions.

Self-test Questions

247. Explain how the markup approach can incorporate all the same issues as the EPVC approach and lead to a price that may be, in the final analysis, net worth maximizing.

248. Explain why the firm will adjust the standard markup rate if some circumstances surrounding the bid are extraordinary.

249. Outline the decision process for bid price determination for a satisficing firm.

250. Explain the relationship between the satisficing firm's standard costs, target capacity, standard price, and its target profitability.

    After writing out your answers, check them against mine in the Answer Key, and proceed.

Practice Problem

251. Read problem 12-4, concerning Stenson Steel, and answer the questions asked. There are a couple of hints, below, if you find you need them.

Hint 1:   The absolute minimum bid will equal the incremental costs of the job. Decide which cost categories will be incurred if the contract is won, as distinct from those that are already sunk or will be incurred anyway.

Hint 2:   There is no "exact" answer for the bid price. Your price should arise from an examination of the situation as you see it, and should be supported by your reasoning.

    When you have finished, check your answers against those in the Answer Key, and continue.

12.4   THE VIEW FROM THE OTHER SIDE - OPTIMAL PURCHASING

Overview of the Text, Section 12.4

When tendering competitive bids or price quotes, or whenever the firm is trying to sell something, its success probability at any price will be higher if it can discern exactly **what the buyer wants** and provide exactly that package of attributes. That is, the decision maker should ascertain the qualitative aspects of the bid which are of importance to the buyer and tailor the bid accordingly. To do this it is important to know the attributes, apart from the price level, which the buyer considers important in making the purchase decision. If we study the problem from the **purchasing agent's viewpoint** we will gain valuable insight into the bidding problem.

Value analysis is a technique the buyer may use to rank bids in terms of price and qualitative attributes of the bids, such as quality, warranty, and delivery schedule. These attributes are given weights according to how important the buyer feels each one to be. Each bid is given a score on each attribute and the weighted scores are added up to find the bid which offers the "best package" of price and the desired attributes. If the seller can ascertain which attributes are desired by the buyer and what weights are attached to these attributes, the seller is able to tailor its bid to exactly what the buyer wants and thus improve the probability of success at every price level.

Collusive bidding, or the joining of all potential suppliers in a conspiracy regarding the bids they tender, may be expected to occur when contracts are large and infrequent and there are only a few suppliers who can easily keep an eye on each other. The firms might submit identical bids and force the buyer to choose on the basis of some other variable (such as perceived quality). Alternatively, the sellers might take it in turns to submit the lowest bid, and thus share the market in an agreeable way. Collusive bidding is illegal, of course, and if the firm is caught participating in such an agreement it can expect severe fines and even jail sentences for its managers.

Disclosure of bids after the successful tender has been announced may not be in the buyer's interests, since it tends to reduce the dispersion of bid prices on the next contract, causing the minimum bid to be higher than it would otherwise have been.

READING: Now read section 12.4 in the text, noting all new terms and concepts. When you have finished the reading, come back to the following questions.

Self-test Questions

252. Describe value analysis as it might be used to arrive at a purchasing decision. What are the benefits of value analysis from the viewpoint of the purchasing firm?

253. What circumstances encourage and facilitate collusive bidding? In what ways might firms bid collusively?

254. Why do purchasing firms prefer not to disclose the bids received?

Check your answers against those in the Answer Key, and continue.

READING: Now read section 12.5, the summary to chapter 12, to refresh your memory of the material in the entire chapter. When you are finished, answer the following questions.

Self-test Questions

Write short answers to each of the ten Discussion Questions at the end of chapter 12.

When you have finished, check your answers against mine in the Answer Key.

Practice Problems

255. Read problem 12-2, concerning Bright Paints, found at the end of the chapter in the text, and answer the questions asked.

When you have written up your answer, compare it with mine in the Answer Key.

256. Now read problem 12-6, concerning the Canino Construction Company's bid on a bridge contract. If necessary, consult the following hints.

Hint 1: Figure out your rivals' expected bids (with high and low estimates) and bid lower than you expect them to bid.

Hint 2: There is no single correct answer for this question;

rather it is designed to elicit from you an analysis of the issues involved. From what you know about this situation, given the data provided, assign success probabilities to various bid levels, using your judgment of the situation. Make sure you qualify your decision with each of the assumptions you introduce here.

When you have finished writing out your answer, check it against mine in the Answer Key.

257. Finally, read problem 12-7, concerning the Milford Power Station, and answer the questions asked.

When you have finished your answers, check them against mine in the Answer Key.

Are you ready for the Quick Quiz?

QUICK QUIZ - CHAPTER 12

Q1. Competitive bid markets are characterized by a _____
     buyer, several potential _____, and _____
     regarding costs and demand.   (3)

Q2. Fixed-price bids assign all _____
     to the seller, whereas cost-plus-fee bids assign it all to
     the buyer.   (2)

Q3. The price paid for the job, after it is completed, under a
     risk-sharing agreement would be equal to _____
     _____ plus or minus the _____
     share of the _____ or _____
                                                                (4)

Q4. Bid preparation costs are not considered an incremental cost
     in the bid pricing decision because _____
     _____
                                                                (2)

Q5. Incremental costs and revenues can be considered in three
     categories, namely _____,
     _____, and _____   (3)

Q6. The expected present value of contribution of a bid price is
     the product of _____
     and the _____(2)

Q7. The certainty equivalent of the fixed-price bid is the
     _____ bid that gives the seller the same
     _____
                                                                (2)

Q8. If the firm knows that its rivals are operating beyond full
     capacity it may decide to _____the markup over its
     standard   costs,   because   it   expects   these   rivals   to
     _____
                                                                (2)

Q9. The satisficing firm will not bid on a contract if _____
     _____
     _____(3)

Q10. Value analysis of the purchasing problem serves to make
     explicit the _____ underlying
     purchasing decisions, and to allow such decisions to be
     subject to _____ by peers and
     superiors.   (2)

Check your answers against those in the Answer Key.

Score: 23 - 25   19 - 22   16 - 18   13 - 15   12 or less
Grade: A   B   C   D   F

CHAPTER 13:   ADVERTISING AND PROMOTIONAL DECISIONS

13.1   INTRODUCTION

Summary

This chapter examines the use of advertising and promotional activity as part of the firm's strategy to meet its profit objectives. Topics include:

1. The **advertising-sales relationship**, which shows how the demand curve shifts in response to changes in advertising. Knowing this, we can find the **optimal amount of advertising**, given a particular price.

2. The **simultaneous adjustment of advertising and price** to find the optimal demand curve and the optimal price on that curve.

3. The **interdependence of advertising** activities for the firms in an oligopoly leads to a problem called the **Prisoner's Dilemma**.

4. The **impact of advertising is always uncertain**. Big budgets can have low impact, and vice versa. Effective advertising is a matter of both art and science.

5. Advertising should be **treated as an investment** in current and future sales, due to its cumulative impacts and its ability to **raise barriers to entry**.

Learning Objectives

When you have finished this chapter, and the associated exercises, you will be able to:

* Explain the rules for optimal advertising expenditures in terms of advertising's marginal impact on sales.

* Demonstrate that increased advertising shifts the demand curve outward and allows the firm to raise price as well, up to a point.

* Discuss the mutual interdependence of advertisers, and the impact another firm's advertising can have on the firm's demand curve and profits.

* Explain why advertising can be regarded as an investment in future sales and profitability.

13.1   OPTIMAL ADVERTISING EXPENDITURES, WITH <u>CETERIS PARIBUS</u>

<u>Overview of the Text, Sections 13.1 and 13.2</u>

Price competition is worrisome and potentially damaging to many firms, and as a result they tend to compete more in other areas, known as **non-price competition.** Vigorous price competition may escalate to price wars, firms facing kinked demand curves find it hard to raise prices again after they reduce them, and price cuts do not work as well for experience and credence products, since the demand for these goods tends to be less elastic.

In this chapter the term **advertising** is used to represent all attempts to **shift the demand curve** by promotional efforts. The impact of advertising on the demand curve may be large at first and then become smaller at higher advertising levels due to **diminishing returns to advertising.** The existence of diminishing returns to advertising will be captured by the **sales-advertising function,** which plots advertising against sales volume, <u>ceteris paribus</u>. This function may be linear over the relevant range, but diminishing returns mean that it is more likely a quadratic, power, or cubic function over a wider range, and that diminishing returns may be evident within the relevant range.

If prices are held constant, advertising should be taken to the point where the last dollar spent on advertising generates only one dollar in contribution toward overhead (which includes advertising expense) and profit. Thus, if the contribution margin is, for example, $0.33, the last dollar spent on advertising must increase sales by at least 3 units to be worthwhile. That is, the **rule for optimal advertising,** given price and all other things constant, is that the rate of change of sales volume with respect to advertising, dQ/dA, should be equal to the reciprocal of the contribution margin, $1/(P - AVC)$.

When **prices and advertising can be adjusted simultaneously,** the demand curve shifts outward and a higher price becomes profit maximizing. But how far should advertising and price increases be taken? You should by now expect the optimal condition to involve a **marginal equality,** and it does. The advertising expense should be taken to the point where the marginal revenue (due to both the shift of the demand curve and the increase in the price level) is just equal to the marginal cost (due to both the change in advertising expense and the change in production cost arising from the extra units produced). A graphical model, which culminates in this rule, is developed in the text.

READING: Now read sections 13.1 and 13.2 in the text, noting all new terms and concepts. Then answer the following questions.

Self-test Questions

258. The major advertisers of consumer goods tend to be the sellers of soft drinks, fast food, beer, and pet food. Why?

259. If there are diminishing returns to advertising, what forms might the advertising-sales function take?

260. Explain the rule for the optimal level of advertising, supposing that price is restrained by market conditions.

261. Explain in words how the firm should adjust both advertising and price to maximize its profits.

When you have finished, check your answers against those in the Answer Key, and proceed.

Practice Problems

262. Suppose that the sales-advertising function has been estimated to be $Q = 42,400 + 10 A - 0.5 A^2$, where A represents thousands of dollars monthly. Given that the product's price and AVC are constant at $18 and $12, respectively, what is the optimal level of the advertising budget?

263. Use graphs to demonstrate the solution of the joint advertising and price adjustment problem.

(a) On one graph, show the derivation of the LASC and LOP curves.

(b) On a second graph, show the curves that are marginal to each of these curves, and the optimal price and advertising level that are implied by their intersection.

(c) Finally, on a third graph, add the marginal costs of production into your analysis.

Check your answers against those in the Answer Key, and proceed to the next section.

13.3   ADVERTISING WHEN MUTUAL DEPENDENCE IS RECOGNIZED

Overview of the Text, Section 13.3

When firms **recognize their mutual dependence** in the non-price arena, they will know that their advertising will have adverse impacts on the sales of their rivals, and that their own sales will suffer if a rival launches a new advertising campaign. Accordingly, firms will monitor their rivals' advertising efforts and attempt to at least offset those efforts with advertising efforts of their own.

But **advertising campaigns require a significant lead time.** Unlike price competition, which can erupt at a moment's notice, non-price competition requires prior planning, creative work, coordination with media availability and publication dates, and so on. Thus, the firm cannot respond immediately to a new advertising campaign by a rival, and might lose a significant share of its market before it can respond. To be sure, hurried responses can be made within a week or so, as did PepsiCo when Coca Cola announced their new Coke in 1985, but successful campaigns that result in a significant gain of market share, or that successfully counter another firm's campaign, typically require creative genius, detailed art and photography, and market testing before they are launched onto the market.

Thus firms that advertise tend to have an ongoing involvement with advertising, with **new campaigns** always in the pipeline. But advertising expense does not always translate into **advertising effectiveness.** Sometimes an advertising dollar goes a long way, other times it has little impact. Thus firms have successful campaigns and less-successful campaigns, depending on the advertisement itself, its timing, and the simultaneous efforts of rivals. In the soft drink, beer, and fast food markets we continually see the pendulum swinging as first one firm, then another, strikes gold with an advertising campaign. At the same time we see shortlived rival campaigns being suspended because they had minimal impact on sales.

Advertisers often get caught in what has been called a **prisoner's dilemma.** This is a situation in which parties making independent decisions are motivated to act in a way that leads to a sub-optimal outcome. In this case, all participants might earn more profits if they simultaneously reduced advertising efforts to a lower level. But fearing that a rival might secretly revert to the higher level of advertising and gain an advantage that might not be recouped, the rivals choose the **maximin strategy** and spend more on advertising than is efficient.

Advertisers could enter into an **agreement to limit advertising competition,** and thus jointly increase profits, but are unlikely to, for several reasons. First, it constitutes an illegal conspiracy in restraint of trade, subject to punishment under the provisions of the Sherman Act. Second, the long lead times involved in successful campaigns leave the firm vulnerable to any firm that reneges on the agreement and increases their advertising efforts. Third, advertising is often seen as an honorable and appropriate forum for competitive effort, where market shares are gained by hard work and creative genius, unlike price competition where the stroke of a madman's pen could precipitate a price war!

READING: Now read section 13.3 in the text. Then answer the following questions.

Self-test Questions

264. Why can a new advertising campaign "get the jump on" rivals and lead to significant gains in market share?

265. Explain the prisoner's dilemma, in which advertisers may find themselves.

266. Why don't firms coordinate their advertising expenditures?

Practice Problem

267. Suppose Big Blue Company and Little Red Company compete in the personal computer market. Given Big Blue's current price and advertising levels, Little Red expects to make $5m in profits with $1m in advertising, or would make $8m profits with $2m advertising. But if Little Red increases its advertising to $2m, it expects that Big Blue will also increase its advertising by another million, or Big Blue may do that anyway. If so, Little Red's profits would be only $3m and $4m, at advertising levels of $1m and $2m, respectively .

(a) Set this up as a payoff matrix showing the profits for Little Red, given the four combinations of the advertising levels.

(b) Explain which strategy is the maximin strategy for Little Red.

(c) What do you advise Little Red to do?

When you have finished your answers, check them against mine in the Answer Key, and continue.

13.4   UNCERTAINTY IN ADVERTISING

Overview of the Text, Section 13.4

Simply spending money on advertising does not mean that the demand curve will shift outward and the firm will make more profits. It is the **effectiveness** of each dollar spent that counts, and this may be increased by careful analysis and planning, creative and entertaining promotional material, not to mention the appropriate choice of media, timing, and target audience.

The **predictability** of advertising's impact can be increased by testing the message content and other aspects of the promotional material on focus groups and in regional markets. Studies can be undertaken to find whether or not a product sells more when advertised in conjunction with a particular TV program, or in wet weather, or on weekends, and so on. Target consumers should be identified and the media, message, and timing should be chosen to gain maximum impact on those target consumers.

Rather than treat advertising as a current period expense, many would argue that advertising has an impact on sales in future periods as well, and is like any other **investment** that gives rise to a stream of earnings in the present and future periods. Persuasive advertising tends to be cumulative, perhaps not inducing a purchase until some time in the future. Similarly, informative advertising may not be acted upon by a consumer until later when the need to purchase the item arises.

Advertising that builds the product's brand name awareness, and informs consumers about the service network and other features of the company, **may raise the barriers to entry** facing potential entrants, since they would have to spend substantial amounts on advertising themselves just to offset the accumulated information and preference that consumers may have attached to existing brands.

READING: Now read sections 13.4 and 13.5 (the chapter summary) in the text. Then answer the following questions.

Self-test Questions

Answer the ten Discussion Questions at the end of chapter 13.

Check your answers against those in the Answer Key, and proceed to the following practice problems.

Practice Problems

268. Read problem 13-1, concerning the Thompson Textile Company, and answer the questions asked. Some hints are available below, if you need them.

Hint 1: The formula for advertising elasticity includes the dQ/dA term. You can solve for it given the data provided.

Hint 2: The advertising elasticity refers to a point on the sales-advertising curve, hence the dQ/dA term is its slope at that point. Whether the slope is constant, increasing, or decreasing, we cannot say.

Check your answers against those in the Answer Key, and continue.

269. Read problem 13-4 (Record Breakers), and answer the questions asked. There are some hints below, if you need them.

Hint 1: Condense the demand function into an expression for the demand curve, using the average value of S = 2.5, and find the profit-maximizing price, output, and profit levels.

Hint 2: Repeat this exercise for other values of S to see if profit rises or falls, until you zero in on the profit-maximizing levels.

Hint 3: Use the other regression equation provided to find the number of records to be put on sale each week. Round this to a whole number.

Check you answers against mine in the Answer Key, and continue.

270. Read problem 13-8, concerning Concord Microwave Systems, and answer the questions asked.

When you have finished, check your answers against mine in the Answer Key.

Now try the Quick Quiz on the next page.

QUICK QUIZ - CHAPTER 13

Q1. Advertising for experience and credence goods may be more effective than price competition because _____
     _____ (2)

Q2. We should expect diminishing returns to advertising because _____
     _____ (2)

Q3. If there are diminishing returns to advertising, increases in advertising shift the demand curve _____ at a _____ rate.   (2)

Q4. In the fixed price case, advertising should be increased until the rate of change of _____ with respect to _____ is equal to the _____
     _____ (3)

Q5. When both price and advertising can be adjusted, advertising should be increased until the _____
     _____ is equal to _____
     _____ (4)

Q6. In the prisoner's dilemma situation, the firms' profits fall when they both increase advertising, because _____
     _____
     _____ (3)

Q7. Firms are unlikely to coordinate their advertising efforts because _____, _____
     _____, and _____
     _____ (3)

Q8. Market testing of promotional material should be expected to reduce the _____ (2)

Q9. Advertising may be regarded as an investment rather than a present period expense because _____
     _____ (2)

Q10. Advertising may raise the barriers to entry by _____
     _____
     _____ (2)

Check your answers against those in the Answer Key.

Score: 22 - 25   18 - 21   15 - 17   13 - 14   12 or less
Grade: A   B   C   D   F

CHAPTER 14:   PRODUCT QUALITY AND COMPETITIVE STRATEGY

14.1   INTRODUCTION

Summary

This chapter is concerned with the firm's decisions about product design, or quality, and the wider issues of competitive strategy. Topics to be discussed include:

1. There are three **generic competitive strategies**, namely the cost-leadership, differentiation, and focus strategies.

2. Product design considerations for the **cost leadership strategy** imply that **search products** may be best suited for this strategy.

3. The quality decision for the firm pursuing a **differentiation strategy** will lean towards experience and credence products.

4. The **joint determination of quality, price, and promotional strategies** will depend on the firm's chosen generic strategy and the nature of its product.

5. **Focus strategies** are of either the cost-leadership or differentiation type, and are **focused on a niche**, or market segment, within the broader market.

Learning Objectives

When you finish this chapter you will be able to :

*   Explain why search goods are more suitable for cost leadership strategies, while experience and credence goods are more suitable for differentiation strategies.

*   Outline the types of product the firm should develop under each type of competitive strategy.

*   Explain why firms following the differentiation strategy spend higher proportions of their sales revenue on advertising than do cost leaders.

*   Explain why informative advertising and price competition are relied on for search goods while persuasive advertising is predominant for experience and credence goods.

14.2   PRODUCT DESIGN FOR A COST LEADERSHIP STRATEGY

Overview of the Text, Sections 14.1 and 14.2

We are concerned with the joint determination of product quality, price, and promotional efforts. The firm will design its product, and set pricing and advertising policy, according to the **competitive strategy** it chooses to follow. There are three generic strategy types. **Cost leadership** is a strategy whereby the firm attempts to be the lowest-cost producer in the market, and as a result obtain superior profitability.

Differentiation is a strategy whereby the firm attempts to differentiate its products so that they more closely suit buyers' preferences. We can think of this as **quality leadership**, since the firm tries to incorporate the quality attributes that buyers will find more desirable. Following this strategy the firm expects to incur higher costs, but hopes to raise price by a greater proportion such that it achieves superior profitability.

Focus strategies involve the identification of a target market, or niche, and focusing the firm's attentions on that particular segment of the market. A **cost-focus** strategy involves attempting to serve the target market at lowest cost, while a **quality-focus** strategy involves serving the target market with the best product they are willing to pay for.

The firm will pursue a cost leadership strategy if that role is vacant or can be wrestled from an existing firm, and if its products lend themselves to this strategy. We argue that search goods are ideally suited to a cost leadership strategy.

Search goods are products comprised primarily of search attributes, meaning quality characteristics that consumers can evaluate and verify prior to purchase. Examples are stereo and video equipment, the quality of which can be seen, heard, and read (the specifications) before buying. It is difficult to differentiate search products, since any superior features are quickly copied by rivals. Consequently, search goods tend to have relatively high price elasticities, since consumers know what they are getting for the money and jump at the chance to buy the product when its price is reduced. Since price elasticities are relatively high, markups are relatively low, and it is necessary to keep costs as low as possible in order to make superior profitability. Thus, given a search product, the cost leadership strategy is probably the best strategy.

But given a cost leadership strategy, is a search product the best type of product to produce? In order to attain cost leadership the firm would like to benefit from long production runs of a single product, rather than shorter production runs of several variants of the product. It would achieve cost savings from learning in production and from economies of plant size. To expand the market to achieve these cost savings it would need elastic demand responses to lower prices. Search goods would allow the firm to pursue a cost leadership strategy much more effectively than would experience or credence goods, which tend to be more highly differentiated and face a less elastic demand.

The cost leader's products should **cover the bases**, meaning they should have all the features considered necessary to compete in the market. Next, they should **trim the fat**, meaning there should be no superfluous features that add to cost without allowing cost to be raised at least as much. Finally, the cost leader may **product proliferate** by developing several brand names of what is essentially the same product. Doing so will increase total sales, because search goods tend to be symmetrically differentiated and buyers will tend to spread equally across brands.

The **pricing strategy** to complement cost leadership would include promotional pricing and price leadership. **Promotional pricing** would allow the firm to sell larger volumes and benefit from learning effects, pecuniary economies, and economies of plant size. **Price leadership**, as in the low-cost firm price leadership model, would allow the firm to choose the price that maximizes its profits or otherwise best serves its objectives.

The **advertising strategy** to complement cost leadership would be to stress the low prices and the quality features of its products. This is primarily **informative advertising**. One would not expect the advertising elasticity to be very high, since there is little scope for persuasive advertising with search goods, and informative advertising may simply be telling consumers what they already know, and, in any case, could confirm prior to purchase.

READING: Now read sections 14.1 and 14.2 in the text, noting all new terms and concepts. When you have finished, answer the following questions.

Self-test Questions

271. What is meant by the term "competitive advantage"?

272. Why is the cost leadership strategy likely to be the best strategy for search products?

273. Why will price elasticity tend to be relatively high for search goods?

274. What are the implications of the cost leadership strategy for product design?

275. What are the pricing and advertising strategies that would best complement the cost leadership strategy?

When you have finished, compare your answers with those in the Answer Key.

14.3 PRODUCT DESIGN FOR A DIFFERENTIATION STRATEGY

Overview of the Text, Section 14.3

The differentiation strategy may be called **quality leadership**, since the firm attempts to offer the buyers the best quality for the price. Buyers will usually pay more for a product that more-closely fits their needs or desires, but higher quality costs more to produce. Thus the quality leader attempts to better serve the buyer's needs, while raising the price by more than its cost per unit has increased.

If the firm produces **experience** and/or **credence goods**, it will find that a quality leadership strategy is probably more effective, although it could adopt the cost leadership role if it were vacant and there were no differentiation opportunities open. Following a differentiation strategy, experience and credence goods allow more latitude for quality claims, since these cannot be verified until after purchase (experience goods), or can then be only partially verified (credence goods). Thus a firm can ask a higher price and get it, at least the first time. If the quality claims are false, the buyer will not come back for a repeat purchase, but this will not worry the firm with a short planning period, or where repeat purchase is not a factor.

The product's **brand name** can be regarded as a stock of information pertaining to product quality. Consumers transfer this perception of quality to any new products the firm might market. Brand name items typically command a price premium, which can be regarded as an insurance premium paid to assure the buyer of higher quality. From the seller's viewpoint, the brand name is a forfeitable bond that will erode if the product's quality does not live up to the buyers' expectations. (Brand names are not very important with search goods, where quality can be verified before purchase in any case).

The implications of a differentiation strategy for a firm's product design are as follows. The firm will tend to offer a broad **product line** of different products, each catering to particular tastes and preferences. The firm will tend to sell its products in **bundles** as well as separately. The products will need to incorporate the latest **technical innovations** and improvements. Finally, development of a brand name advantage requires **consistent quality**, so strict quality control is imperative.

The **pricing implications** for the differentiation strategy do not include vigorous price competition or promotional pricing because the price elasticity will tend to be relatively low. Rather the firm will be a price follower, practicing product line pricing, bundle pricing, and profit-maximization on any new products it discovers. The differentiating firm's motto may be characterized as SOQNOP, meaning "sell on quality, not on price."

The **advertising implications** are much stronger. The differentiating firm will tend to utilize mostly **persuasive advertising**, with informative advertising being confined to unique features of the product. The advertising elasticity of demand is likely to be relatively high, since quality claims are not verifiable <u>a priori</u>. In fact, the firm following a differentiation strategy with experience and credence goods will tend to spend a substantially higher proportion of its sales revenue on advertising, as compared to a cost leader advertising search products.

READING: Now read section 14.3 in the text, carefully noting all new terms and concepts. When you have finished, write short answers to the following questions.

Self-test Questions

276. Could a firm follow a differentiation strategy on the basis of search attributes in its product? Why? For how long?

277. What's in a brand name? Why is consistency of product quality important to the building of brand name awareness?

278. What does the differentiation strategy imply for the firm's product design?

279. What pricing policies would best complement a different-iation strategy utilizing experience and credence goods?

280. What advertising strategy best complements the quality leadership strategy? What is the "elasticities rule"?

Check your answers against mine in the Answer Key, and continue to the next section.

14.4   PRODUCT DESIGN FOR A FOCUS STRATEGY

Overview of the Text, Section 14.4

The **focus strategies** are simply the cost leadership and the differentiation strategies applied to a **market segment**, rather than to the market as a whole. The firm identifies its target market for each product, and then attempts to be either a cost leader, or a quality leader, with that product in that market segment (or niche).

The **cost-focus** strategy involves providing a product to target buyers at lowest cost, such that the firm achieves superior profitability. Small orders for printing provides a good example of a market segment where small firms can prosper by a cost-focus strategy. Larger firms, with larger overheads, are preoccupied with large orders, and typically have higher costs for small orders than do the smaller firms. Thus a small firm might quote a lower price but still make a good profit on small orders.

The **quality-focus** strategy involves offering a better product and better service to those segments of the market that appreciate and are willing to pay for higher quality. Custom-made clothing, custom-built houses, specialty automobiles, high quality business education, and so on, are examples of quality-focus strategies in the real world.

A focus strategy, rather than a broad-based strategy, is indicated for **new firms entering a market**. Rather than a frontal attack on existing firms, the entrant can confine its attack to a particular flank, and gain a foothold for later advancement.

The **pricing and advertising implications** for focus strategies are similar to those for the broad-based strategies of each type. Cost-focus firms will use promotional pricing and tend to be the price leader in their target market, and will use informative advertising that stresses price and quality features. Quality-focus firms will use product line pricing, bundle pricing, and will be price followers rather than leaders. Their advertising will be primarily persuasive, and they will spend relatively large fractions of sales revenues on advertising, since advertising elasticity will tend to be relatively high while price elasticity will tend to be relatively low.

READING: Now read sections 14.4 and 14.5 (the summary to chapter 14) and consolidate your understanding of competitive strategy. Then answer the following questions.

Self-test Questions

Write short answers to each of the ten Discussion Questions at the end of chapter 14.

When you are finished, check your answers against those in the Answer Key, and proceed to the problems.

Practice Problems

281. Read problem 14-1, concerning Dixieland Ice Cream, and answer the questions asked. There are a couple of hints below, if you need them.

Hint 1: Consider the four different competitive strategies (including two focus strategies) in turn, and evaluate Dixieland's chances of successfully pursuing each strategy.

Hint 2: It does not seem they will make much progress until they get better equipment. This should be purchased to suit their new strategy.

Check your answers against mine in the Answer Key, and continue.

282. Read problem 14-3, concerning Richard Koster Legal Associates, and answer the questions asked.

Check your answers against mine in the Answer Key, and continue.

283. Read problem 14-6, concerning Main Street Plumbing and Heating, and answer the questions asked.

I'm sure you're getting the hang of this by now. Check your answers against those in the Answer Key. Then try one more.

284. Read problem 14-9, concerning Whaleback Mountain Ski Resort, and answer the questions asked.

Check your answers against those in the Answer Key. Then proceed to the Quick Quiz.

QUICK QUIZ - CHAPTER 14

Q1.   Competitive advantage, in Porter's lexicon, means _____
_____ (1)

Q2.   A firm would adopt a differentiation strategy in a market
for search products if _____
or if _____ (2)

Q3.   The cost leader will seek cost reductions through several
sources, including _____
_____ (4)

Q4.   Price elasticity will be relatively high for search goods
because rivals _____
and consumers _____ (2)

Q5.   If the firm is a cost leader it will want to develop
products that _____, _____,
and _____. (3)

Q6.   The pricing policy of a cost leader will include _____
_____ and _____. Advertising
will stress _____ (3)

Q7.   Differentiation on the basis of search attributes is likely
to be _____, but differentiation on the
basis of experience and credence attributes is _____
_____ (2)

Q8.   Brand name advantage means that price _____
_____, and that the quality of new products will
_____ (2)

Q9.   The differentiating firm's advertising will be primarily
_____ in nature, stressing _____ not
_____. The advertising budget will be a relatively
_____ proportion of total sales revenue.   (4)

Q10. A quality-focus strategy means that the firm _____
_____
_____
_____ (2)

Check your answers against those in the Answer Key.

Score: 23 - 25   19 - 22   15 - 18   13 - 14   12 or less
Grade: A   B   C   D   F

CHAPTER 15:   CAPITAL BUDGETING AND INVESTMENT DECISIONS

15.1   INTRODUCTION

Summary

This chapter examines the firm's decision whether or not to invest funds in investment projects, and how to choose between mutually exclusive projects. Such projects involve either cost reduction, revenue generation, or a combination of these. Such decisions were first examined in chapter 1, and we return to this topic to clarify and extend some of the issues. Issues include:

1.   With **unlimited availability of funds**, the firm might apply any one of the **net present value, internal rate of return, or the profitability index** criteria, to make its choice.

2.   Simple investment decision criteria, like the **payback period** and the **average rate of return criteria**, may be seriously deficient guides for the firm wishing to maximize the NPV of its net worth.

3.   **Depreciation** is tax deductible and therefore generates a stream of **opportunity revenues** that must be incorporated into the analysis. **Accelerated depreciation methods** increase the NPV of projects compared to straight line depreciation.

4.   For **mutually exclusive investments** the NPV criterion is superior to all others for a firm wishing to maximize the NPV of its net worth.

Learning Objectives

When you finish this chapter you will be able to:

*   Explain why the NPV criterion, the Internal rate of return, and the Profitability index criteria, are equivalent for the case of unlimited availability of capital.

*   Explain why the NPV criterion is superior to all others for the case of mutually exclusive investments to maximize the net present value of net worth.

*   Explain why depreciation and other tax deductible expenses, as well as tax credits, must be included as opportunity revenues in capital budgeting analysis.

15.2   CAPITAL BUDGETING WITH UNLIMITED AVAILABILITY OF FUNDS

Overview of the Text, Section 15.2

Net present value analysis must proceed on the basis of **net cash flow after taxes**, or NCFAT, because investment projects typically have tax consequences. Investment expenditures that involve the purchase of a depreciable asset can be charged against revenues over several years. This **depreciation expense** is tax deductible, and thus reduces tax payments in the present and subsequent years. If **accelerated methods** of depreciation are allowable, more of the depreciation expenses is deducted in earlier years, and this increases the net present value of the **opportunity revenue stream** that depreciation expense represents.

Although we simply speak of NPV analysis in this chapter, the analysis extends easily to **expected present value** (EPV) analysis, as we saw in chapter 1. We abstract from uncertainty in this chapter in order to focus on the new issues introduced.

The **internal rate of return (IRR) criterion** ranks the investment projects on the basis of the rate of discount that would reduce the present value of the revenue stream to equality with the initial cost of the project. The decision maker would then compare each project's IRR with the firm's **cost of capital**, and implement those projects with IRR greater than the cost of capital. If the NPV is positive at the opportunity discount rate, then the IRR exceeds the opportunity discount rate, and thus the NPV and the IRR criteria agree that the project should be implemented.

The **profitability index**, also known as the benefit-cost ratio, evaluates each project in terms of the ratio of the present value of the revenue stream to the initial cost outflow. It measures the relative efficiency of each project in generating present valued revenues per dollar of cost outlay. When funds are unlimited, the decision maker would implement every project that had a profitability index (PI) greater than one. This corresponds to an NPV greater than zero, so the NPV and the PI criteria are in accord.

The **payback period** criterion ranks the projects in ascending order of the time it takes to recoup the initial costs. In crude form this criterion uses nominal cash flows, but it is easily modified to incorporate the present value of the cash flows. But this ignores the cash flows that may continue to arrive after the payback period and before the end of the firm's planning period. Thus, using the payback criterion will not maximize the firm's NPV of net worth, except under limited circumstances.

The **average rate of return** criterion ranks projects in order of the ratio of the average annual revenue streams to the initial cost. Using undiscounted cashflows this criterion is inferior to the ones discussed above. If cashflows are discounted it is equal to the profitability index divided by the number of years, so adds little to the analysis. **Accounting return on investment** (AROI) is even more unsatisfactory, since it also suffers from the deficiencies (for decision making) of financial accounting data.

READING: Now read section 15.2 in the text, carefully noting all new terms and concepts. When you have finished, answer the following questions.

Self-test Questions

285. Why should depreciation charges be included as if they are revenues in the net present value analysis of an investment decision?

286. Explain the difference between the straight-line, sum-of-the-year's-digits, and the double-declining-balance methods of depreciation.

287. What is the impact on the net present value of using an accelerated depreciation method? Why?

288. Explain the relationship between the NPV and the IRR.

289. Explain the relationship between the profitability index and the NPV criteria.

290. Define the payback period criterion, and explain why it may not best serve the firm's objectives.

291. What is the average rate of return criteria, and what is wrong with it?

Now check your answers against those in the Answer Key, and proceed to the following problem.

Practice Problem

292. Read problem 15-1, concerning the Omega Investment Corporation, and answer the questions asked.

Check your answers, and continue.

15.3   MUTUALLY EXCLUSIVE INVESTMENTS

Overview of the Text, Section 15.3

In this section we consider investment projects that are
alternative ways of solving the same problem, such as Plant A
versus Plant B decisions, or alternative uses of the same funds,
when funds are limited.

When investment alternatives are mutually exclusive, a
conflict may arise among the NPV, IRR, and PI criteria. The
latter two may indicate acceptance of a project which would not
raise the firm's expected present value of net worth by as much
as the project indicated by the NPV criterion. Thus, if the
firm's objective is the maximization of its net worth, the NPV
(or EPV) criterion is the best rule. Risk considerations may
cause a trade-off between NPV and reduced risk, as we saw in
chapter 2, of course.

The **IRR criterion may be inferior** to the NPV criterion
because the NPV curves (plotting NPV against the discount rate)
of alternative projects may cross. If so, there is a critical
discount rate at which both projects have equal NPV, but at
higher discount rates one project is preferred while at lower
discount rates the other is preferred. Since the IRR is the
(relatively high) discount rate at which the NPV is zero, it may
disagree with the NPV criterion if the opportunity discount rate
(ODR) is relatively low. Essentially the conflict arises because
the IRR method assumes that the cash inflows can be re-invested
at the internal rate of return, whereas the NPV method assumes,
properly, that the funds are re-invested at the ODR.

The **PI criterion may be inferior** to the NPV criterion
because the PI measures simply the **relative efficiency** of each
project in generating revenues. That is, the PI is the ratio of
revenues generated per dollar of outlay. Smaller initial outlays
may generate more revenues per dollar of outlay, but larger
projects may generate more revenue in total. This "size
disparity" problem means the PI criterion is unreliable for
ranking mutually-exclusive investments when the firm's objective
is to maximize its net worth in NPV or EPV terms.

When the firm or the decision maker is **risk averse**, and this
decision is not simply one of many (where they can afford to act
as if they are risk neutral), the EPV must be adjusted for risk,
as we saw in chapter 2. To reiterate, the firm might use the
coefficient of variation criterion, or the EPV-with-different-
ODR's criterion, or the certainty equivalent criterion, or the
maximin criterion, to find the preferred investment alternative.

READING: Now read section 15.3 in the text, carefully noting all the finer points made. When you have finished, write answers to the following questions.

Self-test Questions

293. Explain why there is a potential crossover of the NPV curves of two alternative investment projects.

294. Could this crossover occur and yet the NPV and IRR criteria still agree which was the preferred investment alternative? Explain.

295. What is the "size disparity problem" that might cause the NPV and the PI criteria to disagree on the ranking of mutually exclusive projects?

296. Given uncertainty, the decision maker may wish to adjust the decision for risk. List the ways this might be accomplished.

297. Considering the criteria that adjust for risk, outline the advantages and disadvantages of each criteria. (The question will require recall from material in chapter 2. If you are having trouble with it, go back to chapter 2 and skim through that material again.)

When you are finished, check your answers against mine in the Answer Key, and continue.

READING: Now read section 15.4, the summary of chapter 15, to refresh your memory of the entire chapter, and then answer the following questions.

Self-test Questions

Write short answers to each of the ten Discussion Questions at the end of Chapter 15.

When you have finished, check your answers against those in the Answer Key, and proceed to the practice problems.

Practice Problems

298. Read problem 15-4, concerning Marilyn Monibaggs, and answer the questions asked.

Check your answers against mine in the Answer Key, and proceed to the next problem.

299. Read problem 15-8, concerning Dimmock Dry Dock Services, and answer the questions asked.

When you have finished, compare your answers with those in the Answer Key, and continue to the next problem. (You didn't think I could stop at number 299, did you?)

300. Read problem 15-10, concerning the Hilltop Raceway Corporation, and answer the questions asked.

Check your answers against mine in the Answer Key.

Now, go to the Quick Quiz on the next page and give it your best shot!

QUICK QUIZ - CHAPTER 15

Q1. The NPV and the PI rankings of projects agree, when funds are unlimited, because while one of these is the _____ of two magnitudes, the other is the _____ of the same two magnitudes. (2)

Q2. The NPV and the IRR criteria agree, when funds are unlimited, because if the _____ exceeds the _____ the NPV is positive. (2)

Q3. Part of depreciation expense is included in NPV analysis as a(n) _____ because _____ _____ (2)

Q4. The internal rate of return is the rate _____ _____ (2)

Q5. The firm's cost of capital is likely to rise with the amount of borrowing because _____ _____ (1)

Q6. The payback period criterion is not likely to best serve the objective of net worth maximization over the firm's planning period because _____ _____ (2)

Q7. The payback period criterion and the NPV criterion would rank projects the same if _____ and if _____ (2)

Q8. The NPV and IRR criteria may indicate different preferred investments due the latter's assumption that the funds received can be _____ _____ (2)

Q9. The profitability index measures the _____ of each alternative in generating revenues per _____ _____ , but may rank mutually exclusive projects differently due to the _____ problem. (3)

Q10. The NPV and EPV criteria assume risk _____ on the part of the investor, or that the investor makes many such decisions and can act as if he/she is risk _____ (2)

Check your answers against those in the Answer Key.

Score:	18 - 20	15 - 17	12 - 14	10 - 11	9 or less
Grade:	A	B	C	D	F

ANSWERS TO QUESTIONS 1 THROUGH 300

Warning: Looking at these answers before you stop to write down your own formulation of the answers will seriously diminish the learning impact of this exercise.

Note: These answers may not be exhaustive or completely accurate in particular cases. Your comments and corrections are welcomed. Write to me at Bentley College, Waltham, MA. 02254.

1.   Managerial economics deals with the application of economic principles and methodologies to the decision-making process of the firm operating under conditions of risk and uncertainty.

2.   Positive economics is descriptive, describing what is, whereas normative economics is prescriptive, prescribing what should be in order to achieve some goal or objective.

3.   There are scale models, analogue models, and symbolic models. Symbolic models comprise verbal models (descriptive speech), diagrammatic models, and mathematical models.

4.   Pedagogical and predictive models should not strive to be realistic at the expense of their purpose. An explanatory model, on the other hand, must be sufficiently realistic since its purpose is to explain what happens within a complex system.

5.   Jargon is a set of verbal models or definitional terms with special meanings. Economists uses jargon to facilitate communication because jargon is both more precise and more concise than regular speech.

6.   Future value is the present value plus the compound interest that can be earned on that present value. $FV = PV(1+r)^t$ where FV is future value, PV is present value, r is the opportunity rate of interest per period, and t is the number of periods between the present and the future period.

7.   A sum of money held today would earn compound interest at the opportunity rate and build to a future value equal to $PV(1+r)^t$. The present value of that future value is found by discounting that future value at the opportunity rate.

8.   The appropriate discount rate is the opportunity discount rate, which is the best alternative rate of interest or return that can be obtained, given the same amount of risk.

9. Daily cash flow discount factors should be used when the actual cash flow pattern is better approximated by a daily stream than it is by the lump-sum-at-yearly-intervals presumption of the year-end discount factors.

10. The firm's time horizon is the end of its planning period, beyond which the firm does not explicitly consider the cash-flow implications of its decisions. If the time horizon falls outside the present period, the firm should use present-value analysis to properly value cash flows occurring within its planning period.

11. (a)

Year	Cash Flow	Discount Factor	Present value (at 14%)
0	2,500,000	1.0000	2,500,000
1	4,000,000	.8772	3,508,800
2	5,000,000	.7695	3,847,500
		Total	$9,856,300

(b) With regard to your intention to accept the so-called $11.5 million grant, rather than the $10 million grant, may I draw to your attention that the present value of the former option is only $9,856,300. The present value of the $10 million grant is, of course, $10 million. These calculations are based on the current availability of 14% interest rates in risk-free securities.

(c) At 12%, NPV of the $11.5 million grant is $10,057,600, which would make it preferable to the $10 million grant. At 16%, the present value is $9,664,400, and it remains inferior to the $10 million received immediately.

12. (a)

Year	Discount factors	Company A Funds	PV	Company B Funds	PV
0	1.0000	10,000	10,000	5,000	5,000
1	.9174	15,000	13,761	10,000	9,174
2	.8417	10,000	8,417	12,500	10,521
3	.7722	5,000	3,861	15,000	11,583
			$36,039		$36,278

(b)

Year	Discount factors	Company A Funds	PV	Company B Funds	PV
0	1.0000	10,000	10,000	5,000	5,000
1	.900	15,000	13,514	10,000	9,009
2	.8116	10,000	8,116	12,500	10,145
3	.7312	5,000	3,656	15,000	10,968
			$35,286		$35,122

Company A's proposal is worth more in present-value terms when the opportunity discount rate is 11% rather than 9%. Thus, if the opportunity rate of interest is expected to be 11% rather than 9%, then company A is preferred to company B.

(c) B is preferable at opportunity discount rates of 10% and below, while A is preferable at ODR's above 10%. Since the firm's opportunity interest rates in the foreseeable future are above 10%, Company A's proposal appears preferable.

13. Certainty exists if the exact outcome of a decision is known in advance, whereas risk and uncertainty exist if there is a prior probability distribution of outcomes associated with each decision.

14. It is the joint probability of getting heads on both coins separately. It is thus 0.5 x 0.5 = 0.25.

15. Subjectively-determined probabilities are assigned on the basis of experience, judgment, and intuition, when the decision maker has no objective basis for assigning the probabilities. Objectively-determined probabilities must be assigned on the basis of past experience in similar circumstances, assuming that all other things are equal.

16. The probability for each cost level is equal to n/20, where n equals the "times observed".

Cost per batch	Probability	Expected value
$		$
800	0.05	40
825	0.20	165
850	0.40	340
875	0.25	218.75
900	0.10	90
	1.00	853.75

17. EV = $11.90, found by converting the observations to percentage frequencies, or probabilities. Note that $6.25 appears twice while all other sales figures appear once only.

18. Profits are the difference between revenues and costs. Revenues add to asset accounts, such as "cash at bank" and "accounts receivable" if the sale is made but the buyer has not yet been paid. Costs detract from the "cash" account and add to liability accounts such as "accounts payable" and "short and long term loans." The effect is to increase net worth by exactly the amount of profits. Thus, maximizing profits maximizes net worth.

19. The most likely scenario for a business firm is that the firm faces uncertainty in a planning period extending beyond the present period. The second-most-likely scenario is that a firm faces uncertainty and its time horizon falls within the present period. (This latter scenario may be envisioned for firms near bankruptcy or for managers who don't plan to stay in their current job for very long).

20. See the chart on page 24 of the text.

21.(a)
Machine A

Year	Cash Flow ($)	Type	D.F. at 16%	Present value ($)
0	-100,000	Lump	1.0000	-100,000
1	60,000	Daily	.9293	55,758
2	80,000	Daily	.8011	64,088
3	40,000	Daily	.6906	27,624
4	20,000	Daily	.5954	11,908
End of 4	20,000	Lump	.5523	11,046
				$70,424

Machine B

Year	Cash Flow ($)	Type	D.F. at 16%	Present value ($)
1	70,000	Daily	.9293	65,051
End of 1	-120,000	Lump	.8621	-103,452
2	60,000	Daily	.8011	48,066
3	50,000	Daily	.6906	34,530
4	30,000	Daily	.5954	17,862
End of 4	30,000	Lump	.5523	16,569
				$78,626

(b) Management should select machine B because of its greater NPV and the advantage it offers for cash flow by virtue of its allowing the initial cost to be deferred for one year.

22. (a)

	Rebuild			Buy New		
Cost $000	Prob.	E.V. $000		Cost $000	Prob.	E.V. $000
25	.05	1.25		35	.05	1.75
30	.15	4.50		36	.10	3.60
35	.40	14.00		37	.30	11.10
40	.25	10.00		38	.35	13.30
45	.10	4.50		39	.15	5.85
50	.05	2.50		40	.05	2.00
		36.75				37.60

(b) Rebuild EPV: $36,750 x 0.9373 = $34,445.78.

Buy-new EPV: $35,000 x 0.8772 = 30,702.00
2,600 x 0.9373 = 2,436.98
$33,138.98

(c) The new engine option is cheaper in EPV terms, due to the deferred payment for the engine.

23. It is the joint probability of getting a head the first time and a head the second time. That is, 0.5 x 0.5 = 0.25.

24. There are 36 possible outcomes.

25. It is half the cost of lunch for both parties.

26. It ignores the probabilities of each outcome's occurrence.

27. (i) Calculate the EPV; (ii) find the deviations of each potential outcome from the EPV; (iii) square these deviations; (iv) multiply each squared deviation by its joint probability of occurring; (v) sum these products; and, finally, (vi) take the square root of that sum.

28. A risk averter will take risks whenever he or she is sufficiently compensated for so doing.

29. The risk averter would choose the more risky alternative if that alternative promises greater utility.

30. The degree of risk aversion is measured by the marginal rate of substitution of risk for return, which is the additional return that just compensates for a one-unit change in risk.

31. (a) Decision tree

Year 0	Year 1		Year 2		
	Demand	Profits	Entry?	Probab.	Profits
			Yes	0.8	$2,500
	Heavy	$10,000			
	(0.3)		No	0.2	$20,000
Initial			Yes	0.5	$1,250
cost	Medium	$5,000			
$4,000	(0.5)		No	0.5	$10,000
			Yes	0.1	$250
	Light	$1,000			
	(0.2)		No	0.9	$2,000

(b) Calculation of expected present value

Year 0 PV	Year 1 PV	Year 2 PV	Total PV	Joint prob.	EPV
		2,029	7,362	0.24	1,767
	9,333				
		16,231	21,564	0.06	1,294
		1,014	1,681	0.25	420
-4000	4,667				
		8,115	8,872	0.25	2,196
		203	-2,864	0.02	-57
	933				
		1,623	-1,444	0.18	-260
					5,360

(c) Calculation of standard deviation (in thousands).

X_i	EV	X_i-EV	$(X_i-EV)^2$	P_i	$(X_i-EV)^2 P_i$
7.362	5.360	2.002	4.0080	0.24	0.9619
21.564	5.360	16.204	262.5696	0.06	15.7542
1,681	5.360	-3.679	13.5350	0.25	3.3838
8.782	5.360	3.422	11.7101	0.25	2.9275
-2.864	5.360	-8.224	67.6342	0.02	1.3527
-1.444	5.360	-6.804	46.2944	0.18	8.3330
				Variance	32.7131
				Standard deviation	5.71953

32. Risk-adjusted return is the EPV divided by the standard deviation, giving a measure of return for each unit of risk. Return-adjusted risk is the standard deviation divided by the EPV and this gives a measure of risk for each dollar of return.

33. The EVDDR criterion requires extensive search activity to find the correct ODR for each decision alternative. The coefficient of variation criterion uses the same discount rate for all alternatives to find the EPV, and later adjusts for risk by dividing by the standard deviation. Firms tend to use their cost of capital, which they already know, as the discount rate.

34. The CE of a decision alternative is the sum of money, available with certainty, which the decision maker feels would give the same utility (lie on the same indifference curve) as the risk/return combination of the decision alternative.

35. The potential conflict arises because the CV criterion assumes a constant trade-off of risk for return, whereas the CE criterion recognizes that the marginal rate of substitution will more likely increase as the individual bears progressively more risk. There is no conflict when one alternative has both greater return and less risk when compared to all other alternatives.

36. It is potentially misleading whenever no alternative has both greater return and less risk as compared to all other alternatives. Our recommendation should be to choose the one with the lowest CV but to warn that this is subject to the decision maker's degree of risk aversion. The slightly risk-averse person might prefer an alternative that has a higher CV.

37. The maximin criterion is appropriate when the decision maker must avoid the worst possible payoff, due to impending bankruptcy for example, or where the decision maker puts personal gain (e.g. a promotion) ahead of the firm's objectives.

38. The simple EPV criterion is appropriate for risk-neutral decision makers, and it is appropriate for risk-averse decision makers when the decision is repeated many times because the law

of averages will ensure that over many trials the firm will be better off than it otherwise would have been.

39. (a) Decision-tree analysis indicates that the medium-price strategy promises the highest ENPV.

High Price

Year 1		Year 2		Total	Joint	Weighted
Profit	PV	Profit	PV	NPV	prob.	NPV
		25,000	19,750	13,308	.02	266.15
17,500	15,558	20,000	15,800	9,358	.03	280.73
		15,000	11,850	5,408	.05	270.38
		25,000	19,750	8,863	.06	531.75
12,500	11,113	20,000	15,800	4,913	.09	442.13
		15,000	11,850	963	.15	144.38
		25,000	19,750	4,418	.12	530.10
7,500	6,668	20,000	15,800	468	.18	84.15
		15,000	11,850	−3,483	.30	−1,044.75
		Expected net present value				$1,505.00

Medium Price

Year 1		Year 2		Total	Joint	Weighted
Profit	PV	Profit	PV	NPV	prob.	NPV
		24,000	18,960	10,295	.06	617.70
15,000	13,335	19,500	15,405	6,740	.08	539.20
		15,000	11,850	3,185	.06	191.10
		24,000	18,960	7,628	.15	1,144.20
12,000	10,668	19,500	15,405	4,073	.20	814.60
		15,000	11,850	518	.15	77.70
		24,000	18,960	4,961	.09	446.49
9,000	8,001	19,500	15,405	1,406	.12	168.79
		15,000	11,850	−2,149	.09	−193.41
		Expected net present value				$3,806.30

Low Price

Year 1		Year 2		Total	Joint	Weighted
Profit	PV	Profit	PV	NPV	prob.	NPV
		18,000	14,220	5,555	.12	666.60
15,000	13,335	13,500	10,665	2,000	.20	400.00
		11,250	8,875	210	.08	16.80
		18,000	14,220	2,221	.09	199.91
11,250	10,001	13,500	10,665	−1,334	.15	−200.06
		11,250	8,875	−3,124	.06	−187.43
		18,000	14,220	−1,113	.09	−100.13
7,500	6,668	13,500	10,665	−4,668	.15	−700.13
		11,250	8,875	−6,458	.06	−387.45
		Expected net present value				$−291.88

(b) No, The ENPV of the bonds is zero when discounted at 12.5%. The principal plus interest earned on the bonds (at 12.5%) discounts back to a sum equal to the principal. Subtract the initial cost of the bonds from this and you have ENPV = 0. Thus, positive ENPV's indicate better alternatives, while negative ENPV's indicate inferior alternatives, as compared to the bonds.

(c)	Rank	Strategy	Standard Deviation
	1	Medium price	4,290.53
	2	High price	3,405.71
	3	Low price	3,385.40

Standard deviation is a measure of absolute risk, showing the extent of the dispersion of the possible outcomes around the expected value of each strategy.

(d)	Rank	Strategy	Coefficient-of-variation
	1	Medium price	0.89
	2	High price	2.85
	3	Low price	-11.67

The coefficient of variation shows the risk per dollar of expected return. Ranking the strategies in the reverse order of their coefficient of variation thus puts them in order of their risk-adjusted return.

(e) Not for a risk-averse decision maker. The medium-price strategy has both the higher expected return and the lower risk, compared to the high-price strategy. Thus the medium-price strategy would be on a higher indifference curve for all risk averters regardless of their degree of risk aversion.

40. Search activity includes surveys, investigations, interviews and other means of deriving raw data, as well as the processing of this data to find averages, expected present values, standard deviations, coefficients of variation, and so forth. So, search activity is both the gathering and the processing of data.

41. Given each state of nature, select the alternative with the best payoff. Weight each payoff by the probability of that state of nature occurring. The sum of these is the EPV with full information. Subtract from this the best EPV without the additional information to find the value of the information.

42. (a)

Hot dogs alternative			Ice cream alternative		
X_i $	P_i	EV_i $	X_i $	P_i	EV_i $
300	.15	45.00	75	.15	11.25
250	.55	137.50	150	.55	82.50
100	.30	30.00	400	.30	120.00
		EV = 212.50			EV = 213.75

(b)

State of nature	Best alternative	Payoff $	Prior probability	EV $
Rain	Hot dogs	300	.15	45.00
Cloud	Hot dogs	250	.55	137.50
Sun	Ice cream	400	.35	120.00
				EV = 302.50

The value of information is the difference between the expected value with full information, $302.50, and the expected value with incomplete information, $213.75. It is thus $88.75.

43. Was search activity taken to the point where the cost of further search would have exceeded the value of information? Was all information properly processed and interpreted? Was the appropriate decision criteria used, in view of the firm's objectives and attitudes toward risk?

44. Don't procrastinate - work through the decision as soon as you can, but be ready to modify this if new information is forthcoming before the time comes for implementation. Do not implement it until you have to, or until it is clear that more is lost than gained by waiting further.

45. Sensitivity analysis is concerned with the robustness of your decision with respect to its underlying assumptions. Would a different assumption have led to a different decision? If so, your decision is very sensitive to its assumptions.

46. (a) Lease alternative

Year 1 NPV	Year 2 NPV	Total NPV	Joint prob.	Expected value
	3,780.50	−567.50	.075	−42.56
−4,348	7,561.00	3,213.00	.125	401.63
	11,341.50	6,993.50	.05	349.68
	3,780.50	8,128.50	.12	975.42
4,348	7,561.00	11,909.00	.20	2,381.80
	11,341.50	15,689.50	.08	1,255.16
	3,780.50	16,824.50	.105	1.766.57
13,044	7,561.00	20,605.00	.175	3,605.88
	11,341.50	24,385.50	.07	1,706.99
		Expected net present value		$12,400.55

Buy alternative

Year 1 NPV	Year 2 NPV	Total NPV	Joint prob.	Expected value
	7,561	−1,134	.06	−68.05
−8,696	11,342	2,647	.10	264.65
	15,123	6,427	.04	257.09
	7,561	7,561	.15	1,134.22
0	11,342	11,342	.25	2,835.54
	15,123	15,123	.10	1,512.29
	7,561	16,257	.09	1,463.13
8,696	11,342	20,038	.15	3,005.67
	15,123	23,819	.06	1,429.11
		Expected net present value		$11,833.64

(b) The standard deviation for the lease alternative is 7,185 compared with 6,637 for the buy alternative.

179

(c)

Criterion	Alternative	Reason
EPV	Buy	$16,521 vs. $11,834
C. of V.	Buy	0.303 vs. 0.561
Maximin	Buy	$3,213 vs. $-1,134
CE	Buy	More return and less risk

(d) We are assuming management is risk averse; that all data are accurate and complete; and that _ceteris paribus_ holds, particularly for customer tastes and incomes and for rivals' actions and reactions.

47. An indifference curve is a line joining combinations of products that give the consumer equal utility. The properties of indifference curves are (i) combinations on higher curves are preferred, (ii) negative slope throughout, (iii) no intersecting, and (iv) convexity from below.

48. The assumptions are that (i) consumers can rank preferences in order of utility received, (ii) preferences are transitive, (iii) more is always preferred to less, and (iv) there is diminishing marginal utility for all goods.

49. The MRS is the ratio of the MU of the product being acquired over the MU of the product being given up. MU diminishes as more of a product is acquired, and it rises as less of a product is retained. Thus, the MRS is a ratio of a declining numerator and an increasing denominator, as more X is substituted for Y. Therefore, MRS declines as we move down an indifference curve.

50. The budget-constraint line is a straight line because the prices of the products are assumed fixed, regardless of how much or how little of each product the consumer purchases. Thus there is a linear tradeoff between the two products.

51. The utility-maximizing rule is to spend until the last dollar spent on each product generates the same increment to utility. Symbolically, set MRS or $MU_x/MU_y = -P_x/P_y$, given that the entire budget is spent. Generalizing to n products, spend until the ratio of MU/P is the same for all products and the budget is exhausted.

52. The price effect is the change in quantity demanded induced by a change in the price level, for a particular product, given that all other factors remain unchanged.

53. The law of demand is an empirical law which states that the price and the quantity demanded of a particular product will be inversely related, given _ceteris paribus_. The price consumption curve in indifference curve analysis provides the theoretical support for this phenomenon.

54. The income effect is negative if the quantity demanded of a product and the consumer's income move in opposite directions, _ceteris paribus_. This would happen when the consumer substitutes in favor of an inferior good when income falls, or oppositely, substitutes away from an inferior good when income rises.

55. The consumer will demand less of product X than before, because the indifference curves will swing outward to the right, causing a new point of tangency between the budget constraint and a new indifference curve at a product combination that includes less of product X (and more of product Y). If product Y represents all other products, the consumer has substituted away from X and in favor of some or all other products.

56. An attribute is a benefit or service provided by a product. Different products typically provide attributes in different ratios. Products are represented in attribute space as a ray from the origin, where the slope of that ray reflects the ratio in which that product provides the two attributes.

57. The length of an attribute ray from the origin to the efficiency frontier depends on (i) the price of the product, (ii) the consumer's income constraint, and (iii) the consumer's perception of the attribute content in each unit of the product.

58. The consumer can attain any attribute combination by mixing products in consumption. When products are indivisible and can't be mixed, the efficiency frontier is simply a series of points, these being the outer ends of the product rays where the budget constraint becomes binding.

59. Price reductions are represented by a lengthening of the product ray. Changes of perceptions are represented by a change in the length and/or the slope of a product ray. Changes of taste are reflected by changes in the slope of indifference curves.

60. Design the product and price it such that the ray pushes out the efficiency frontier in an area where it can capture as many customers as possible from adjacent products. Seek low-cost production to allow a lower price and better market penetration.

61. Market segments are groups of consumers who share similar taste and preference patterns. Thus their indifference maps would be similar and would exhibit similar marginal rates of substitution between attributes at any particular combination of attributes.

62. Given a price increase for product X, the budget line swings inward, leading to a new tangency point on a lower indifference curve, and reduced consumption of product X. The price increase

causes real income to fall, causing the consumer to be able to afford less of product X (the income effect), and the price increase also causes the consumer to substitute away from product X toward cheaper substitutes (the substitution effect).

63. Advertising may improve consumers' perceptions of the attributes in company A's product. This would cause the product ray to lengthen, push out the frontier, and cause consumers to buy more of that product than before. A subsequent price increase would cause the frontier to shrink back along the product's ray, and it would lose some of these new customers. The marketing manager apparently feels that the advertising will cause the frontier to move out further than the price increase would shrink it back.

64. (a) The product ray representing the Snackers bar would become flatter (assuming protein is on the vertical axis) with a new slope (attribute ratio) of 0.5. The efficiency frontier would change to reflect this change of perceptions.
    (b) Hopefully the repositioning of Snackers has resulted in a greater number of buyers whose indifference curves are sloped such that Snackers will allow the highest curve to be achieved. From the data supplied, however, it is not clear that Snackers will improve its market share or not. Perhaps a price reduction, or a further change in attributes will be necessary to attract more buyers.
    (c) As always, we assume data accuracy and that all other things, such as consumers' incomes, tastes, expectations, and rivals' products, prices and promotion efforts, remain the same. We also assume that consumers will accurately perceive the change in attribute content.

65. (i) Show the initial situation at the point of tangency (point A) between the budget line and the highest-attainable indifference curve. (ii) Rotate the budget line to reflect the change in the price of product X. Identify the new tangency point (between this new budget line and the highest-attainable indifference curve) as point B. (iii) Shift the new budget line in a parallel fashion until it is tangent to the initial indifference curve and call this third point of tangency point C. (iv) The income effect is the horizontal distance (along the X axis) between points C and B. (v) The remainder of the price effect (the horizontal distance between points A and C) is the substitution effect.

66. If X is regarded as an inferior good, the indifference curves will be closer together as they approach verticality and further apart as they approach horizontality, as compared to when X is regarded as a superior good. (See the graphs on pages 84 and 97, and the footnote on page 97, in the text.)

67. Your graph should show an initial tangency point (point A) between an indifference curve and a budget line. Then, a new budget line that represents the increased price of X will swing inward from the same intercept point on the Y axis. It will be tangent (at point B) to a new indifference curve that is not parallel to the first indifference curve, but rather is closer together near the top of your graph. The new budget line is then shifted up in a parallel fashion until it is just tangent (at point C) to the initial indifference curve. The income effect (C to B) should be negative - that is, cause more X to be consumed when its price increased. The balance of the price effect (A to C) is the substitution effect, and can be seen to outweigh the income effect such that the consumer buys less of X after its price increase (presuming it is not a Giffen good).

68. For a Giffen good the indifference curves must reflect the extreme inferiority of product X. Thus they should diverge quite substantially along their length, being very close together at the top and quite distant at the bottom. Then, when the price of the Giffen good falls, the substitution effect will be to buy more, but this will be outweighed by the income effect which will be to buy much less, so that the net effect is to buy less.

69. The demand curve relates quantity demanded of a product to the price of that product, with all other determinants of demand held constant. The demand function relates quantity demanded to all its determinants. Thus the demand curve is a special case of the demand function where only price is permitted to vary.

70. The demand for ice cream no doubt depends on its price, consumer incomes, tastes, and preferences, prices of substitutes, prices of complements, advertising expenditures, product design (e.g. flavor, consistency, composition), place of sale, temperature, and various other variables you might think of.

71. Movement along a demand curve occurs when there is a price change but all other determinants of demand remain unchanged. Shifts of the demand curve occur when there is a change in one or more of the other determinants of quantity demanded.

72. Total revenue is the product of price per unit and quantity sold. Marginal revenue is the change in total revenue due to the sale of the marginal unit. The marginal revenue curve has the same intercept as, and twice the slope of, the demand curve.

73. (a) $Q_X = 28,550.82 - 1,931.6P_X$, or $P_X = 14.79 - 0.0005177\ Q_X$
    (b) $Q_X = 14,284$ and $P_X = \$7.395$
    (c) $Q_X = 12,353$ and $P_X = \$8.395$.

74. Price elasticity of demand measures the relative responsive-

ness of quantity demanded to changes in price. It is the ratio of the percentage change in quantity demanded to the percentage change in price. It is the reciprocal of the slope of the demand curve weighted by the ratio of price to quantity demanded.

75. When price elasticity, e, is greater (less) than one in absolute terms, MR is positive (negative), and TR would be increased (decreased) by a price reduction. Oppositely, a price increase will reduce (increase) TR when MR is positive (negative) and e is greater (less) than one. When e = 1, MR is zero, and TR will not change for small price changes in either direction.

76. Point-price elasticity is the appropriate concept when the slope of the demand curve is known and we wish to know the price elasticity at a particular price level. Arc elasticity is the appropriate concept when we wish to know the average price elasticity for all prices included in a discrete interval (or arc) on the demand curve. Similarly, for other elasticity measures, if the slope term is known we can use point elasticity and reserve arc elasticity for situations where an average elasticity over a range of quantity levels is called for.

77. (a) dP/dQ = -0.0016, P = 18 - 0.0016Q, and MR = 18 - 0.0032Q. Setting MR= MC we find the profit-maximizing quantity is 4,375 units, and from the demand curve we find the profit-maximizing price is $11.00.
    (b) The revenue maximizing price is found where MR = 0. Setting the MR expression equal to zero and solving for Q we find Q = 5,625. The associated price for this volume $9.00. (If you don't know how the above answers were calculated, see the text, pages 136-137, where a similar problem is worked through).

78. e = -0.4373. Note that this is less than one (in absolute terms), confirming that the price is lower than the revenue-maximizing level, which we calculated to be $7.395.

79. The income elasticity of demand measures the relative responsiveness of quantity demanded (of a particular product) to a change in the consumer's discretionary income. Or, it is the percentage change in quantity demanded divided by the percentage change in income. Symbolically, it is equal to dQ/dB x B/Q.

80. A positive sign indicates that quantity demanded and incomes move in the same direction - such products are known as normal or superior goods. A negative sign indicates that quantity demanded and incomes move in opposite directions and that the product is an inferior good.

81. (a) Solving for Q = 33,500 we find the income elasticity of demand is 1.0746. (b) A luxury good, but only slightly.

82. The cross-price elasticity of demand measures the relative responsiveness of quantity demanded for one product to a change in the price of another. The cross-advertising elasticity of demand measures the relative responsiveness of the quantity demanded for one product to changes in the advertising efforts of another.

83. For substitutes, we would expect the cross-price elasticity to be positive and the cross-advertising elasticity to be negative. But one firm's advertising may increase consumer appreciation of the attributes involved in the product, giving rise to spillover benefits to other firms. This could make cross-advertising elasticity positive. For complements, we expect negative cross-price elasticity and positive cross-advertising elasticity. Cross-advertising elasticity between complements would only be negative if the advertising turned consumers off the product and its complements.

84. (a) The current level of demand is 116,415.6 units.
    (b) Price elasticity is -0.437, cross elasticity is 0.439, and advertising elasticity is 2.044.
    (c) No cost information is given, but we can infer from the price elasticity that a price increase would increase total revenues, and therefore must also increase profits, _ceteris paribus_.

85. (a) Arc price elasticity = -3.0768. (The price-elasticity measure is an arc measure since we have two significantly different price and output levels. To find the current output level, divide total profits by the profit per unit, and find Q_1 = 81,652. From this deduce that total fixed costs must be 81,652 x 1.57 = $128,193.64. To find Q_2, the projected output level when price is $3.99, we know that Profit = TR - TVC - TFC. Thus, 15,000 = 3.99Q - 2.74Q - 128,193.64 and Q_2 = 114,555
    (b) The product's demand curve is P = a + bQ where b = dP/dQ = 0.46/32,903 = 0.00001398. To find the intercept term a, we substitute known values for P and Q in the demand curve. Thus,
           4.45 = a - 0.00001398(81,652)
      or   a = 5.5915
    Now, since MR = a + 2bQ, and setting MR = MC = 2.74, we have
           2.74 = 5.5915 - 0.00002796Q
      or   Q = 101,985
To find the profit-maximizing price
           P = 5.5915 - 0.00001398(101,985)
              = 4.16575, or realistically $4.17, at which price only 101,681 units will be demanded. To find the maximum profit level,
      Profit = TR - TVC - TFC
              = 4.17Q - 2.74Q - 128,193.64
              = 1.43(101,681) - 128,193.64 = 17,210.19

Thus the price reduction to $3.99 would have been too far since maximum profits of $17,210.19 could be earned with a price reduction to only $4.17. This price is even less likely to cause a price reduction by competitors.

(c) Data is assumed to be accurate, but since the ability of the $3.99 price to attain the $15,000 profit target is simply based on management "feeling" we should be cautious before recommending a price reduction. If the profit target is the over-riding consideration, price could be reduced as a first step to around $4.17 in order to confirm or deny the model of the demand curve we have constructed. If profits in fact exceed the target, then a further price reduction can be taken at that time. Ceteris paribus is assumed, particularly with respect to rivals' prices, product offerings, advertising and promotion, hours of sale, and so on. Also, consumer taste and preferences, incomes, and expectations are assumed to remain constant. We also assume that there will be no changes in overhead costs and that variable costs will remain constant per unit at the higher output levels.

86. Demand estimation is concerned with finding values for the coefficients and independent variables in the demand function for the current period, such that we may calculate the expected impact on quantity demanded of a change in any of the independent variables. Demand forecasting is concerned with the values of all variables and coefficients in future periods.

87. (i) Non-representative sample; (ii) Interviewer bias; (iii) Questions might be confusing or unanswerable; (iv) Intentions may not carry through to actions.

88. Consumer clinics are simulated market situations in which groups of people are given "play money" and asked to allocate this as they see fit among various products presented in the simulated market situation. Different groups are exposed to different values of the controllable variable under examination, with ceteris paribus. The different reactions of the different groups are then tabulated and conclusions are drawn concerning the impact of the controllable variable on the quantity demanded. To organize a consumer clinic, one would assemble several randomly selected groups of individuals and expose them to the simulated shopping environment at separate times, having varied the price of the product under review each time, with all other factors held constant.

89. Direct marketing is an ideal vehicle for market experiments because different offers can be made to different consumers at the same time, without the consumers being aware of the differences. Given representative samples, the results should be more reliable than consumer clinics or market experiments, but may not be generalizable to other marketing channels.

90. (a) The intercept on the price axis is approximately $12.84 and the slope is about -1/5 or -0.2, or about -$2 for every 10 units of additional quantity demanded. (The exact line of best fit is P = 12.838 - 0.2063 Q).
    (b) The intercept term remains the same but the slope term dP/dQ changes. For every dP there will be 10,000 times dQ. Hence the slope of the market demand curve is -0.00002063, and the full expression is P = 12.838 - 0.00002063Q.
    (c) Since P = 12.838 - 0.00002063Q, MR = 12,838 - 0.00004126Q. Setting MR = 0 and solve for Q and then P, we find Q = 311,197.28 and P = 6.42
    (d) Price elasticity = dQ/dP x P/Q = 1.0

91. (a) Sketching in the line of best fit should indicate a price intercept value close to 262 and a slope term of about -0.008, or -$8 for every 1,000 extra units sold. (The exact line of best fit to the data is Q = 161.369 - 0.615P, or in terms of price, P = 262.389 - 1.626Q). Dividing the slope term by 200 (since for every dP there will be 200 times dQ) we arrive at the estimated demand curve for the 500,000 subscribers, namely: P = 262.389 - 0.00813Q.
    (b) At $179.95 we estimate Q using the demand curve. Thus, Q = 10,140, and price elasticity = -2.183. Similarly, at price $199.95, e = -3.202; at price $219.95, e = -5.183; and at price $239.95, e = -10.693.
    (c) MR = 262.389 - 0.01626Q. Set MR = MC = $150, solve for Q and then P:

$$150 = 262.389 - 0.01626Q$$
thus   Q = 6,912
and   P = 206.19

    (d) Ceteris paribus is expected to hold for all other variables, including promotion, prices of all related products, consumer tastes, incomes, and expectations, and so forth. We assume that the four sub-samples are each representative of the subscribers in general and that there were no systematic differences in the circumstances surrounding the offer to each of the four sub-samples (except for the price level).

92. Time-series data is a set of Y and X observations collected from the same place at intervals over a period of time, such as weekly observations of the quantity demanded and price at a particular store during the past six months. Cross-section data is a set of Y and X observations collected from different places at the same point of time, such as quantity demanded and price observations at each branch of a chain store for a given week.

93. The line of best fit is the line which minimizes the sum of the squares of the deviations of the Y observations from the predicted Y values, given the associated X values. It is a line which characterizes the apparent statistical relationship between

the two variables, abstracting from the assumed random deviations of the observed Y values from their predicted values. It is an estimate of the "true" relationship between Y and X after removal of the random disturbances evident in the actual observations.

94. The coefficient of determination is the ratio of the variation in Y which is explained by X to the total variation in Y. It thus tells us what proportion (or percentage) of the total variation in Y is explained by the variable X.

95. The confidence interval is calculated as a multiple of the standard error of estimate, S_e. The multiple depends on the degree of confidence required. The S_e is in turn a measure of the residuals evident in the scatter of the observations around the line of best fit. Assuming that the residuals are normally distributed around the line of best fit with an expected value of zero, 68% of the observations are expected to lie within one S_e each side of the predicted Y value; 95% of the observations are expected to lie within the range Y plus or minus $2(S_e)$; and 99.7% of the observations will lie in the range Y plus or minus $3(S_e)$.

96. The standard error of the coefficient, (S_c), allows us to express confidence intervals for the values of the coefficients estimated by the regression program. Assuming the residuals are normally distributed, we assert that the true slope will lie within the confidence interval of beta plus or minus $2(S_c)$ at the 95% confidence level. The smaller the S_c the more confident we can be that the estimated beta is an accurate estimate of the true marginal relationship.

97. (i) The form of the function may be misspecified; (ii) A significant determining variable may be omitted from the function; (iii) The wrong variable may be included in situations where both Y and the included X_i variable are functions of the excluded variable.

98. The simultaneous relationships problem arises when the observed variables Y and X are the result of two or more relationships changing simultaneously. The regression program assumes that a single equation can explain the relationship between Y and X. If in fact two functions, such as the supply and the demand curves, are shifting, the regression program is unable to identify the cause because it simply assumes that a single equation model explains the relationship.

99. Multicollinearity exists when there is a significant correlation between the values of two or more independent variables. It can be tolerated when the purpose of the regression equation is simply predictive, and no importance is placed on the individual independent variables or their coefficients.

100. Heteroscedasticity exists when the residual or error terms do not occur randomly with respect to any one of the independent variables. You may discover it in your data by plotting the residuals against each independent variable.

101. Autocorrelation is the serial correlation of the residuals. That is, when the residuals are arranged in chronological order of the observations, a pattern will be evident. Autocorrelation may occur in time-series data but not in cross-sectional data since the latter are collected at the same point of time.

102. (a) Your graph should show the demand curve intercepting at approximately P = 41 with a slope term of approximately -0.5.

(b) X_i	Y_i	XY	X^2	Y^2
10	64	640	100	4,096
15	53	795	225	2,809
17	43	731	289	1,849
20	37	740	400	1,369
27	29	783	729	841
30	23	690	900	529
119	249	4,379	2,643	11,493

Mean X = 9.8333; Mean Y = 41.50; Slope term = -1.9782; and intercept term = 80.73424. Thus Y = 80.73424 - 1.9782 X and P = 40.816 - 0.505 Q.

(c) 35.2356 hours, or 35 hours and 14 minutes.

(d) Q = 30.48 and P = $25.41. It hardly seems worth raising price from $25 to $25.41, since there are likely to be some costs associated with changing prices (such as reprinting brochures) which would probably outweigh any gains.

103. (a) Given Q = 38,658.235 - 8,667P we find P = 4,460.394 - 0.11538Q and hence MR = 4,460.394 - 0.23076Q. Setting this equal to marginal cost we find Q = 12,828.867 and P = 2,980.197.

(b) Set MR = 4,460.394 - 0.23076Q = 0 to find Q = 19,329.147 and P = 2,230.197.

(c) e = dQ/dP x P/Q = -8.667 x (2,980.20/12,828.867) = -2.0134. This indicates that demand is price elastic and that total revenue would increase for a price decrease or, alternatively, decrease for a price increase.

(d) Add and subtract 2(3,251.625) to and from 12,828.667 to find 19,332.12 and 6,325.62.

(e) The regression statistics are not very encouraging. The R^2 indicates that price explains only 72.3% of the variation in demand, and the standard error of the coefficient indicates that we cannot be confident at the 95% level that price is a significant determinant of quantity demanded. We assume the absence of the six major pitfalls in regression analysis but should suspect that at least some of them were present, given the results. Omitted variables, as well as autocorrelation, are most

189

likely. We also assume data accuracy and _ceteris paribus_.

104. (a) S = 34,732 units.
    (b) 95% confidence interval is 32,254 to 37,210 units.
    (c) The R^2 is reasonably high, at 86%, and the standard error of estimate is a relatively small fraction of the predicted value of sales, at 3.57%, so these bode well for reliability. But the standard error of the INT variable is too high, which casts doubt on the negative relationship between INT and Sales.
    (d) Advertising efforts, retail outlets, product design and quality features, consumer tastes, consumer expectations concerning their future incomes and future prices, and so on.

105. (a) Trend value of Q is 21,943.2 and predicted value of Q = 25,634.75.
    (b) 95% confidence interval is 20,169 to 23,717.
    (c) 25,457.35 to 25,813.15.
    (d) The relatively high coefficient of determination, 0.933, and the relatively small ratio of standard error to the predicted value, 3.46%, indicates that this is a quite reliable predictive model. Things we especially require to have remained constant are consumers' incomes, tastes, and expectations, rivals' prices, advertising, and distributional strategies vis-a-vis Huberts' strategies, and so on. Six years is a long time for _ceteris paribus_ to hold. Each one of the pitfalls should be considered to see if one or more of these would jeopardize the reliability of the results.

106. The short run is a production situation in which some factors of production are fixed and others are variable, and the fixed factors constrain the output to some upper limit. The long run is a hypothetical situation in which all factors of production can be varied and the firm can choose a larger or smaller size of plant.

107. (a) Raw materials are variable inputs and therefore qualify under the rubric of "labor". (b) Casual labor, if it can be hired or fired as production needs dictate, is "labor." If not, it would tend to be invariant with respect to output and would be "capital." (c) Usually, highly-skilled labor is not hired and fired as production levels fluctuate, and therefore it is "capital." (d) Typically, management personnel is not variable with output and is therefore "capital." (e) Electric energy comes from the plug as demanded, and is therefore "labor." (f) Buildings and machinery are "capital," since they don't vary with output.

108. The state of technology determines the productivity of the inputs. Improvements in technology are exemplified by more efficient machines, computer-assisted assembly, increases in

skill and training levels of workers, and other improvements embodied in the inputs to the production process. These improvements allow the productivity of the inputs to improve.

109. The law of variable proportions states that as units of the variable inputs are added to the fixed inputs, the marginal product of the variable factors may be expected to rise at first, then perhaps be constant over a range, and finally decline and become negative. The law of diminishing returns states simply that, after some point, the increment to total product will decline progressively as more and more of the variable input is added to the fixed inputs in the production process.

110. A point of inflection is the point on a line where the curvature of that line changes from concavity to convexity, or vice versa. On the TP curve the point of inflection signifies the onset of diminishing returns, because the rate of change of the TP (that is, MP) has reached its maximum and has started to fall.

111. (a) Increasing returns up to 5 divers employed, constant returns from 6 to 12 divers employed, and diminishing returns for the 13th and subsequent divers employed. (b) 5 divers. Average product of the variable factor is at a maximum (6.4 pounds per diver). (c) 14 divers. Total product is maximized.

112. The AVC is equal to the ratio of TVC to Q by definition. The ray joining a point on the TVC curve and the origin has a slope which is equal to the ratio of the TVC and the Q values represented by that point on the TVC curve. Thus the slope of the ray is the value of the AVC at that output level.

113. Marginal costs are defined as the rate of change of TVC with respect to output and can thus be represented by the slope of a tangent to the TVC curve at any particular output level. AVC are at their minimum when a ray from the origin is just tangent to the TVC curve. Since the slope of this ray (AVC) and the slope of the tangent to the TVC curve (MC) are the same at this point, MC = AVC at the minimum point of the latter.

114. When the marginal product of the variable factors is rising, the marginal cost of output is falling. If MP is constant, so is MC. When MP is falling (diminishing returns) the MC curve will be rising.

115. The SAC curve converges toward AVC as Q increases because SAC = AVC + AFC, and AFC becomes progressively smaller as fixed costs are spread over more and more output units.

116. SAC continues to fall for a short range of outputs after AVC begins to rise because over that range AVC is rising more slowly

than AFC is falling.

117. If some of the machines that labor works with directly can be left idle when labor input is reduced, we say that capital is divisible. When AVC is minimized, there is a particular ratio of labor to these machines which is the optimal ratio.   By maintaining this ratio as labor inputs are reduced (by leaving machines idle rather than having the reduced labor force operate all machines), the firm can keep AVC at its minimum level over an extended range of labor input (and output) levels.

118. In the short run the firm will produce and supply output as long as TR exceeds TVC. Alternatively, if price exceeds AVC the firm is able to cover its discretionary costs and make some contribution to its fixed costs which are not discretionary and must be paid in any case.   If there is a reduction in price (below AVC) which is thought to be temporary, the firm may elect to leave the plant idle until price rises above AVC again.   The firm will liquidate the plant if it feels the expected present value of the firm's net worth would be maximized by liquidation.

119. The LAC curve is smooth without kinks when plant size can be varied by very small increments.   The LAC curve is the envelope curve of the SAC curves representing each of these slightly different plant sizes; it is a smooth curve because the SAC curves differ only slightly from each other as capital input is increased.

120. Economies of plant size are evident when the minimum point on the SAC curve falls as the size of plant is increased. Constant returns are evident if the SAC curves associated with larger plant sizes are simply displaced horizontally and each has the same level of minimum SAC.   Diseconomies of plant size are indicated by successively higher minimum points on the SAC curves representing progressively larger plants.

121. The TP curve should be drawn concave from above at first; then it should be linear as constant returns continue; finally the TP curve is convex from above after diminishing returns set in.   The TVC curve is a mirror-image of this, giving rise to an AVC curve that falls at first, then has a horizontal section, and then rises again. The MC curve would similarly fall at first, then rise to equal AVC along the latter's horizontal section, and then rise above AVC when diminishing returns set in. The SAC curve will lie above the AVC, separated by a constantly declining distance equal to the average fixed costs.

122. (a) Plot the SAC curves from the calculations (rounded to the nearest dollar) shown on the next page.

Plant 1

Q	30	52	80	110	130	145	155	162
AFC	667	385	250	182	154	138	129	123
AVC	333	385	375	364	385	414	452	494
SAC	1000	769	625	545	538	552	581	617

Plant 2

Q	50	80	120	164	200	220	235	248
AFC	800	500	333	244	200	182	170	161
AVC	200	250	250	244	250	273	298	323
SAC	1000	750	583	488	450	455	468	484

Plant 3

Q	80	124	175	226	260	274	282	287
AFC	750	484	343	265	231	219	213	209
AVC	125	161	171	177	192	219	248	279
SAC	875	645	514	442	423	438	461	488

Plant 4

Q	100	150	218	272	302	320	335	345
AFC	800	500	367	294	265	250	239	232
AVC	100	125	138	147	166	188	209	232
SAC	900	625	505	441	430	438	448	464

(b) Plotting these on a graph (and interpolating) shows that there are economies of plant size up to and including the third plant size, and diseconomies of plant size for plant 4.

(c) (i) Plant 1, since its per unit costs are the lowest of all available plants at this output level. (ii) Plant 3, since it allows average costs to be minimized at this output level. (iii) Without any probability information, we must weight each possibility equally. It is probably sufficient to divide the range into several classes and use the midpoint of each class as follows. (The average cost at each output level is estimated from the graph.)

Output level	Plant 3 Average costs	Plant 4 Average costs
205	470	530
215	455	510
225	445	495
235	435	480
245	425	465
255	425	455
265	435	450
275	440	440
285	485	435
295	550	430
Expected value	456.6	469
Standard deviation	38.08	33.81
Coeff. of variation	0.0834	0.0721
Worst outcome (maximum)	550	530

Plant 3 is indicated by the expected-value and coefficient-of-variation criteria, and there is little difference in the worst outcome.

123. (a) The SAC curves are plotted from the following calculations, where the figures represent thousands of dollars.

Plant 3

Q	40	90	140	170	180	185
AFC	67.50	30.00	19.29	15.88	15.00	14.59
AVC	17.50	15.83	15.36	16.62	19.17	21.96
SAC	85.00	45.83	34.65	32.50	34.17	36.55

Plant 4

Q	60	120	180	220	230	236
AFC	60.00	30.00	20.00	16.36	15.65	15.25
AVC	12.50	12.50	12.50	13.41	15.54	17.75
SAC	72.50	42.50	32.50	29.77	31.19	33.00

Plant 5

Q	100	170	230	250	260	268
AFC	45.00	26.47	19.57	18.00	17.31	16.79
AVC	8.50	9.56	10.33	12.10	14.04	15.93
SAC	53.50	36.03	29.89	30.10	31.35	32.72

Plant 6

Q	170	200	240	270	280	289
AFC	31.76	27.00	22.50	20.00	19.29	18.69
AVC	6.03	8.50	10.00	11.39	13.20	14.96
SAC	37.79	35.50	32.50	31.39	32.50	33.65

(b) Economies of plant size are evident as we move from plant 3 to plant 4. Plants 4 and 5 appear to reach almost the same minimum SAC level, when these are interpolated. Thus returns to plant size are virtually constant from plant 4 to plant 5, and there are diseconomies of plant size thereafter.

(c)

Units Q	Probability	EV [Q]	Plant 4 SAC	Plant 4 EV[SAC]	Plant 5 SAC	Plant 5 EV[SAC]
100	0.2	20	50	10	53.5	10.7
150	0.5	75	37.5	18.75	38.5	19.25
200	0.2	40	30	6	32	6.4
250	0.1	25	40	4	30.1	3.01
Expected values		160		38.75		39.36

(Note that most of these SAC figures are interpolations from a graph - yours may differ slightly). We can conclude that plant 4 has a slight edge, offering the lowest expected value of SAC, and hence the highest profits, given the price level. Alternatively, you might have worked out the expected profits, which are $1.8m for plant 4 and $1.7024m with plant 5.

124. (a) An isoquant curve is a locus of input combinations which give rise to the same output level. (b) Technical efficiency is a situation in which no part of any input to the production process can be withdrawn without the output level falling. (c) The MRTS is the rate at which one input can be subtracted from the production process as another input is added to the production process such that the output level is kept

constant. (d) Economic efficiency is a situation in which the inputs to the production process have been selected to minimize the cost of producing a particular output level. (e) An isocost line is a locus of input combinations which cost the same amount. (f)´ The long-run expansion path is the locus of points of economic efficiency (least cost) for all output levels when the firm is free to vary the inputs of all resources.

125. Isoquants may bend back because we allow for negative marginal products of both labor and capital when too much of one of those inputs is combined with too little of the other. Indifference curves were negatively sloped throughout due to our assumption of non-satiation, which meant that although marginal utilities diminish they never reach zero.

126 - 128. No questions, no answers!

129. Your graph should show an initial equilibrium situation where the 2,000-unit isoquant curve is tangent to an initial isocost curve. Then the isocost curve would swing downward to reflect the increased cost of labor. To continue producing 2,000 units in the short run, the firm must spend more money than before on the same capital and labor inputs, as indicated by a new isoquant that reflects the new input-price ratio but passes through the initial equilibrium point. In the long run the firm would reduce total costs (shift the isocost line back) by substituting in favor of capital and away from labor until a new tangency point is attained between the 2,000-unit isoquant curve and an isocost line reflecting the new input-price ratio.

130. Although the cost of capital is similar in both countries (due to the international mobility of capital), the cost of labor is substantially greater in America than in Taiwan. Thus the isocost curve will be steeper in the American case than in the Taiwanese case. The isoquant curves will be more or less the same shape in both countries due to the international mobility of technology. The tangency between a particular isoquant curve and the appropriate isocost curve will occur at a higher capital-labor ratio in America than in Taiwan. Since the cost of capital is the same in both cases, the higher intercept on the capital axis of the American isocost curve means that the output will require a greater budget in America than in Taiwan.

131. For a given budget, B, more yards of cotton can be purchased (B/P_C) than yards of silk (B/P_S), since $P_S > P_C$. The same amount of labor can be purchased (B/P_1) regardless of which material is to be used. Thus the isocost line for a given budget is steeper (slope $-P_1/P_C$) for cotton shirts than it is (slope $-P_1/P_S$) for silk shirts. Thus the tangency point with any given isoquant will occur at a more labor-intensive input combination for silk shirts

than for cotton shirts. (Material and labor are substitutable in the production of shirts because more labor used will result in less wastage of material due to more careful marking and cutting of the material). Morover, the production of silk shirts is also more expensive for any given output level, than is the case for cotton shirts. In effect, the firm substitutes labor for material when materials are more expensive, _ceteris paribus._

132. (a) Using the input-output data supplied, plot on a grid the output levels for each input combination. Then sketch in several isoquant curves by joining input combinations that have the same output, and by skirting points that have higher or lower outputs. (b) The isocost line corresponding to the initial factor price situation is $K = 3,200 - 0.4L$. The highest attainable isoquant curve represents approximately 127,000 units, using approximately 4,500 labor hours and 1,400 machine hours. (Your answer should be close to this, and will depend on your artwork). c) If labor cost increases to $15/hour, the new isocost line will be steeper, intercepting at $L = 5,333.33$. The highest attainable output is approximately 117,000 units, using approximately 3,700 labor hours and 980 machine hours.

133. (a) 2,833 pounds of fish cakes and 8,603 pounds of fish meal. (b) $8,289. (c) The shredding and packing processes.

134. (a) 90 bags of the sandy mixture, 145 bags of the pebbly mixture, and 115 bags of the rocky mixture. (b) $868.75. (c) All are binding.

135. (a) Direct costs are those that can be identified with the production of each unit of output, such as raw materials, labor, and energy. (b) Indirect costs are the other costs associated with the production process which cannot readily be attributed to the production of particular units of output but which are joint costs or overhead costs of production. (c) Explicit costs are those outflows of funds made during a particular production period in exchange for the purchase, lease, rental or hire of inputs to the production process. (d) Opportunity costs are the imputed value of resources which are owned by the firm and used in the production process. The imputed value is the foregone contribution these resources could have made in their next-best-alternative employment. (e) Historic costs are the nominal dollar figures paid for assets or resources at the time these were purchased.

136. The economic costs of production are the total opportunity costs of all inputs to the production process. Inputs purchased at their market values during the current period should be properly valued at their opportunity costs, while the opportunity costs of owned resources must be imputed.

137. Normal profits are earned when total revenue equals total (economic) costs. Thus normal profits mean that all resources are earning as much as they could in their next-best-alternative employments. There is a _ceteris paribus_ caveat to normal profits, which includes the degree of risk. Thus, more-risky businesses will need to earn greater total revenues in order to earn normal profits, since their economic costs will be higher than those of less-risky businesses.

138. The economic costs are comprised of explicit and implicit costs as follows:

Drivers' wages	$ 32,000
Secretary's wages	12,500
Office expenses	2,800
City taxes	4,200
Fuel and repairs	28,600
Opportunity costs of trucks	8,000
Opportunity cost of plant and buildings	10,000
Opportunity cost of manager	20,000
Miscellaneous expenses	1,400
Economic costs	$119,500

Since total revenues are $122,500, Mr. Winstell is making an economic or pure profit of $3,000 by operating his trucking business rather than working for the other firm and investing the funds involved. Thus we recommend that he stay in business subject to the qualifications that his expectations for next year's costs and revenues are accurate, that the opportunity cost figures used are in fact the best-alternative use of the resources involved at equal risk, and that wages and other explicit expenses reflect the market value of those resources.

139. Incremental costs are all those costs that arise as a consequence of a decision being made.

140. Explicit present period costs, opportunity costs, and future incremental costs.

141. Future incremental costs must be calculated in expected present value terms, since they occur in the future and are subject to uncertainty.

142. Incremental revenue categories, and examples, are as follows: (i) Explicit present-period revenues, such as cash deposits received, sales revenues, and cash refunds. (ii) Opportunity revenues, or cash outflows which will be avoided as a result of this decision, such as layoff costs, penalties for late delivery, and training costs avoided by hiring a previously trained person. (iii) Future revenues, such as the EPV of future

contributions which arise as a result of this decision and such as the EPV of revenues from the present sale which accrue in future periods. Incremental cost categories, and examples, are as follows: (i) Explicit present period costs, such as wages, costs of raw materials and energy, variable overhead. (ii) Opportunity costs, such as foregone contribution due to the diversion of resources as a result of the contemplated decision. (iii) Future costs, such as the EPV of loss of contribution or lawsuits which may occur in the future as a result of this decision.

143. If we assume that a cost category is entirely fixed, then this assumption must be stated explicitly as a qualification to the final recommendation, and the sensitivity of the recommendation to that assumption should be investigated. For example, if the decision would be changed if the cost category was partly or wholly variable (rather than fixed, as assumed), the maximum variability of this cost category (before the decision would change) should be noted.

144. The "make" alternative allows the firm to oversee quality control and adherence to delivery schedules, whereas the "buy" alternative means this control is relinquished. The "make" alternative means that the production experience will be gained by our firm rather than by a rival producer and will not facilitate a rival becoming a stronger competitor in the future. On the other hand, the "buy" alternative avoids the risks of design problems and cost overruns if the contract price is fixed.

145. Future business with the client (or other firms) as a result of this sale should be considered. The probable impact of this deal on relations with regular clients or consumers in general, should also be examined. Labor relations may also be aggravated if the deal involves unusually stringent standards, irregular hours, or other features that are undesirable from labor's viewpoint.

146. **Alternative No. 1:** Produce extra 160,000 units of A by reducing production of B by 80,000 units.

Incremental revenues (160,000 @ $2.50)	$400,000
Incremental costs	
Materials costs (160,000 @ $0.46)	-73,600
Foregone contribution to labor and	
overheads (160,000 @ $3.77)	-301,600
Contribution	$ 24,800

Alternative No. 2: Buy from D.D.D.

Incremental revenues (160,000 @ $2.50)	$400,000
Incremental costs (160,000 @ $2.25)	-360,000
Contribution	40,000

Thus, C.C.C.'s best option is to buy from D.D.D., subject to the following qualifications: (a) How reliable is D.D.D. for quality and meeting delivery schedules? Inferior quality and/or delivery delays could easily erase the cost advantages of the "buy" alternative. (b) Is D.D.D. the cheapest and/or the best source of supply? (c) What is likely to be the competitive impact of the extra supply? Will it invite price competition and drive prices down? Is our implicit assumption of excess demand a reasonable one? (d) Is the demand estimate accurate? If demand falls below the estimated one million units, C.C.C. will be stuck with a contract with D.D.D. which will result in forced inventory buildup or other costs. (e) Other factors which should be considered include cash-flow considerations, labor relations, future relations with D.D.D. and other competitors, loss of goodwill in connection with the reduced supply of product B if C.C.C. decides to produce the extra units of A in-house, and so forth. All of these issues should be investigated and quantified in EPV terms. If the EPV of these eventualities exceeds the apparent cost advantage of the "buy" alternative (viz. $15,200), then the "make" decision is indicated.

147. The first consideration is whether the XYZ Co. has the capacity to produce the February demand of 1,888,827 units, plus the special order of 10,000 units. Given maximum capacity of 200,000 units it can, but with little room to spare.

Take-it alternative:

Incremental revenue	(10,000 @ $5)	50,000
Incremental costs	(10,000 @ $4.9037)	49,037
Contribution		963

Note that indirect factory labor was treated as a fully-variable cost as a "worst-case" assumption. To the extent that some part is not variable, the contribution of the "take it" alternative would increase. But we are neglecting the fact that next month, March, demand will probably exceed capacity and XYZ will forego $6 (or higher) prices on these units. Thus it seems better to produce these items now and put them in inventory for sale in March, and meanwhile plan to expand capacity, perhaps also raising prices to reduce quantity demanded. That is, the "leave it" alternative looks best.

148. Note that some of the cash flows occur on a more-or-less daily basis while others are lump sum.

The "make" alternative

Cost	Cash flow	Type	D.F.	PV
New equipment	- 23,000	Lump	1.0000	-23,000
Variable-Year 1	-153,000	Daily	0.9284	-142,045
Variable-Year 2	-238,000	Daily	0.7991	-190,186
Present value of incremental cost				$-355,231

199

The "buy" alternative

Cost	Cash flow	Type	D.F.	PV
Purchase-Year 1	-146,250	Lump	0.8696	-127,179
Storage-Year 1	- 26,000	Daily	0.9284	-24,138
Purchase-Year 2	-227,500	Lump	0.7561	-172,013
Storage-Year 2	- 40,000	Daily	0.7991	-31,964
	Present value of incremental cost			$-355,294

Thus, the "make" alternative is slightly less expensive in present-value terms, and it also offers the advantages of having no major lump-sum payments to make, control over quality and delivery schedules, and can be suspended if demand does not materialize, whereas the "buy" alternative presumably involves a contract for the entire job. On the other hand, the "make" alternative may cause labor problems, or unanticipated variations in fixed or variable costs. On balance, the "make" option looks more promising, assuming data accuracy and _ceteris paribus_.

149. The incremental cost of undertaking the contract is composed of four elements:

Expected cost of driver:	
$50 per day x 20 days	$1,000.00
Incremental running expenses:	
Gasoline (13.67 cents/mile x 4000 miles)	
Oil, grease etc. (6 cents/mile x 4000 miles)	
Repairs (14.5 cents/mile x 4000 miles)	
Total (34.17 cents/mile for 4,000 miles)	1,366.80
Cost of installing loading ramp:	400.00
Opportunity costs:	
Contribution foregone is daily rental charge ($25), plus contribution per mile (0.35 - 0.3417) times expected daily mileage (50) by 20 days, times 200/300, which is the probability that the truck could in fact have been rented out.	338.87
Incremental Cost	$3,105.67

150. (a) The breakeven volume Q = 120/(45 - 12.5) = 3.692. Your graph should show TR and TC as straight lines intersecting at 3,692 units. (b) Given P = 80 - 10Q, quantity demanded is expected to be 3,500 units when price is $45. Thus the breakeven volume appears to be unattainable and we advise the firm to consider other price levels. Plotting the (estimated) total revenue curve against the total cost curve we see that there is no profitable volume, since TR lies below TC at all output levels. Losses are minimized at price $46.25 and output 3,375 units. Our advice should be to reconsider the design of the product, and/or consider the promotional opportunities which exist to shift the demand curve, and hence the TR curve, upwards.

151. (a) <u>Expected value of profits</u>:

Output	Plant A	Plant B	Plant C
10,000	0	-150	-350
15,000	500	0	-1,125
20,000	3,600	2,700	0
30,000	18,000	20,250	15,750
40,000	15,000	18,750	17,500
50,000	4,000	5,250	5,250
60,000	<u>1,000</u>	<u>1,350</u>	<u>1,400</u>
	<u>42,100</u>	<u>48,150</u>	<u>38,425</u>

(b) The standard deviations are 18,563 for Plant A; 27,845 for Plant B; and 32,933 for Plant C.

(c) The coefficients of variation are 0.44 for A, 0.58 for B, and 0.86 for C, thus favoring Plant A, unless the decision maker has only a relatively slight aversion toward risk, being willing to take on the additional $9,282 of risk for the additional $5,650 of expected present value.

152. Extrapolation proceeds on the basis of an assumption regarding the behavior of costs outside the range of the data base. If a trend is apparent, one can assume that this trend will continue. The risk is that our assumption will be inaccurate (because diminishing returns set in, or because diminishing returns accelerate, for example) and the trend which was apparent does not, in fact, continue over the range of extrapolation.

153. The gradient of total costs is the ratio of the change in TC to the change in output over a particular output range. The gradient is equal to marginal cost when the change in the output level is only one unit. For larger changes in output, the gradient is the average MC over the output range.

154. Measurement error means that the cost and/or the output observations contain inaccuracies or changes which are not due to output changes. Specification error means that the regression equation takes an inappropriate mathematical form, or includes the wrong variables, or excludes significant variables. Cost curves derived from such data and by such means might either overestimate or underestimate the actual costs per unit at any particular output level.

155. The standard error of estimate allows us to calculate the confidence interval around the predicted cost level for any given output level. The 95% confidence limits, for example, are two standard errors above and below the predicted cost level.

156. The engineering technique involves the estimation of the physical production function and the conversion of the production data into cost data. The production function is represented by a matrix showing the requirements of each variable input for each

of several output levels. This data is then multiplied by the input prices to find the costs of each input at each output level. Adding these costs at each output level, we find the TVC. TFC will be known and added to find TC at each output level. AVC and SAC are found by division by the appropriate output level, and MC are estimated as the gradient of TVC.

157. Most studies report data only from the "relevant range" of output levels at and around the firm's usual output level. This is typically at a point less than full capacity where we would expect the MC curve to be relatively flat around its minimum point. If capital is divisible to some degree, this will also allow MC to be relatively constant over a range.

158. (a) Marginal costs would have to be estimated as the gradient between June and July, namely $3.25 per unit.

(b)

Output	AVC	Gradients (at midpoints)
1,850	10.55	2.20
3,050	7.27	4.75
3,850	6.74	1.81
4,900	5.69	4.99
5,700	5.59	0.87
7,000	4.71	0.48
8,100	4.14	2.20
9,000	3.94	1.21
10,650	3.52	9.98
11,150	3.81	4.49
12,600	3.89	7.89
13,050	4.03	

(c) Your plot of the AVC and MC values will show the AVC as a U-shaped curve, but the MC curve will show several reversals. This possibly indicates the presence of measurement errors, or it may simply be random disturbances in the data.

(d) Sketching a line of best fit will indicate that TVC is about $33,000 at 7,000 units and about $37,000 at 10,000 units. Thus the incremental cost of increasing output from 7,000 to 10,000 is expected to be $4,000.

159. (a) Given the demand function, $P = 9.24 - 1.09769Q$, and hence $MR = 9.24 - 2.19539Q$. Your graph should show both curves intercepting the vertical axis at 9.24. The horizontal intercept is 8.42 for the demand curve and 4.21 for the marginal revenue curve, where Q represents thousands of dozens.

(b) Gradient analysis of the cost data proceeds as follows:

Period	Quantity	TC	AC	MC (at midpoint)
August	1,500	8,700	5.80	
October	3,300	14,520	4.40	3.23
September	4,650	24,645	5.30	7.50

When these are plotted, the MC estimates should be plotted in the middle of the output range which they represent (i.e., at

202

2,400 units and at 3,975 units). Care should be exercised such that the interpolated MC curve cuts the minimum point on the interpolated AC curve.

(c) The intersection of MC and MR on the graph occurs at approximately Q = 2,500 and P = $6.50.

(d) We assume that all changes in the TC figures were due to changes in the output level. Also, we assume the absence of any learning curve effect, and that the demand data is accurate, although we note that the coefficient of determination is only 0.86 and that the standard error of estimate is relatively large.

160. It depends on the signs of the intercept term and the coefficients, since over the relevant range the cost curve may be concave from below, above, the left, or the right. The important thing is whether the TC/Q ratio declines or rises as Q rises. If declining, economies of plant size are evident throughout the range, and if rising diseconomies are evident.

161. If _ceteris paribus_ does not hold, the data might reflect different plant vintages, different labor productivities, different input prices, and different managerial effectiveness, and thus the results will be meaningless. The LAC curve should represent the various short-run cost situations available to the firm at a particular point of time, given the current state of technology and factor prices. The above-mentioned differences are essentially measurement problems. Specification problems, the identification problem, multicollinearity and hetero-scedasticity should also be avoided. (Autocorrelation cannot occur with cross-sectional data.)

162. All plant sizes will reflect the latest technology and the the latest appropriate (local) input prices and productivities can be inserted into the calculations, to update them.

163. (a) Done Brown

Output	TC	SAC	MC
6,000	124,700	20.78	
			16.50
6,500	132,950	20.45	
			16.00
7,000	140,950	20.14	
			15.50
7,500	148,700	19.83	
			15.00
8,000	156,200	19.53	
			20.10
8,500	166,250	19.56	
			25.40
9,000	178,950	19.88	
			30.20
9,500	194,050	20.43	
			41.30
10,000	214,700	21.47	

Competitor

Output	TC	SAC	MC
8,500	176,275	20.74	
			16.35
9,000	184,450	20.49	
			11.23

9,500	190,065	20.01	9.57
10,000	194,850	19.49	13.25
10,500	201,475	19.19	18.25
11,000	210,600	19.15	21.45
11,500	221,325	19.25	26.25
12,000	234,450	19.54	30.30
12,500	249,600	19.97	

(b) Estimating the TC figures by interpolation (when necessary, and assuming that Done Brown will not supply more than 10,000 units even if demand is greater, we have the following:

Done Brown's (smaller) plant: (Dollar figures in thousands)

Demand	TR	TC	Profit	Prob.	EV
8,000	180.0	156.20	23.80	0.05	1.190
9,000	202.5	178.95	23.55	0.20	4.710
10,000	225.0	214.70	10.30	0.50	5.150
11,000	225.0	214.70	10.30	0.20	2.060
12,000	225.0	214.70	10.30	0.05	0.515
		Expected value of monthly profit			$13.625

Competitor's (larger) plant:

Demand	TR	TC	Profit	Prob.	EV
8,000	180.0	176.00*	4.00	0.05	0.200
9,000	202.5	184.45	18.05	0.20	3.610
10,000	225.0	194.85	30.15	0.50	15.075
11,000	247.5	210.60	36.90	0.20	7.380
12,000	270.0	234.45	35.55	0.05	1.778
		Expected value of monthly profit			28.043

*estimated from the graph to be $22 per unit. The expected value criterion thus indicates the larger plant. The maximin criterion indicates the smaller plant. To calculate the coefficient of variation we proceed as follows.

Smaller plant: (Thousands of dollars)

X_i	X_i-EV	$(X_i-EV)^2$	$(X_i-EV)^2 P_i$
23.80	10.175	103.531	5.1765
23.55	9.925	98.506	19.7011
10.30	-3.325	11.056	5.5278
10.30	-3.325	11.056	2.2111
10.30	-3.325	11.056	0.5528
		Variance	33.1694

Standard Deviation = 5.759, and Coefficient of Variation = 0.423

Larger plant:

X_i	X_i-EV	$(X_i-EV)^2$	$(X_i-EV)^2 P_i$
4.00	-24.0425	578.0420	28.9021
18.05	-9.9925	99.8500	19.9700
30.15	2.1075	4.4416	2.2208
36.90	8.8575	78.4553	15.6911
35.55	7.5075	56.3626	2.8181
		Variance	69.6021

The standard Deviation is 8.343, and the coefficient of variation is 0.2975. The coefficient of variation criterion indicates the larger plant. But since it has both the larger return and the larger risk, a risk averter may not prefer the larger plant. The relevant question is whether or not the management of Done Brown will accept the additional $2,583.50 in risk for an additional $14,417.50 in expected profits. They will, unless they are highly risk averse.

164. If wages rise faster than the cost of capital, the firm will, in the long run, substitute in favor of capital and away from labor, because the least-cost combination of capital and labor will be a more capital-intensive combination than before. In terms of isoquant-isocost analysis, the isocost curve will be steeper, and the expansion path (locus of tangencies with successive isoquants) will pass through each isoquant curve at a higher (more capital-intensive) point.

165. If the productivity of capital grows more quickly than that of labor, the isoquant curves will sink towards the labor axis, since it will now take less capital than before, in conjunction with any particular amount of labor, to produce a given level of output. Given ceteris paribus, the isocost curves will have the same slope but will be tangent to the new isoquant curves at a more capital intensive (higher K/L) ratio. Thus the firm will, in the long run, substitute in favor of capital and away from labor, if capital's productivity grows faster than labor's and relative factor prices remain the same.

166. The learning curve is a locus of per-unit production costs and cumulative output levels. It shows that per-units costs of producing a given output level per period tend to decline as cumulative production grows, as a result of cost-saving procedures, more-efficient workers and machines, and better organization of production. Typically the learning curve indicates that per-unit costs will decline by about 20% each time cumulative output doubles.

167. The increasing efficiency of the production process due to learning will be reflected in a downward sinking of the firm's SAC, AVC and MC curves, since any particular output level per period can be produced at progressively lower costs.

168. This means that costs per unit have been observed to (and are expected to) decline by 21.5% each time cumulative output doubles. For example, if costs per unit are $20 after the first 10,000 units, at 20,000 units we expect costs to be $20 - (20 x 0.215) = $20 - 4.3 = $15.70 per unit.

169. (a) The final calculations are shown below:

Output level	500	650	800	950	1,100
TVC ($)	9,583.55	12,240.20	14,959.00	17,719.70	20,853.00
AVC ($)	19.17	18.83	18.70	18.65	18.96
MC ($)		17.71	18.13	18.40	20.89

(b) A graphical interpolation indicates that AVC is minimized at about 920 units per week. Minimum AVC corresponds to maximum average product of the variable factors, indicating maximum average efficiency of those factors.

(c) Graphical interpolation indicates that MC = MR = $20 at about 1,000 units per week. Contribution is maximized when profit is maximized since the difference between these (fixed costs) is a constant.

170. (a) Multiplying the input quantities by their costs per unit, we find the following cost data:

Output	TVC $	TC $	AVC $	AC $	MC $
1,000	7,520	31,520	7.52	31.52	5.68
2,000	13,200	37,200	6.60	18.60	4.14
3,000	17,340	41,340	5.78	13.78	3.26
4,000	20,600	44,600	5.15	11.15	2.75
5,000	23,350	47,350	4.67	9.47	2.45
6,000	25,800	49,800	4.30	8.30	2.55
7,000	28,350	52,350	4.05	7.48	3.65
8,000	32,000	56,000	4.00	7.00	5.62
9,000	37,620	61,620	4.18	6.85	9.38
10,000	47,000	71,000	4.70	7.10	12.95
11,000	59,950	83,950	5.45	7.63	15.89
12,000	75,840	99,840	6.32	8.32	

When plotting the MC values, you should have plotted them in the middle of the output range which each represents. Otherwise the MC curve will be displaced and will not pass through the minimum point on the AVC and AC curves.

(b) We compare the expected value of the contribution in each of the "take it" and "leave it" options. Alternatively you might compare the expected values of profits, whereby your answers would be lower by $24,000 in both cases.

Leave it alternative

Output ($)	TR ($)	TVC ($)	Contribution	Prob-ability	E.V. ($)
5,000	50,000	23,500	26,650	0.10	2,665
6,000	60,000	25,800	34,200	0.15	5,130
7,000	70,000	28,350	41,650	0.20	8,330
8,000	80,000	32,000	48,000	0.25	12,000
9,000	90,000	37,620	52,380	0.20	10,476
10,000	100,000	47,000	53,000	0.10	5,300
				Expected value	$43,901

Take it alternative

Output ($)	TR ($)	TVC	Increm. fixed	Contri-bution	Probab-ility	E.V. ($)

7,000	68,000	28,350	6,000	33,650	0.10	3,365
8,000	78,000	32,000	6,000	40,000	0.15	6,000
9,000	88,000	37,620	6,000	44,380	0.20	8,876
10,000	98,000	47,000	6,000	45,000	0.25	11,250
11,000	108,000	59,950	6,000	42,050	0.20	8,410
12,000	118,000	75,840	6,000	36,160	0.10.	3,616
				Expected value		$41,517

Thus the expected value of profits is $2,384 less if the firm takes the special order, or the contribution of the special order is negative by that amount. Thus we advise the sales manager to "leave it," subject to the following qualifications.
   (c) We assume data accuracy in all the cost estimations and the probability distribution of demand. We treat the $3,000 set-up costs and the $3,000 packing and shipping costs as fully incremental - if at least $2,384 of this is part of the fixed costs, or if the customer can be persuaded to pay at least $2,384 toward set-up, packing, or shipping costs, our recommendation would be reversed. We assume _ceteris paribus_, particularly with respect to the sales of the regular paddles. That is, there will be no substitution between the specially imprinted paddles and the regular paddles. On this assumption, the incremental costs of the "take it" alternative would be reduced. We assume no change in customer relations - that the regular demand will not be reduced as a result of this deal for a new customer. Also, and perhaps most importantly, we assume the absence of any future costs and benefits. If this deal would lead to future repeat sales to this customer (goodwill) with expected present value of contribution greater than $2,384, then our recommendation would be reversed. The manager should also consider a counter-offer.

171. SAC = $4.23198Q^{-0.345}$. (a) When Q = 10,000, SAC = $711.19, and when Q = 20,000, SAC = $559.92. (b) R^2 = 0.9964 and S_e = 0.0101. Thus the learning curve fits the data points very well. The 95% confidence interval is thus 0.0202 each side of the predicted value. (c) We assume _ceteris paribus_, data accuracy, absence of the six pitfalls, and so on.

172. The critical difference between "few" and "many" firms is whether or not the pricing actions of any one firm will cause the general price level to change. If there are few firms, the firm expects its price change to cause a change in other firms' prices and hence in the general price level. If there are many firms, there are enough other firms that any one firm can expect _ceteris paribus_ to hold when it adjusts its price.

173. In pure competition the cross elasticity of demand approaches infinity, since an infinitesimally small change in firm X's price would lead to a small (but much greater than infinitesimal) change in the quantity demanded of any firm Y.

(If firm X raises its price infinitesimally, it loses all of its customers, who account for, let us say, 1% of total customers. These customers then go and spread themselves across the other 99 firms. These firms therefore each gain an insignificant amount of sales, i.e. 1/99th of 1%.) In monopoly the cross elasticity of demand is zero, or insignificantly small, since the monopolist does not have any significant competition in the market for its product. In oligopoly, cross elasticity may range from very high to very low, depending on the degree of product differentiation. In monopolistic competition, cross elasticity is relatively high but less than infinite, since the firms' products are only slightly differentiated.

174. Conjectural variation is the expected change in rivals' prices which would be induced by a change in the firm's own price. Algebraically, and more generally, it can be expressed as the percentage change in firm Y's price over the percentage change in firm X's price.

175. In pure competition we have many sellers; cubic total cost curve; many buyers; zero product differentiation; short-run profit maximization; adjustment of quantity (unless price is not at the equilibrium value, in which case it too is adjusted); and zero conjectural variation. Full information is assumed on the cost side such that all firms have access to the same technology and the lowest factor prices. Full information is assumed on the demand side such that all consumers will know the attributes of all products (and that they are identical) and will know the prices of each seller.

176. Monopolistic competition differs from pure competition because products are slightly differentiated rather than being identical across firms. Monopolistic competition is difficult to find since it requires that a buyer have more or less equal access to all sellers. Thus the sellers must be concentrated in a compact area, such as at a fruit and vegetable market, a swap meet, or an arts and craft show.

177. A firm might become a monopoly by controlling the supply of a necessary raw material or by inventing a new product or new production process and holding the patent or by merging with and taking over its rivals (a natural monopoly) or by government mandate. A firm will remain a monopoly only if these barriers to entry are maintained and it is able to successfully prevent any other firm from becoming established in the market.

178. Your graphs should show the market demand curve shifting outward and the equilibrium price rising to a new level. The firm's demand and marginal revenue curve thus shifts upward, allowing a higher profit-maximizing output level (where the MC

curve cuts the new MR curve). Thus the reaction of the firm is to produce a larger output at the higher price level.

179. Your graph should show the monopolist experiencing a downward shift of the cost curves due to learning in the production process. The new MC curve will cut MR at a larger output, indicating that a lower price is now profit maximizing.

180. In a kinked-demand curve oligopoly we have few firms; cubic total cost curve; many buyers; product differentiation of some degree; short run profit maximization; price and output adjustment; conjectural variation equal to zero for price increases and equal to unity for price reductions.

181. A _mutatis mutandis_ demand curve is a locus of the firm's prices and the quantity it expects to sell at each of those prices, taking into account the reactions of rival firms.

182. The MR curve associated with a kinked demand curve consists of two tangible sections and an intervening intangible gap (or vertical discontinuity). The upper tangible section will relate to the _ceteris paribus_ demand curve above the current price, having the same price intercept and twice the slope. The lower tangible section will relate to the _mutatis mutandis_ demand curve below the current price, having twice the slope and the same price intercept (if both curves were to be extended up to the price axis). Since the two demand curves have different slopes, there will be a kink at the current price level and the length of the gap in the MR curve will be a function of the sharpness of the kink. If the kink is very sharp, and/or the _mutatis mutandis_ demand curve particularly steep, the lower tangible section of the MR curve could lie completely below the quantity axis.

183. The KDC model is not a complete model of price determination since it takes the current price as given. It can only predict price changes from the current level, or that prices will not change from the current level in some circumstances. The KDC model has been called a model of price rigidity because it shows that prices will not change in response to changes in costs and demand as long as the MC curve passes through the gap in the MR curve. In other cases, for larger cost and demand shifts, it will explain or predict price adjustments in response to those shifts.

184. It would "travel" up the _mutatis mutandis_ demand curve to the extent that other firms were also raising their prices, and would encounter a kink and travel along a _ceteris paribus_ demand curve if it continued to raise price alone.

185. The conjectural variation for a price leader is unity for both price increases and price decreases. For price followers it

is zero for price increases and unity for price decreases since these firms expect that nobody would follow a price increase they initiate but that all others would follow a price reduction.

186. A barometric price leader has the ability to sense that the time is right for a price adjustment, the willingness to risk loss of market share if others don't follow price increases, and the respect of the other firms for its judgment.

187. The low-cost firm selects the price which maximizes its own profits, taking into consideration that all other firms will adjust the price to the same price level. It thus equates its marginal costs with the marginal revenues it expects from its share-of-the-market (_mutatis mutandis_) demand curve.

188. The price leader will raise its price by a certain percentage and the followers will raise price by a similar percentage in order to preserve their relative prices vis-a-vis the price leader's and all other firms' prices.

189. The dominant firm selects the price level which will maximize its profits from the residual demand. The residual demand is the demand left over, at each price level, after the smaller firms have supplied all they want to at that price level. Residual demand is thus equal to market demand less the sum of the quantities supplied by all the smaller firms. The dominant firm lowers price until the falling marginal revenue from the residual demand is just equal to the firm's marginal cost.

190. Your graph should show an initial KDC and MR curve, and an MC curve that passes through the gap in the MR curve. Then, the KDC will be shifted to the right as far as it can go while still allowing the MC curve to pass through the MR gap in the new KDC. Any greater demand shift would induce a price increase.

191. The profit generated each period by the proxy policy must be no less than the EPV-maximizing profit minus the search costs which would otherwise need to be expended.

192. Short-run sales maximization (subject to a minimum-profit constraint) is a proxy for long-term-profit maximization because it tends to limit entry of new firms, to increase repeat sales in future periods, and to increase sales of complementary goods and services. The minimum-profit target is chosen to prevent shareholders from selling their shares (possibly inviting market takeover and a change of managers) or voting for a new board of directors at the annual meeting (who would change the managers).

193. An oligopolist could deter the entry of a high-cost firm by setting the price at a level just below the minimum point on the

potential entrant's SAC curve. Thus, the potential entrant would foresee making only losses and would therefore not enter.

194. When the potential entrant is a low-cost firm, the existing firms threaten that they would maintain output levels at current levels, such that any production by a new firm would depress the market price below the costs of the new firm (and all existing firms). If this threat is believed, the potential entrant expects only losses and will not enter. But if the entrant calls the bluff of the existing firms and does enter, it is likely that the existing firms would soon relent and reduce production such that prices rise above costs for all firms.

195. A contestable market is one that has minimal barriers to entry, such that entry is always feared by the existing firms. Thus they keep their prices down to avoid earning excessive profits which would attract the entry of new competition.

196. Growth maximization requires profits for spending on new assets, and therefore profits are desirable in the short run. But excess profits might attract entry of new firms, limiting growth possibilities in future periods. Thus prices are kept below the profit-maximizing level with consequent benefits for longer-term profits. Maximization of managerial utility requires consideration of the managers' utility functions. The long-term success, profits and growth of the firm are likely to be an element in any manager's utility function, positively related to utility. Thus, managers maximizing utility will tend to make decisions which augment the longer-term profits of the firm. Satisficing as a policy in the short run typically has profits and sales as goals, as well as other cost-reduction goals like the inventory/sales ratio and labor productivity. Pursuit of these goals, and the periodic revision of these goals, leads to the enhancement of longer-term profits.

197. (a) Struktatuff's (*mutatis mutandis*) demand curve will have the same intercept and 1.5 times the slope of the market demand curve (that is, divide the slope by two-thirds). At any price level Struktatuff's demand curve will lie two-thirds of the horizontal distance to the market-demand curve. Steeldeal's demand curve will have the same intercept and three times the slope (divide by one-third) of the market demand curve.
    (b) Struktatuff's demand curve will be $P = 36,384 - 1.875Q$ and its marginal curve will be $MR = 36,384 - 3.75Q$. Marginal costs are constant at \$4,850 per unit. Setting $MR = MC$ and solving for Q we find $Q = 8,409.067$ or 8,409 homes. Substituting for Q in the demand curve we find Strukatuff's preferred price to be \$20,617.
    (c) At price \$20,617, market demand is 12,613 units. Struktatuff produces 8,409 and Steeldeal produces 4,202 units.

198. (a)   Plot the demand curve with intercepts 100 on the price axis and 80 on the quantity axis. The small firms' marginal cost curves are each MC = 15 + 22.5Q. Since there are twenty of these, we divide the slope term by 20 to find the horizontal addition of the MC curves, namely 15 + 1.125Q. This curve intersects the demand curve at 35.789 units. Hence the residual-demand curve intercepts the vertical axis at P = 100 - 1.25(35.789) = $55.26 and slopes down to cut the market-demand curve when P = 15. At this price, residual demand equals market demand, equals 68 units. The slope of the residual demand between these two co-ordinates is -40.26/68 = -0.5921. Thus the residual demand curve is P = 55.26375 - 0.5921Q.
    (b)   The dominant firm's marginal revenue is MR = 55.26375 - 1.1842Q and its marginal cost curve is MC = 10 + 0.5Q. Solving for Q when MR = MC we find Q = 26.875 and P = $39.35. The smaller firms will equate this price to MC and sell 1,802.22 units each.
    (c)   The dominant firm's profits will be $108.21 and the profits of each small firm will be $3.18 per period.
    (d)   Since the small firms each make pure profits we may expect them to expand facilities, and we may expect that new firms will enter, such that the residual-demand curve will shift to the left (given constant market demand) and price will fall. The industry may change from a dominant firm oligopoly to some other form of oligopoly.

199. (a)   The firms should practice limit pricing if the EPV of the contribution stream out to their time horizon (given the limit price) exceeds the EPV of their contribution stream over the same period given the entry of the new firm. To find the limit price, we need to find the average costs for the potential entrant. Its AVC is expected to be constant at $24.00 per ton. TFC are $850,000, which means AFC will be $8.50 over the first year's expected sales of 100,000 units. SAC is thus $32.50 and the entrant could therefore not make a profit initially. When it achieves an equal share (166,667 units), its AFC will fall to $5.10, implying SAC = $29.10. Thus it can make a profit (at price $32) in the future, but these profits must be converted to present value for comparison with its earlier losses. The answer will depend upon the time horizon of the entrant, how quickly it attains an equal share, and its opportunity rate of discount. The absolute minimum level of the limit price will be $29.10, presuming an infinite time horizon, zero discount rate, and an almost immediate attainment of equal market share. At lower prices, market demand will be increased and this should be taken into account. You might consider several scenarios and will probably find the limit price to be in the area of $30 per ton.
    (b)   The market demand is P = a + bQ where P = 32, Q = 1,000,000 and b = dP/dQ. Since E = -0.2, dP/dQ = -0.00016. Solving for a, we have P = 192 - 0.00016Q. Each firm's _mutatis mutandis_ demand curve will have the same intercept and six times

the slope, or P = 192 - 0.00096Q. Each firm's MR curve is thus MR = 192 - 0.00192Q. Since the MC for the first five firms is lower, we set MR = MC = 20 to solve the profit-maximizing values Q = 89,583.33 and P = 106.00. This answer relies upon all firms simultaneously setting this price, and it would only be set if there were no more potential entrants or the firms' time horizons are very short. In practice, of course, we should expect the firms not to expect the absence of other potential entrants, and, wishing to maximize the present value of contributions over a time horizon exceeding the short run, they are likely to set a price somewhat lower and probably near the perceived limit price.

200. (a) Here are the algebraic calculations to check your graphical answers against. To find the combined MC curve we must add the two MC curves in the form Q = f(MC) to achieve horizontal addition. Since MC_a = 1.5 + $0.01Q_a$ and MC_b = 1.2 + $0.006Q_b$, we transpose these to read Q_a = 150 + $100MC_a$ and Q_b = 200 + $166.67Q_b$ and then add them to find SQ = 350 + 266.6667 SMC, or SMC = 1.3125 + 0.00375SQ, where S represents sigma. Setting this equal to MR = 68.5 - 0.01Q, we solve for Q = 4,886.3636. Thus the profit-maximizing total output is 4,886.3636 pounds.
    (b) Production should continue in each plant up to the point where MC = MR. MR = 68.5 - 0.01(4,886.36) = 19.63636 when SMC = MR. Setting MC = 19.63636 in each plant we find 1,813.636 pounds from plant A and 3,072.727 pounds from plant B.
    (c) Using the demand curve expression and substituting for Q = 4,886.36 we find P = $44.07.
    (d) Total costs of producing 4,886.36 pounds will be $63,280, since TC_a = $25,017 and TC_b = $38,264. Allocating 100 pounds from plant A to plant B we have TC_a = $23,103 and TC_b = $40,256, totalling $63,359. Thus, total costs increase by $79 (and contribution decreases by the same amount) if the last 100 pounds are produced in plant B instead of plant A.

201. (a) I will show the algebraic solutions here. If you attempted this graphically, your answers should be close to these answers. First we find the firm's MC curve by adding vertically the MC curves of its two divisions. Hence MC_f = 300 + 0.875Q. Setting this equal to MR = 1,000 - 1.25Q we solve for Q = 329.41. Insert this value of Q in the manufacturing division's MC (MC_a) expression to find MC = $323.53, which is the transfer price.
    (b) Since the external price is $350, set MC_a equal to $350 and solve for Q = 400. Then find the expression for net marginal revenue NMR = MR_f - MC_b = 900 - 1.75Q and set this equal to $350 to find Q = 314.29. Thus the manufacturing division makes 400 units, transfers 314.29 to the marketing department, and sells the remaining 85.71 units on the outside market.
    (c) First we transpose the MR curves to facilitate their horizontal addition. Given MR_e = 1,200 - 1.6Q and NMR = 900 - 1.75Q we have Q = 750 - $0.625MR_e$ and Q = 514.29 - 0.574NMR.

Adding these and transposing back again we have SMR = 1.056.72-0.8358Q. Setting this equal to MC_a we find Q = 707.55, which is the total production. Substituting in the MC_a expression we find MC_a = \$465.33, which is the transfer price. Substituting that figure in the NMR expression we find Q = 248.38 is the amount transferred. To confirm, we substitute 465.33 in the MR_e expression to find Q = 459.17, which is the amount sold externally, and that 248.38 + 459.17 = 707.55. Finally, substituting 459.17 in the external demand curve we find \$832.67 as the external market price.

202. P = AVC + [-1/(e + 1)]AVC, where the term in the square brackets is the markup rate. This markup rate is the profit-maximizing rate because the profit-maximizing condition (MC = MR) is embedded in the above derivation. It also assumes MC = AVC.

203. The markup rate can deviate from -1/(e + 1) yet still allow the firm's profits to be maximized if the loss of contribution is no more than the search costs avoided (opportunity revenues).

204. The range of markup rates which allows profits to be at least equal to maximum profits after search costs will be wider the greater are search costs, the more inelastic the firm's demand, and the lower the firm's marginal costs, _ceteris paribus_.

205. Where the firm has had enough experience to confirm that it is located on the negatively sloping section of the profit curve, it need not incur any expenditures on search because these will only reduce profits below target and require a reduction in sales to re-attain the profit target. Rather, the firm may proceed simply by raising price if profits are below target, or lowering price if profits exceed the target, in order to achieve its sales maximization objective.

206. Since (P - AVC)/AVC is an expression for the markup rate, and since the profit-maximizing markup is -1/(e + 1), we can equate these two expressions and solve for e = [-AVC/(P-AVC)]-1. The resultant value is what price elasticity would need to be for the present price to be profit maximizing. We then ask whether that is likely to be reasonably close to the truth.

207. If the demand shift is an isoelastic shift, the price elasticity will remain the same (at each price level) as it was before the shift. Thus the markup rate -1/(e + 1) will be unchanged and the current price will remain optimal.

208. The markup rate remains optimal if both the firm's costs and the consumers' incomes have risen (in nominal terms) by the same proportion. If so, then in real terms the price level will be constant if the same markup is applied.

214

209. If markup pricing is an accepted practice in a market, and if each firm expects all other firms to continue to use markup pricing whenever common costs change, then each firm can confidently pass on cost increases to consumers by using their established markup rates on the new cost levels. Thus all firms raise prices at about the same time and to the same extent (or proportion, if price differentials exist), expecting that all other firms are doing the same thing. Markup pricing facilitates this conscious parallelism because it involves a simple decision rule for each firm, and allows firms to confirm that the other firms are also following this simple pricing rule.

210. (a) Using the formula supplied in the text (on page 420) we find e = -4.0.
   (b) We find P = 51.4285 - 0.038095Q by using e = -3.5 to find dP/dQ = -0.038095 and solve for the intercept value given P = 40 and Q = 300. Setting MR = 51.4285 = 0.07619 = MC = 30) we find that contribution is maximized when Q = 281.25 per week (or 1,125 every four weeks) and price is $40.71, implying a markup of 35.7%. By plotting TR, TVC, and Contribution curves, or using algebra you could find that the range of acceptable markups is from 21% to 50%. Thus the present markup rate was well within the acceptable range.
   (c) No it was not, as it will take almost a year to earn enough extra contribution (in EPV terms) to cover the search costs, and by then something will almost certainly have changed to cause the demand curve to shift.

211. (a) Given P = $750, Q = 60, and e = -1.1 we can solve for P = 1,431.8182 - 11.3636Q. TR = P.Q and TC = 8,000 + 600Q.
   (b) For several values of P within the relevant range, we find the associated Q, TR, TC, and profit figures, as follows.

P	Q	TR	TC	Profits
750	60.00	45,000	44,000	1,000
760	59.12	44,930	43,472	1,458
770	58.23	44,837	42,938	1,899
772.31	58.04	44,825	42,824	2,000
775	57.80	44,795	42,680	2,115

Thus the price level which maximizes sales volume subject to the profit target of $2,000 per month is $772.31, (implying 58.0369 jobs for $2,000.34 profits). The implied markup rate is (772.31 - 600)/600 = 28.72%.
   (c) Demand shifts must be isoelastic with costs constant, or inflation must increase clients' discretionary incomes (on average) by the same proportion as variable cost are shifted upwards.
   (d) If demand shifts cause demand to be more elastic, ATS should lower the markup rate; if less elastic, then ATS should raise it. If costs increase by a greater proportion than clients' incomes, ATS should reduce the markup, but if costs increase by

less than clients' incomes, ATS should raise the markup rate.

212. The price of the product should be selected with regard to the relative value offered by this product compared to others - nearer the top of the price range if it is generally superior, or nearer the bottom if it is generally inferior to other firms' offerings. This price positioning involves an implicit estimate of the value of each attribute contained in the product, as perceived and valued by the consumers in the marketplace.

213. (i) For complements, the more elastic the demand, the lower the markup. The product which forms the basis of the line of complementary products probably faces considerable competition, and is therefore priced using a lower markup, and the more esoteric the accessory or complementary good, the higher the markup we would expect, since these will typically be designed specifically for the basic product and will have fewer substitutes. (ii) For substitutes, the product offering the least quality, performance, durability, and other desirable features should be given a lower markup, while the better quality products with additional features should be given progressively higher markups, with adjustments made to reflect the intensity of competition at various points in the price-quality range.

214. A higher price will convey information suggesting higher quality if the consumer cannot immediately refute that suggestion by examination of the product or by reference to past experience, comparative product tests, or other sources of information. New products often meet these criteria, at least initially. High-technology products, even in established product markets, are often difficult to rank qualitatively and are thus also candidates for higher price suggesting higher quality.

215. A person will spend more than otherwise if the bundle permits that person to obtain an additional item (or unit of volume) at an incremental price that is less than that person's reservation price for that item or unit.

216. Larger quantities can be regarded as larger bundles of the basic unit of measure. Additional units are bundled in at progressively decreasing incremental prices per basic unit of measure (such as per ounce, gallon, or hour).

217. The firm may use promotional pricing to reduce inventories, to broaden market share, to avoid loss of market share, as a loss leader, or simply as part of their promotional strategy to keep their name and low-price image in the minds of consumers.

218. Possible disadvantages of promotional pricing are that demand may prove inelastic, consumers may stockpile and wait for

sales, consumer price awareness might be increased (to the firm's detriment), and it may damage the product's quality image.

219. Search goods typically have higher price elasticities of demand. Since they are easily evaluated, consumers know what they are getting for the money and there are no negative inferences about quality associated with the price reduction.

220. Demand has been shifting at the rate of 10% per month and may be expected to continue this trend to reach 2990 units in April at the same price level ($6.88). Given e = -2.5, we can derive the demand curve at the March price and output levels, as follows. Since e = dQ/dP x P/Q where e, P, and Q known, dQ/dP = -987.65 and dP/dQ = -0.0010125. Since P = a + dP/dQ(Q) where P, dP/dQ, and Q are known, a = 9.632. Thus the demand curve for March is P = 9.632 - 0.0010125Q. Presuming the April demand curve to be parallel to the March curve we find its intercept by substituting P = 6.88 and Q = 2,990 to find a = 9.90738. The marginal revenue curve is consequently MR = 9.907 - 0.002025Q. To estimate marginal costs we use the gradient method to find $4.11 per unit between January and February and $4.41 between February and March. (We ignore the change in light and heat costs as probably not being an output-related change, given the winters in Pittsburgh.) Plotting these two MC points (in the middle of each range) against the demand and MR curves we see that MR = MC at approximately 2,720 units, which would be demanded at price $7.15. Thus, (a) the optimal price for April is $7.15, and (b) 2,720 units are expected to be sold at this price. (c) These answers are subject to the usual qualifications concerning data accuracy, continuation of trends in demand and costs, the assumption of a parallel shift in the demand curve, the absence of competitive reactions to this price change, and so forth.

221. (a) $499.99 (Anywhere in the range $495-505 is reasonable).
(b) The price must be selected with reference to the value of the attributes involved in the Valhalla unit vis-a-vis the other refrigerators available. The four attributes shown, plus the implied fifth one (brand name and its associated quality and after-sales service) appear to be the ones operating to cause product differentiation. The new Valhalla is physically identical to the GE model which sells for $525 but lacks the brand image of the latter, although the department store has a strong reputation for quality and after-sales service. The value of a major brand name is indicated by the price difference between the Kelvinator K-7742 and store B's BK-7742 which should be recognized as the same refrigerator. The price difference, $30, is presumably due to Kelvinator's brand image. This suggests a starting price for Valhalla of $495. But the Valhalla has wheels, four trays, and larger capacity than some of the other refrigerators.
(c) Qualifications largely relate to the assumptions made

and the need for more information concerning consumers' evaluation of the various attributes and the service reputations of the stores.

222. (a) $775, or perhaps a little higher if Emerson's brand name and quality are considered equal to Quasar's. Emerson's model A is most similar to Quasar's model 5254, the Hitachi, and the Magnavox VR8530, with some differences, and this price seems to reflect the differences.
(b) $1,199 or a little higher if Emerson's quality is considered to be as high as JVC's. Again, this price reflects the presence of desirable attributes as compared with rival products.

223. If the firm has a short time horizon, if barriers to entry are insurmountable, if it expects a positive price-quality association, and if the demand will be short-lived, we expect to see the firm set the short run profit-maximizing price.

224. If it can establish a higher-quality image by setting a high price initially, this will cause its demand curve to lie further to the right in later periods, as compared to a lesser-quality image, since quality is a shift variable underlying the demand curve. The firm would sacrifice profits initially in order to earn greater (EPV of) profits in later periods.

225. It would if that strategy promised to maximize the EPV of its profit stream. The limit price simply keeps out new firms, while a lower price may do more for future profits by stimulating present sales volume such that future repeat business and sales of complementary goods is maximized.

226. Since search goods may be copied quite closely by new entrants, the firm cannot expect to keep a disproportionate share of the market after entry occurs. Thus it should make hay while the sun shines, and set a skimming price. With experience and credence goods, on the other hand, the firm may anticipate a disproportionate share of the market following entry and would thus prefer to limit entry to a lesser number of firms.

227. The limit price is a skimming price when it is high, relative to the firm's unit costs, whereas it is a penetration price when it is low, relative to the firm's unit costs. It will be both a limit and a skimming price if barriers to the entry of new firms are relatively high, giving the existing firm a substantial unit cost advantage.

228. (a) Strategy B with NPV = $203,211, compared with strategy A's NPV = $186,276. (b) No, strategy B's NPV is still higher than A's ($164,011 compared to $150,344). (c) Yes. After four years, at 14%, NPV = $148,020 for A and $142,099 for B, and at

10%, NPV = $170,753 for A and $163,923 for B.

229. Not unless potential entrants are able to gather information about production that would allow them to reduce their unit costs of production if they did enter.

230. A reduction in unit costs would increase profit beyond the target level, possibly attracting entry. The firm would reduce price because it wants to expand its present customer base in order to increase its sales in the future through repeat business and complementary sales.

231. Price would remain the same if there was static market demand, constant marginal costs, and an isoelastic demand shift for the innovating firm as it becomes a price leader following the entry of new firms.

232. In the introduction and growth stages the market demand will shift outward, at an increasing rate at first and later at a decreasing rate. In the maturity stage, the market demand reaches a peak and begins to fall. Thus the market demand curve begins to shift inward at that time, and continues to do so during the decline stage.

233. If market demand grows faster than entrants are able to capture market share from the innovating firm, that firm's demand curve(s) will shift outward. Oppositely, if entrants capture market share faster than the market grows, the firm's demand curve will shift inward.

234. The two major first-mover advantages are the initial monopoly profits, and the ongoing cost advantage (and superior profits) the firm will enjoy as a result of having moved further down the learning curve.

235. Presuming the slope of the demand curves to be similar, your graph will show both price and output being reduced, as the new MR curve cuts the upward-sloping MC curve at a smaller output.

236. (a) Profit maximizing prices are $17.75 the first year, $17.50 the second year, and $14.50 the third year, approximately. The marginal cost data points are found using gradient analysis, and the marginal revenue curves are deduced from the demand curves. Plotting the D and MR curves against the MC curves (estimated by interpolating between the gradient points) we find the profit-maximizing prices for each year.
    (b) Penetration pricing would be recommended if entry of competing products was expected to take place more quickly, if substantial product differentiation could be built into the product such that sacrificed profits early in the product's life

are more than compensated for by later profits from repeat sales, and/or if the penetration price allows substantially increased sales of profitable accessory items, such as brushes.

237. (a) $129.88 and 25,371 units, found by setting MC = MR and solving for Q, then substituting in the demand curve.
(b) The minimum SAC for the entrant firm is $78.82, found algebraically or graphically. This is the limit price. At that price BB would sell 47,580 units, found by substitution for P in the demand curve.
(c) $135.20, found by increasing the intercept term of the demand curve by 10%, and dividing the slope term by 2/3, to find the price leader's *mutatis mutandis* demand curve, and so on. Its output level will be 20,827 and its profit will be $1,496,490.
(d) No. Setting the limit price of $78.80 would have caused BB to incur a loss of $1.556 million in the first year alone if it had attempted to serve the market demand at that price.

238. (a) $190 and 22,000 units. (b) $180 and $172.50, and 9,600 and 10,200 units. These are found by adjusting the slope of the firm's demand curve (dividing by its market share) and by reducing the marginal costs due to the learning effect.
(c) $124, found graphically or algebraically as the point where the entrant's SAC curve would cross its demand curve from below. Any higher price would allow a profit to be made. Note that we do not need to set price equal to minimum SAC of the entrant in this case.
(d) The limit pricing strategy promises EPV = $4,745,953 compared to $3,845,925 for the skimming strategy.
(e) Data accuracy, particularly with regard to demand, the potential entrant's costs, and the firm's own costs. We are also assuming that the entrant would not be willing to sustain a loss in the first year.

239. A competitive bid market is characterized by few sellers and a single buyer for each particular contract put up for tender. Uncertainty underlies both the cost and demand estimates, the degree of uncertainty being greater the more differentiated this product is compared to past production experience, and the more firms that are expected to bid on the contract.

240. With fixed-price bidding, the seller bears the entire risk of cost variation. With cost-plus-fee bidding, the buyer bears the entire risk of cost variation. With incentive bidding, the risk of cost variation is shared in pre-arranged proportions.

241. The firm's minimum bid price is equal to the EPV of all incremental costs associated with the contract minus the EPV of any incremental revenues (other than the bid price) associated with the contract. This is the minimum-bid price because the

contribution to overheads and profits will be zero in EPV terms and the firm should not tender a lower bid price, since this would result in a negative contribution.

242. We first calculate the minimum-bid price by estimating all incremental costs and revenues (other than the bid price). We then select arbitrary prices above this minimum price and estimate the probability of success at each of these prices. The contribution for each bid price level is equal to the bid price less the minimum bid price. The EPVC at each price level is the product of the contribution and the success probability. The optimal bid price is the one with the highest EPVC, and we find this price level by interpolating between the arbitrarily-chosen price levels to find the price with the greatest EPVC.

243. The firm might bid above or below the EPVC-maximizing price after considering non-monetary factors such as aesthetics, politics and risk. In effect, the monetary equivalent of these factors is subtracted from, or added to, the EPVC-maximizing price to arrive at the bid price.

244. Since risk averters are willing to trade off risk for return, the seller will have a series of bids that promise the same utility. The certainty equivalent of the fixed-price bid is the cost-plus-fee bid. In between these two extremes there is a variety of risk-shares and expected profits which the supplier will consider equivalent.

245. If the buyer is risk averse, he/she will prefer the fixed bid over all risk-sharing bids, with cost-plus-fee bids least preferred. Within the risk-sharing possibilities, the risk-averse buyer will prefer a lower risk share, _ceteris paribus_.

246. (a) $4,700, $7,200, $6,750, $3,600, and $1,500.
(b) A 23.25% markup will mean a bid price of $61,625 and EPVC of $ 7,349.91, given a simple interpolation between the 20% and 30% markup rates.
(c) Data accuracy and _ceteris paribus_. You should outline which data is especially critical to the decision, and which things in particular must remain unchanged, for the analysis to remain sound.

247. The markup approach incorporates all the incremental costs and incremental revenues (which were not estimated or calculated) in the size of the markup finally selected. The standard markup over the standard cost base covers all the usual incremental but not-easily-measurable costs and revenues, and the adjustments made to that standard markup to arrive at the final markup reflect all the extraordinary incremental costs and revenues involved in this particular contract.

248. If extraordinary future costs (or revenues) are expected to be associated with the contract, the firm will adjust its markup upward (or downward) to reflect this. In effect the firm adjusts the bid price in the direction that will maximize the EPVC.

249. The satisficing firm proceeds through a number of yes/no decisions before it actually decides to bid. It will bid if it has the technology and capacity to handle the job; if it seems worthwhile to prepare a bid; if the firm is desperate for work or considering diversification into this particular line of work; if it is necessary to maintain a relationship with this buyer; if the capacity utilization target is not being achieved; or if the profitability target is not being achieved. Having decided to bid, the firm calculates the standard costs of the contract, applies the standard markup, and adjusts the resultant price upward or downward in order to meet its capacity and profit targets or to compensate for extraordinary incremental costs or revenues associated with this particular contract.

250. The satisficing firm's standard costs are equal to its SAC at the target capacity output level. Its standard price is equal to SAC plus target profit per unit of output. Its target profitability is the firm's required rate of return on investment, or the opportunity cost of the resources owned by the firm. Its target capacity will be the desired rate of capacity utilization, something less than full capacity, leaving some excess capacity available to allow the firm to take advantage of opportunities which may arise.

251. (a) The incremental costs are direct materials $18,600, direct labor $33,200, and variable overhead $14,400 for a total of $66,200.
   (b) We should expect rivals to bid somewhat lower than usual, so our bid should be lower in order to maintain the one-third probability of success. It is more important than usual to gain this contract, since later contracts may be few and far between and subject to vigorous competition. Your bid price will reflect your assessment of the situation (and degree of risk aversion) and should fall somewhere between the incremental costs and full cost plus 15%.
   (c) Further information is desirable on the likely bids of rivals, their previous bidding patterns and the likelihood that they will submit lower bids on this contract.

252. The salient attributes of the bid are each given a score, these scores are weighted, and the bid with the highest total weighted score is offered the contract. Value analysis helps purchasers evaluate and compare competing bids on a quasi-scientific basis.

253. If there are few firms that usually bid, and contracts are both infrequent and of high value, the firms will have both the opportunity and motive to collude. They may collude by taking it in turn to submit the lowest bid, by submitting identical bids, or by agreeing not to bid on particular contracts.

254. Disclosure of bids allows all firms to know what prices other firms tendered. The low bidder will see how much money was "left on the table" - the difference between its bid and the next lowest bid. Next time it will try to narrow this margin, and the buyer will pay a higher price as a result.

255. (a) Presumably it was desperate for the jobs at the time, or it foresaw other incremental or opportunity revenues that would make it worthwhile. It lost some of these contracts because other firms' must have bid lower, presumably because their costs were lower.
   (b) $87,630, found by calculating the EPVC at each markup level over the minimum bid price.
   (c) We assume that this situation is similar in all important respects to the situations that make up the data base, including number of firms bidding, degree of capacity utilization for all firms, and so on.
   (d) The fixed-price mode is likely to be quite acceptable to the supplier because the risk of cost variation is very small, given the firm's experience in this production process.

256. (a) If we must win, we should bid below A's lowest expected price, and hence bid $396,500 or something in this area.
   (b) A bid of about $428,000 appears likely to have a relatively high success probability while at the same time contributing nicely to overheads and profits. Your answer will depend on the reasoning you followed and the assumptions underlying your reasoning, all of which should be made explicit.

257. (a) Our absolute minimum price would be the incremental cost level of $437,000, comprising only direct materials, direct labor, variable overhead, and the special equipment costs.
   (b) Full costs plus 25% suggests our bid price should be $655,625. Supposing we are bidding to win, our greatest competition comes from firm B, whose capacity utilization is quite low. Normally we might expect B to bid to be $663,493, but it could be somewhat lower this time. B's full costs are $576,950, ten percent higher than ours. Suppose B applies a 10% markup to these to arrive at a bid price of $634,645. B might feel confident of winning at that price if it expects us to maintain our bidding policy. Thus a bid of $630,000, representing a 20% markup on our full costs, would probably win the contract.
   (c) Will deviating from our normal policy cause a longer term decline in bid prices? Will goodwill be served by obtaining

this contract at a lower than normal bid? How do relative qualities compare? Do the other firms also have to purchase the specialized equipment?

258. The "elasticities rule" indicates that experience goods, with relatively high advertising elasticities and relatively low price elasticities, will tend to have relatively large advertising budgets as a proportion of sales.

259. Diminishing returns will be captured in a quadratic, cubic, (or power) function, if the appropriate coefficient (or exponent) has a negative sign.

260. Spend on advertising until, at the margin, the change in revenue is just equal to the change in production and advertising costs.

261. Increase advertising to shift the demand curve outward and adjust price to maximize profit given that demand curve. Continue this procedure until the change in revenue just equals the change in production and selling costs.

262. $9,833.33, Since $dQ/dA = 10 - A$, and the contribution margin is $6 per unit. See text, page 523, for a similar problem.

263. Your graphs should look like the ones in the text on pages 525 and 527. Drawing them yourself, working them out as you go, will really help you understand them, and help you remember them.

264. Advertising campaigns take a substantial period of time to conceptualize, organize, create the advertisement copy or film, await the availability of media time and space, and so on.

265. The prisoners' dilemma occurs when two or more parties, each acting in his or her own self-interest without information as to the simultaneous actions of others, are each motivated to choose strategies that have inferior outcomes as compared to the outcome of a cooperative strategy.

266. Firms tend not to coordinate the advertising expenditures because it would be difficult to do so, it would remove a desirable outlet for their competitive instincts, and it would leave any firm vulnerable to the cheating of another.

267. (a) Payoff Matrix for Little Red

	Little Red's Strategies	
Big Blue's strategies	$1m	$2m
Status Quo	$5m	$8m
Extra $1m	$3m	$4m

(b) The maximin strategy for Little Red is to spend $2m on advertising, since the worst outcome of that strategy, $4m, is better than the worst outcome of the alternate strategy, $3m.

(c) Little Red should estimate the probability of Big Blue raising its advertising budget and calculate the expected values of each strategy. It should also consider the jump it could get on Big Blue by raising its advertising first. With this additional information it can make a more informed decision.

268. (a) No. The profit maximizing level is where dQ/dA equals the reciprocal of the contribution margin. We find $dQ/dA = 12.62$ from the advertising elasticity value, since $a = dQ/dA \times A/Q$. Since the contribution margin is one dollar, Thompson could increase advertising to increase profits.

(b) We cannot say how much more should be spent on advertising, since the elasticity figure gives us only a point estimate of the slope of the advertising-sales curve. Thompson might make a series of increments, noting the magnitude of dQ/dA after each increase in the advertising level.

269. (a) Profit contribution appears to be maximized with $S = 5.5$ and $P = 6.55. This can be verified algebraically.

(b) Two records per week on sale will reduce the average price to $6.55. Quantity demanded will be 772 records and contribution will be $1,090.60 per week .

270. (a) 52,501 units, TR = $15,487,730, Profit = $2,307,574, found by substituting for A in the advertising-sales function.

(b) $242,812, found by equating dQ/dA with the reciprocal of the contribution margin and solving for A.

(c) Q = 53,207, TR = $1,569,616, Profit = $2,311,884.

271. Competitive advantage is used by Porter to mean superior and sustained profitability - profitability exceeding the industry average on a continuing basis.

272. With search products, price elasticity tends to be relatively high. Thus the profit-maximizing markup will be relatively small. Given elastic demand, the best way to increase the price-cost margin is to reduce unit costs.

273. Since information on search products is easy to acquire, consumers tend to be aware of more substitutes. There tends to be more substitutes, as well, because search goods are relatively easy to copy. With search goods, consumers recognize good value when price is reduced, and tend to switch more readily. Thus, demand tends to be relatively elastic.

274. In short, cover the bases, trim the fat, and proliferate brands, to the extent that costs can be saved without causing a

greater loss of revenue.

275. Price leadership and promotional pricing, and informative advertising relating to price, quality features, and the product's availability.

276. If the product has a search attribute that is unique, and desirable, the firm should differentiate its product on that basis, and make hay while the sun shines, for other firms will attempt to incorporate the same feature in their products at the earliest opportunity.

277. A brand name acts as a stock of information about product quality. Past experience with a brand-name product can be used as a strong predictor of quality for the next purchase of the same brand. Consistent quality means that the consumer's uncertainty about quality is reduced - a lesser variance means a smaller confidence interval around mean quality expected.

278. The differentiating firm will tend to offer a relatively broad product line and product bundles within that line. It will strive to be first with new features that it can use as a basis for differentiation, and it will pay particular attention to consistency of product quality through stringent quality control.

279. Since a quality leader sells on quality, not on price, its pricing strategy will tend to be relatively passive, following the price leader when necessary. It will practice product line pricing, bundle pricing, setting higher prices wherever possible and where this may have positive impact on quality perceptions.

280. Advertising will tend to be largely persuasive, concerning unique features of the product and other attributes that are claimed to be present in greater quantity in the product. The advertising budget will tend to be a relatively high proportion of sales revenue, following the elasticities rule, which says that the advertising/sales ratio will equal the ratio of advertising elasticity to price elasticity.

281. (a) Neither cost leadership nor quality leadership seems possible without the purchase of new equipment. When purchased, this equipment should be chosen with the strategy in mind, since different equipment may best serve each strategy.
    (b) You could argue either way here. Their reputation and proclivity for promotional pricing militates for a cost-leadership strategy. But more promising, I think, is the opportunity to be a quality leader, either broad-based or focused, where the price-cost margins tend to be higher.
    (c) What is the cost of new equipment, the costs of other firms, the feasibility of repositioning their product and/or of

introducing a superior quality brand name, and/or of opening up some ice-cream parlors, and so on.

282. (a) A focused differentiation strategy seems optimal, considering all the issues. Mr Koster's particular skills make him particularly suitable for the "immigration" segment of the market, where there is less competition and sufficient work to keep him busy and adequately remunerated.

(b) He should provide immigration law services, priced at a premium to reflect quality, targeting the colleges and high-technology firms who regularly hire foreign professionals. His advertising should be largely persuasive, offering to do the job more quickly, and with fewer problems, than anyone else can.

283. (a) To suit the owners' objectives, a differentiation strategy of some description seems to offer the most promise.

(b) They could open a store catering to the do-it-yourselfer, and from this base offer a service for luxury bathrooms.

(c) Products for the home handyperson, priced at a small premium to reflect the advice that is also available, with promotion targeted at the do-it-yourselfer in the local media. Separate advertisements might be placed in magazines for the luxury bathroom service.

284. (a) Limited capacity precludes cost leadership. A focused differentiation strategy seems the superior alternative.

(b) Focus on the more-affluent, enthusiast skier, by upgrading the trials and installing snow-making equipment. Limit the number of tickets sold daily. Prices should be higher than average, and promotion should stress the uncrowded slopes, the good snow conditions, and the exclusivity.

285. If depreciation is tax-deductible, the depreciation charges multiplied by the tax rate are opportunity revenues associated with the investment. If investment credits are allowed directly against tax liability, the amount of those credits are opportunity revenues. In either case, a cash outflow is avoided.

286. The straight-line method divides the net cost (initial cost less salvage value) into equal parts over the life of the asset. The SYD and DDB methods allocate a greater proportion of the net cost in the earlier years than in the later years, due to the formulas used.

287. The NPV is increased when depreciation is accelerated because a greater part of the tax deduction is taken sooner, and thus is multiplied by a larger discount factor.

288. The NPV is zero when the IRR is equal to the opportunity

discount rate (ODR), positive when the IRR is greater than the ODR, and negative when the IRR is less than the ODR.

289. The profitability index (PI) is equal to one when the NPV is zero, greater than one when the NPV is positive, and less than one when the NPV is negative.

290. The payback-period criterion is to select the investment which recoups its nominal initial cost in the least elapsed time. It may not serve the firm's objectives because the cashflows are not discounted and other cashflows within the firm's time horizon are not considered.

291. The ARR criterion is to select the investment with the largest ratio of cumulative revenues to initial cost. Unless the revenue stream is discounted, this criterion ignores the present value of money.

292. Omega should undertake projects A, B, and C only, since the NPV of these projects is positive. Alternatively, the IRR exceeds 10%, and the PI exceeds unity, for these three projects. Check your calculations against the following, which assume a discount rate of 10% per annum.

	A ($)	B ($)	C ($)	D ($)
Initial Cost	-100,000	-135,000	-85,000	-122,000
Year 1	-11,091	23,909	50,909	-22,728
Year 2	-7,024	28,428	26,445	8,760
Year 3	57,550	36,513	13,974	36,213
Year 4	42,619	38,590	8,469	65,910
Year 5	14,591	13,660	3,415	21,111
Year 6	5,362	5,645	--	10,556
N.P.V.	2,007	11,745	18,213	-2,179

293. The NPV curves of two investments may cross because the NPV calculation implicitly assumes that funds received can be reinvested at the opportunity discount rate, while the IRR calculation implicitly assumes that the funds can be reinvested at the IRR, which may not be readily available in other investment opportunities.

294. Yes, if the crossover point occurs at a discount rate that is higher than the opportunity discount rate.

295. The profitability index measures the relative efficiency of an investment for generating revenues, while the NPV measures the absolute efficiency. Thus a small project might generate more per dollar of initial cost, and leave the remainder of the funds earning the opportunity rate of return, while a larger project might generate more NPV overall.

296. Use the Coefficient of variation, certainty equivalent, or EPV-using-different-discount-rates criteria. Maximin, and the payback criterion, are also crude risk-averter's criteria.

297. The certainty equivalent criterion incorporates all risk and return considerations, but is hard to apply for other people (or a firm) since we cannot know their preference patterns. The coefficient of variation is easier to calculate but is unable to account for degrees of risk aversion. The EPV using DDR criterion requires either an arbitrary choice of discount rates or immense search costs to accurately assign the ODR to each separate project. Maximin ignores the probabilities and all outcomes except the worst one for each project, but is applicable if the firm cannot afford the worst possible outcome. The payback period criterion may not discount the cashflows, and ignores the cashflows occurring after the initial cost is recouped.

298. (a) Location A - Sportswear: $55,351; Location A- Equipment: $49,140; Location B - Sportswear: $59,129; and Location B - Equipment: $45,165.
    (b) Plotting the cumulative payback against months we estimate that the payback periods are: Location A - Sportswear: 18 months; Location B - Sportswear: 21 months; Location A - Equipment: 23.5 months; Location B - Equipment: 25 months.
    (c) Location B - Sportswear has the highest NPV (by $3,777.91) and the second shortest payback period (by 3 months), in both cases compared with Location A - Sportswear. Ms. Monibaggs will choose the former if she thinks that it is worth waiting an extra 3 months for payback, in return for a sum $3,777.91 greater in NPV terms over the life of the project. This in turn depends on her individual time preference for money.

299. (a) Plan A: NPV = $231,174; IRR = 23.26%; and PI = 2.15. Plan B: NPV = $255,177; IRR = 26.47; and PI = 2.34.
    (b) Implement Plan B. It is favored by all three criteria, and involves less risk as well. We assume data accuracy and *ceteris paribus*.

300. (a) Oval circuit EPV = $23,396,753. Road circuit EPV = $28,863,680.
    (b) Payback periods (nominal dollars) are 3.75 years for plan A and 4.6 years for plan B. In present-valued dollars, these are 4.94 years and 5.21 years.
    (c) The road circuit promises a larger EPV by $5.5 million, and only takes three months longer to reach payback in PV terms. It also requires less initial outlay.
    (d) Data accuracy and *ceteris paribus*. All projections of costs, demand, and participant behavior must be reliable, and there must be no changes in consumer tastes, incomes, expectations, or other attractions.

Chapter 1

1-1 Certainty exists when the outcome of an action is known in advance. Risk exists when there are several possible outcomes with a prior probability distribution that can be assigned objectively. Uncertainty exists when there is are several possible outcomes with subjective prior probabilities.

1-2 A model may be based on extremely simplistic assumptions if its purpose is pedagogical or predictive. It would be a good model if it served that purpose well, by either teaching about the main elements of a complex system, or by predicting the outcome of an action. Predictive models may be based on demonstrably false assumptions if a more reasonable assumption is not possible, and yet serve their predictive purpose.

1-3 Graphical and algebraic models offer more precise characterization of the system to be represented, and are typically more concise, with consequent economy of time and effort needed to achieve the same purpose.

1-4 The firm's time horizon is the end of its planning period, and is determined by the magnitude of search costs, the prevailing interest rates, and the preferences of managers and shareholders.

1-5 The opportunity discount rate is the best rate of interest or return available from that subset of alternative uses of funds which has the same risk as compared to the project (or profit stream) under consideration.

1-6 The most accurate measure of present value would be found by using a modified formula recognizing 52 discrete cash flows spaced evenly throughout the year. Using the daily cash flow convention will cause a slight overstatement of the present value because it assumes that weekly revenues are spread evenly over the week, and that funds received early in the week are invested to earn interest during the remainder of the week.

1-7 The firm has a problem when its objective function is not being maximized, and this is a decision problem when there is more than one possible solution to the problem. A decision problem is not necessarily a crisis; it might simply involve falling short of potential performance levels. By reference to its objective function and its performance, the firm will, or will not, perceive a problem to exist.

1-8 Uncertainty, as distinct from risk, exists when there is a probability distribution of outcomes associated with any decision alternative, and the probability associated with each possible outcome must be assigned subjectively - that is, on the basis of the decision maker's experience, intuition, and judgment.

1-9 Presuming that the firm wishes to maximize its present value over its time horizon, the appropriate decision rule, given certainty and time horizon within the present period, is short run profit maximization . Uncertainty requires expected value analysis and hence the objective becomes the maximization of the EV of profits. Longer time horizons require present value analysis, and the objective is then changed to maximization of the PV of profits. With both uncertainty and longer time horizons, the objective is to maximize the EPV of profits.

1-10 The Principal-agent problem exists when there is asymmetric information concerning the agent's actions. Thus the agent may serve his/her own objectives to some degree, rather than the principal's. Incentive contracts may be structured to align the agent's objectives with the principal's.

Chapter 2

2-1 In risk and uncertainty there is a probability distribution of prior possible outcomes associated with each decision. Risk and uncertainty is measured by the standard deviation of the probability distribution. You might argue that measures of downside risk, such as the semivariance (i.e. including only the outcomes below the EV) or measures concerned only with losses, would be more appropriate. You would need to reconcile this with an appropriate measure of value, however, since the EV criterion is based on both sides of the probability distribution and all possible outcomes.

2-2 Risk aversion means getting disutility from risk. Risk averters take risks whenever it is utility-maximizing to do so. They will select the more risky alternative whenever it offers sufficient expected return to compensate for its risk and thus, utility is maximized by selecting that alternative.

2-3 A risk preferrer might choose a high-risk low-stakes gamble to a low-risk, high-stakes gamble because the risk preferrer expects to derive utility from both the risk and the return. Most of you will conclude that you are risk averse, and some of you will be convinced that you are a risk preferrer. You can demonstrate both, depending on the size of the gamble involved. (For example, you might be willing to toss a coin for double or nothing rather than pay back a dollar you owe, but you probably wouldn't take the same chance with your automobile.)

2-4 The degree of risk aversion, or the marginal rate of substitution between risk and return, is reflected by the slope of the indifference curves. Given a set of decision alternatives more-risk-averse decision makers may prefer one alternative, while less-risk-averse decision makers may prefer another, because the preferred alternative, in each case, allows the attainment of the highest indifference curve.

2-5 (a) The expected value of the ticket is the probability of winning times the prize, or 1/100,000 times $10,000, minus the cost of the ticket. Thus it is minus forty cents.

(b) You will if the high-risk, minus-forty-cent alternative puts you on a higher indifference curve than the zero-risk, zero-profit alternative of not buying it. If so, you are a risk preferrer at this level. If not, you are risk averse, or object to gambling on other grounds.

(c) Your answer will vary depending on your degree of risk aversion or preference.

(d) No, the certainty equivalent is slightly higher than the sum that makes you prefer the gamble.

2-6 Although the maximin criterion favors product B, without more information on the expected values, the standard deviations, and on the product manager's degree of risk aversion, we cannot make a definite statement.

2-7 These criteria may disagree when one alternative has both greater expected value and greater risk than another. Which is preferable depends on the decision maker's trade-off between risk and return. The CV criterion assumes that this trade-off is linear and constant and that it converges on the zero-risk, zero-return point; the CE criterion recognizes that this trade-off may change with higher levels of risk, and need not converge on the zero point. There is more likely to be disagreement between these criteria when there is a substantial difference in magnitude between decision alternatives.

2-8 The value of additional information is calculated by identifying the best alternative for each state of nature. The profits from each situation are then weighted by the probabilities to find the EV of the decision given full information. Subtract from this the EV obtainable without further information and the remainder is the value of the information.

2-9 Decisions are evaluated <u>a priori</u> on the basis of their use of the available data, whether sufficient search activity was undertaken, was the appropriate decision criterion used, was the timing appropriate, and was sensitivity analysis used.

2-10 Sensitivity analysis examines the optimality of the decision alternative selected, relative to the assumptions underlying the decision. If different, reasonable, assumptions would not cause a change in the recommended decision, the decision is not sensitive to its underlying assumptions. If it is sensitive to an assumption, additional search activity may be worthwhile to allow management to take the decision based on their own views of the underlying assumptions, once the impact of these have been explicitly brought to their attention.

Chapter 3

3-1 The MRS diminishes to the right along an indifference curve because it is equal to MU_x/MU_y, and MU_x declines as the consumer obtains more of product X, and the MU_y increases as the consumer retains less of product Y.

3-2 The MRS (slope) for the milkshake lover will be relatively high, since she would be prepared to give up a relatively large amount of burgers in order to obtain an extra milkshake while staying at the same level of utility. Conversely the burger lover would give up relatively few burgers for an extra milkshake.

3-3 Using the product approach, increased income is reflected by a parallel shift outward of the budget line. In the attribute approach, the efficiency frontier will move outward in a parallel fashion. In both cases, the new equilibrium might include either more of product X (if a superior good) or less (if inferior).

3-4 A change in tastes and preferences toward the product (or attribute) on the X-axis will cause the indifference curves to steepen, as the MU_x increases for any level of X. The highest attainable curve in the new indifference map will indicate greater purchases of product X (or a product which contains a higher ratio of attribute X) relative to product Y (or a product containing a lower ratio of attribute X).

3-5 With self-service gasoline on the vertical axis, the first person's indifference curves would be relatively flat (low MRS) compared with the person with the opposite traits.

3-6 The consumer who regards both X and Y as normal goods (or attributes) will have indifference curves that are roughly parallel in their curvature, whereas the consumer who regards X as an inferior good (or attribute) will have indifference curves that converge for high Y/X ratios and diverge for low Y/X ratios.

3-7 The flyer might be seeking to save time, avoid the effort of driving and the displeasure of traffic tickets, and to experience the thrill of flying and the pleasure of in-flight service and entertainment. The driver might be seeking economy, the flexibility to stop en route, the lack of anxiety associated with flying, the pleasure of driving, and so on.

3-8 Rationality means pursuing one's objective function, and the consumer would not be maximizing utility by choosing an attribute combination inside the frontier.

3-9 A change in perception causes the consumer to view a product differently - e.g., recognize greater attribute content in the product. A change in tastes causes the consumer to value attributes more (or less) highly without necessarily changing perception of a particular product's attributes.

3-10 New products could be designed to contain attributes in combinations desired by consumers but not offered in competing products. When consumer preferences are concentrated around the products already offered the optimal strategy might be to give more of the desired attribute combination per dollar, rather than to serve a smaller but neglected market segment.

Appendix 3A

3A-1 It is the change in quantity demanded due to the change in real income caused by the price change, ceteris paribus. Yes, the change in real income might cause more or less to be demanded of all products.

3A-2 It is the change in the quantity demanded of a product due to a change in the relative prices of products, with real income and other things being equal.

3A-3 The value of income lies in what it can purchase. Thus if two different nominal incomes produce the same level of utility under two different price ratios, then real income is constant.

3A-4 The budget line is kept parallel while delineating the income effect in order to preserve ceteris paribus, since the slope of the budget line reflects the price ratio.

3A-5 The substitution effect is equal to dQ/dP, with constant real income. The consumer will always substitute toward a product if its price decreases, or substitute away from it if its price increases, ceteris paribus. Thus, either dQ or dP will be negative, and the ratio dQ/dP will always be negative.

Chapter 4

4-1 The factors include the disposable income and tastes and preferences of the population regarding football versus other forms of entertainment, the performance prospects of the team, the presence of superstars, the prices of competing events and entertainment sources, the extent of TV coverage of home games, the scheduling of the games, the promotional efforts of competing events and entertainments, and so on.

4-2 The coefficient to price in the demand function is dQ/dP while the slope of the demand curve is dP/dQ: one is thus the reciprocal of the other.

4-3

	TR increases	TR decreases
e > 1	Price decrease	Price increase
e = 1	(TR constant for small price changes)	
e < 1	Price increase	Price decrease

4-4 Point price elasticity changes at every price as one moves along the demand curve. Thus it underestimates the elasticity above the price used for the calculation of the point elasticity, and overestimates the elasticity for points below this price on the demand curve.

4-5 Since price elasticity can be expressed as E = dQ/dP x P/Q and the demand curve can be expressed as P = a + bQ where b = dP/dQ the elasticity value can be calculated by substituting 1/b and the current values of P and Q into the elasticity expression.

4-6 (a) Soft drinks (as a product class) probably have a relatively low price elasticity since substitute beverages are quite distinctively different and soft drinks typically take only a minor proportion of incomes.
(b) It would be relatively high since several close substitutes are available.
(c) Similar to Coke's.
(d) Quite high, since there are several reasonably close substitutes, and the product takes a relatively large proportion of the consumer's income.
(e) Relatively high, since there are many other brands of jeans and types of apparel, and they probably take a high proportion of buyers' incomes.

4-7 Since e = dQ/dP x P/Q and we are given P, Q, and e we can calculate dQ/dP = -8.333. The expression for the demand curve is P = a + bQ, where b = dP/dQ = -0.12. Given the current values of P and Q and b we solve for a = 7.5. Thus the expression for the demand curve is P = 7.5 - 0.12Q.

4-8 The income elasticity of demand for "luxury" goods exceeds one; hence for any percentage change in incomes the demand for these products will change by a larger percentage. Oppositely for groceries and meat, which may be regarded as necessities, the income elasticity is likely to be positive but less than unity, in which case the demand for these products changes less than proportionately with incomes.

4-9 The positive cross-price elasticity indicates that the two products are substitutes. The positive cross-advertising elasticity indicates that advertising one product benefits the other. Either it was very bad advertising, or there were spillover effects resulting from the advertising that expanded the market for the product class.

4-10 The rainfall elasticity of demand could be defined as the proportionate change in demand for umbrellas divided by the proportionate change in the rainfall level. It may be useful for estimating the required inventory of umbrellas needed to meet demand during an expected rainy period, for example.

Chapter 5

5-1 To form an expectation regarding the impact on sales if one of the uncontrollable variables did change. This data would facilitate planning for production, inventories, and promotion efforts, and alert the firm to areas of possible vulnerability.

5-2 (i) Sample must be representative; (ii) questionnaire must be well designed; (iii) interviewer bias must be avoided; (iv) Ceteris paribus must prevail between the survey period and the implementation period.

5-3 These questions elicit information about the consumer's likely reaction to changes in prices, incomes, taste of the product, claimed advantages, an so on. They should be formulated such that the responses allow estimates to be made of the coefficients to the variables.

5-4 For each person, take the highest price at which the consumer would buy the product. Plot the number of respondents specifying each price level (as the highest they would pay) against that price level. The line of best fit to these observations may be regarded as the estimated demand curve.

5-5 Your experiment should contain adequate controls to ensure that the impact of changes in each variable can be ascertained while ceteris paribus prevails. Thus, repeated trials must be undertaken with one variable being changed each time, with different samples from a population of customers each time.

5-6 The researcher must monitor all factors which may change exogenously and which may have an impact on the quantity demanded. When a control market is used, it must be ascertained that the control market and the experimental market are sufficiently similar in all important respects, and that any changes in uncontrollable variables were present to a similar degree in both markets.

5-7   It would be unreliable because <u>ceteris paribus</u> did not hold over the past twenty years.   The value of the dollar, supply conditions, consumer incomes and tastes, availability of substitutes for newspapers, and other factors have changed significantly, thus rendering such an exercise virtually useless.

5-8 Regression analysis proceeds on the assumption that the residuals occur randomly, are normally distributed, have constant variance, and have an expected value of zero.   These conditions are not met if we have specification errors, heteroscedasticity, or autocorrelation.   The presence of any one of these "pitfalls" means that the coefficients to the independent variables, and the standard errors, will be inaccurate.

5-9 The appropriate functional form would be found by running several variants of the regression equation and choosing the form which generates the highest R^2, with the caveat that for explanatory models all independent variables must be significant at, for example, the 95% level.   An examination of the residuals should indicate whether any important variables have been omitted, considering also the absolute size of the R^2 statistic. Logical analysis should underlie the inclusion of all variables in the regression equation, in order to avoid the "wrong variable" problem.   Multicollinearity should be absent for explanatory models -- if pairs of independent variables are highly correlated the regression equation should be re-specified to exclude the least important of each pair.

5-10   None of the "six major pitfalls" discussed in the text should be present.   The coefficient of determination should be relatively high, and the standard error of estimate and the standard errors of the coefficients should be relatively low.

Appendix 5A

5A-1 Causal forecasting models attempt to accurately model the system and explain the changes occurring in that system. Time-series forecasting models use data from past periods and attempt to predict future values by projection, weighted averages, and similar techniques.

5A-2 A moving average technique will usually be superior if the variable is subject to random fluctuations about a trend.

5A-3 Exponential smoothing models adjust each prior forecast to reflect its forecast error, and require much less data retrieval and calculation.

5A-4 The weight would be adjusted to minimize the sum of the squared deviations when applied to past data.   That is, the squared differences between the predicted values and the actual values would be minimized by the appropriate weight.

5A-5 The data is first deseasonalized, by dividing each observation by its seasonal index. A trend line is then fitted. The ratio of the observed point to the trend line is the cyclical index. Dividing each observation by its cyclical index leaves the trend and irregular components. The latter are expected to occur randomly and have expected value of zero.

5A-6 Leading indicators show turning points in advance of the turning points for GNP or the variable in question. Sales of a product for which your product is a component, accessory, or repair part, are typically leading indicators. Employment, new building permits, and the change in consumer debt also tend to lead the demand for many products.

5A-7 A single leading index rarely performs perfectly well, as it sometimes gives false signals due to random changes. A composite leading index allows these random events to cancel each other out, giving a more reliable indication of what is likely to happen in the future.

5A-8 One might begin with trend analysis and projection of growth rates in order to identify the longer term movement in the demand for the product group. This naive forecast would then be modified on the basis of intention surveys, leading indicator analysis, and consideration of the specific factors influencing demand for that product. Alternatively one could construct a single-equation regression model, or an econometric model, to explain and predict the demand for the product in terms of all the major determining variables.

Chapter 6

6-1 Since only one level of capital is possible in the short run, each row of the table represents the input combinations available in a short-run situation. A long-run situation is one where the firm can choose among several levels of capital (or short-run situations). Thus the entire table represents the input combinations available in the long run.

6-2 The decision to change plant size can be made immediately, but the firm must remain in a short-run situation until the last constraining fixed factor can be varied. This will take six months, if plant is to be expanded and eight months if plant size is to be reduced. In the latter case, it may be worthwhile to give some workers leave with pay for the last two months and begin production in the smaller plant after six months.

6-3 The law of variable proportions covers the three possible stages of increasing, constant and declining marginal physical productivity of the variable factor(s). The law of diminishing returns simply says that after some point there will be declining marginal productivity and thus makes no direct reference to the other two possible stages.

6-4 The point of inflection indicates that the slope of TP has reached a maximum and then begins falling. Since the slope of TP is equal to the MP, the inflection point indicates that MP has reached a maximum and then falls. Thus it is the point where diminishing returns to the variable factor begin.

6-5 The short run AVC curve derives its shape from the TVC curve, which in turn derives its shape from the TP curve, which in turn derives its shape from the specific form of the production function.

6-6 (i) The firm may stabilize its output level at the average demand level and use inventories to balance supply and demand. (ii) It may leave some plant and equipment idle, as demand decreases, to maintain the least cost input ratio. (iii) It may contract with other firms who would supply additional goods when demanded. (iv) It may establish a backlist, or waiting list, which it will satisfy as soon as it gets the chance to.

6-7 It would be erroneous because the SAC value at the expected value of demand may be substantially different from its value at other points in the probability distribution of demand. One should incorporate all values of SAC over the full range of output levels that are possible, by calculating the expected value of SAC given the demand distribution.

6-8 Full capacity refers to the output rate at which MC rise above SAC. Absolute full capacity refers to the output rate at which the SAC curve becomes vertical. Overfull capacity refers to output rates between the full capacity and the absolute full capacity levels. Excess capacity refers to the difference between the full capacity rate and the current (lower) output rate.

6-9 The LAC curve is the envelope curve of all the available SAC curves. It is compromised of those points on the SAC curves that allow the per unit cost of each output level to be minimized, given the choice of any SAC curve. The LMC curve lies below the LAC curve when the LAC is falling and lies above it when the LAC is rising. The LMC curve shows the minimal marginal cost of producing each output unit given the variability of all inputs.

6-10 Economies of scale occur when LAC decreases as a result of all inputs being augmented by the same proportion. Economies of plant size occur when LAC decreases as a result of the fixed inputs being augmented (not necessarily in the same proportion as labor or each other). Economies of firm size occur when the LAC curve sinks downward as a result of more efficient utilization of some fixed factors as another plant is established, or when the firm is able to purchase inputs at lower prices.

Appendix 6A

6A-1 Technical efficiency means that no part of any input can be removed without the output level falling, and thus the MRTS and slope of the isoquant curve at that particular input combination are negative. Economic efficiency is the least-cost input combination, found by the tangency of the isocost line to the highest attainable isoquant curve.

6A-2 If inputs are not completely divisible in a physical sense, they are usually divisible on the basis of time. Thus, inputs may be hired or leased for short periods without the necessity of actually purchasing that input in its entirety. Similarly, although the supplier of labor is not divisible, that person may be hired for short periods in order to provide the fractional units of labor required.

6A-3 Isoquants bend back if the marginal productivity of the variable (or the fixed) inputs becomes negative, causing the MRTS to become positive. At relatively high K/L ratios there is too much capital relative to labor, and at relatively low K/L ratios there is too little capital relative to labor.

6A-4 Inputs should be used such that the ratio of each input's marginal product to its price is equal, or the MRTS is equal to the negative of the price ratio for any pair of inputs, at the desired output or budget level. MRTS = $-P_l/P_k$ = MP_l/MP_k.

6A-5 The relative factor price will differ between countries due to differing labor and capital markets, and labor productivity may be higher in some less-developed countries. Thus, not only is the isocost curve likely to be flatter, but also the isoquant curves are likely to be flatter, in less-developed countries. If the difference in relative factor prices exceeds the difference in relative factor productivities, the less-developed country should use the more labor-intensive technology.

Appendix 6B

6B-1 The objective function and all constraints must be linear in the solution variables.

6B-2 It would be horizontal if the constraint applies only to the variable on the Y axis. Similarly, it would be vertical if the constraint applies only to the variable on the X axis.

6B-3 In the long run there are, theoretically, no constraints on any resources. In the short run, however, fixed inputs act as constraints on the firm's objective function.

6B-4 Arbitrarily, since the isoprofit line and the binding constraint line are coextensive throughout their lengths.

6B-5 Expressing the constraint as an equality allows us to delineate the outer limit to the output possibilities.

6B-6 In algebra we work with equations, and the slack variable allows the equation to remain true at the solution values of the variables, whether or not the constraint is binding.

6B-7 The procedure is to evaluate the objective function at each corner solution, where the number of non-zero-valued variables and the number of constraint equations will be the same. We can limit our search to the corners because no solution on a facet of the feasible region will better serve the objective function.

6B-8 In effect, the constraint is relaxed to some degree. The feasible region will shift outward in the area of the constraint that is relaxed.

6B-9 He/she should enquire whether the resource can be purchased for less than the shadow price per unit. If so, it would be more profitable to add an extra unit of that variable to the production process.

6B-10 In a primal maximization problem, one maximizes the output variable subject to the input constraints. The dual problem is to minimize the value of the unutilized inputs, subject to the constraints concerning the requirements of each output on each input. The solutions are identical, since it is simply two ways to approach the same problem.

Chapter 7

7-1 Indirect costs are those that are not easily separable for individual units of output, but which may, nevertheless, vary to some degree with output. Thus the accountant's indirect costs may exceed the economist's fixed costs.

7-2 The opportunity cost of a fixed factor is the greatest of (i) the contribution the asset could have made in an alternative employment at similar risk, or (ii) the amount the asset's salvage value fall during the production period, or (iii) the amount the funds tied up in the asset could have earned if liquidated and deposited in a security of similar risk.

7-3 The opportunity cost of an input is zero if it has already been paid for, and the input has no alternative usage, no resale value, and would not be replaced in inventory. If an input has several different uses, its opportunity cost is the greatest contribution or revenue it could earn in that subset of these alternative uses which exhibit similar risk.

7-4 Normal profit means that each input is making as much income (or contribution) as it could in its next-best-alternative employment. Pure, or economic, profit means that each input is making as much or more than it could elsewhere. The firm would not liquidate and invest elsewhere when TR = TC because nowhere else offers a better investment at the same level of risk.

7-5 The relevant costs of a particular decision are the EPV of all costs that are expected to be incurred as a result of that decision being taken. Relevant costs thus include those parts of fixed costs which vary as a result of the decision.

7-6 Fixed overhead costs are the result of an earlier decision and are incurred or will be incurred regardless of a later decision. Irrelevant costs do not change the contribution of a decision and can therefore be ignored.

7-7 Future cost and revenue consequences of a current decision should be evaluated on the basis of expected net present value, and added to (if positive) or subtracted from (if negative) the contribution calculation.

7-8 The appropriate discount factor is (i) the one reflecting the opportunity discount rate, and (ii) the one reflecting the cashflow convention that best approximates the actual pattern of cashflows.

7-9 As well as the present-period explicit costs, opportunity costs, and other future costs, one would calculate the expected present value of the legal costs by forming a probability distribution of the costs involved and discounting these expected costs back to present-value terms using the opportunity discount rate. This is no small task, of course, and would most likely involve substantial search costs.

7-10 Opportunity costs are revenues, income, or contribution forgone as a result of the decision to use a factor of production in its present use, whereas opportunity revenues are costs avoided as a result of the decision to use factors of production in their present use.

Appendix 7A

7A-1 Breakeven analysis allows decision makers to calculate the sales volume beyond which total revenues exceed total costs, and to question whether or not this sales volume is attainable at the proposed price level. If not, or if the expected value of the decision is negative, different prices and quality combinations (reflected in different variable costs) may be examined to find the preferable price-quality combination.

7A-2 First, the cost and revenue curves must adequately reflect the true relationships in the vicinity of the breakeven point. Second, the TR and TC curves must reflect only incremental revenues and costs, but musr reflect <u>all</u> incremental revenues and costs, when breakeven analysis is used for decision making purposes.

7A-3 One can derive a measure of "volume elasticity of profit" to reflect the responsiveness of profits to changes in sales volume. It would be represented as the percentage change in profits over the percentage change in volume. Higher elasticity values would indicate higher operating leverage, and hence greater sensitivity of profits to fluctuations in sales volume.

7A-4 The TR and TC curves may be represented as linear functions of output when this is either accurate or represents a reasonable approximation of the actual relationships in the vicinity of the breakeven volume and over the relevant range of output levels.

7A-5 Since $TR = aQ + bQ^2$ and $TC = TFC + cQ$, we set $TR = TC$ and solve for Q. Thus, $aQ + bQ^2 = TFC + cQ$, or $bQ^2 + (a - c)Q - FC = 0$. To solve this for Q requires the quadratic equation,

$$Q = \frac{-B \pm \sqrt{B^2 - 4AC}}{2A}$$

Substituting for $A = b$, $B = (a - c)$, and $C = -TFC$ we find

$$Q = \frac{c - a \pm \sqrt{a^2 - 2ac + c^2 + 4b(TFC)}}{2b}$$

Since b is negative there are two solutions and the relevant one is the larger value for Q. (Note: This may have been a little tough for you unless you remembered the quadratic equation from an earlier course. If not, well, now you know!)

Chapter 8

8-1 Extrapolation from the data base implicitly assumes that the observed relationship will hold at output levels outside those observed. But since the efficiency of the variable factor in the production process may increase, remain constant and later decrease, the relationship between costs and output should be expected to change at different output levels.

8-2 Cross-section observations of total costs and output levels are unlikely to allow accurate estimation of short-run cost functions, since such estimation requires <u>ceteris paribus</u> to hold for factor prices and factor productivities, not to mention that each firm's product be the same (no product differentiation).

8-3 It is important (i) to obtain the best equation for predictive purposes and (ii) to avoid a serious mis-specification of any derived cost relationship such as the MC and AVC curves.

8-4 Essentially the engineering technique seeks to find the physical production function, or the input requirements for each of several output levels. These input requirements are then monetized to find the TVC curve, and the per unit cost curves are then derived from the TVC (and the TFC) data.

8-5 Raw materials usage might become less efficient as output increases, resulting in greater wastage. Labor efficiency might increase at first due to division of labor, specialization and learning by doing, and decrease eventually due to overcrowding, boredom, declining morale, and so on. Repairs and maintenance expense might increase faster than output due to greater wear and tear taking place at higher utilization rates, inspections and services being delayed due to greater activity with consequent higher costs, and so on.

8-6 Problems include cost-and-output measurement and matching problems, overestimation of economies and diseconomies of plant size due to SAC observations not being on the LAC curve, differing factor prices and factor price ratios, and differing technologies due to differences in the skill and productivity of labor and the vintages of the capital equipment involved.

8-7 If the linear relationship has a positive intercept on the cost axis, the ratio of TC to Q declines as Q increases and hence the LAC declines as Q increases. Even then, the data may spuriously indicate economies of plant size if some observations are significantly different from the tangency point between the SAC curve and the true LAC curve.

8-8 The learning curve shows the reduction in SAC as cumulative volume increases, given a particular plant size. SAC falls, for any particular output level, due to increased efficiency in the production process as workers discover shortcuts, improve assembly procedures, become faster with their hands, and so on. Similarly, changes in the composition or arrangement of the plant and equipment may make the fixed factors more efficient.

8-9 There will be no factor substitution only if the factor price ratio(s) remain constant. If all factor prices remain constant, or all change by the same proportion, the same input ratio will remain optimal for each output level, although each output level will require less of both inputs.

8-10 If all factor prices are expected to follow the general trend of inflation, then the SAC at each output level will increase at the inflation rate. If factor prices change at rates different to the rate of inflation, then forecasting factor substitution will also be required when forecasting SAC levels.

Chapter 9

9-1 Monopolistic competition differs from pure competition only because products are perceived as being differentiated rather than as identical across firms. Oligopoly may have either identical or differentiated products, but it differs from both the above cases by virtue of the fewness of sellers in oligopoly compared to many sellers in both of the other two cases.

9-2 (a) Oligopoly, since in particular markets for a particular make or type of automobile, the impacts of one's actions are likely to be felt upon the other's sales and profits. (b) They act like oligopolies in competition for particular students, since student mobility is limited, and not all schools offer all attributes desired by students. (c) A monopoly, since there is no other seller offering a remotely similar product. (d) Pure competition, since there are likely to be hundreds of similar farmers selling similar grain to the flour millers, and the product are virtually identical.

9-3 If MC shifts such that it crosses the upper tangible section of the MR curve, profits will be maximized given the new cost conditions at a higher price, notwithstanding that this involves significant loss of market share. To stay at the old price and output level would cause marginal units to be unprofitable so that profits would be less than those at the higher price.

9-4 When the cost or demand shifts are firm specific, no other firm will have a reason to raise price from the present level. The expectation that the firm will face a relatively elastic ceteris paribus demand curve for price increases will inhibit the firm from raising price unless MC rises so much as to cause the marginal units to be unprofitable. If the cost or demand shift is common to all firms, then they all have similar motivation to change prices.

9-5 Under conscious parallelism all firms adjust prices at about the same time. Thus, all firms are acting like price leaders, each one being confident that the others will do likewise and that it will face a _mutatis mutandis_ demand for the price change contemplated. If a cost change is confined to one firm, that firm will not expect conscious parallelism, because the other firms have no similar reason to adjust prices.

9-6 Some firms may follow the price leader out of fear that the price leader might drive them into bankruptcy with a price war or supplier boycott. Most firms probably follow the price leader to reduce uncertainty, to avoid the risk attached to initiating price changes, and to obviate the time and expense which would otherwise have to be spent on analysis of the pricing problem.

9-7 The price followers face a kinked demand curve, since they expect rivals to ignore their price increases and match their price reductions.

9-8 Sales maximization subject to a profit constraint requires a lower price than does short-run profit maximization. This is consistent with the lower price required for long-term profit maximization, since demand is expected to be more elastic over the longer term. The lower price inhibits entry and broadens the current market share. This in turn lays a foundation for repeat sales, and of complementary items in future periods. Thus the lower current price leads to increased future sales and profits.

9-9   The firms' objective function must be long term profit maximization, and each firm's time horizon falls beyond the short run. Strategic variables are price, promotion, product design, and place of sale. The conjectural variation is as for price leadership or conscious parallelism - for the price leader(s) it is unity for both price increases and decreases, and for the price followers it is zero for self-initiated price increases and unity for price decreases.

9-10 The greater are the search costs necessary to set the price in each period that maximizes expected present net worth, the more "wrong" the actual price can be without current profits being less than the level indicated by the EPNW analysis (given full information). Profits in each period will be higher as long as the search costs avoided exceed the revenues forgone.

Appendix 9A:

9A-1 The multiplant firm's sigma-MC curve represents the least incremental cost of producing each output unit when the firm is free to designate which of its plants should produce that unit.

9A-2 A cartel is an oligopoly operating like a multiplant monopoly. The output of each firm is constrained such that the overall profit is maximized. An individual firm could make greater profits for itself if it undercut the cartel price, since it faces a <u>ceteris paribus</u> demand curve as long as the price cut remains secret. When products are differentiated, there will be an equilibrium structure of price differentials. Cheating on the cartel will still bring increased profits, as buyers align their marginal rates of substitution with the new price ratios.

9A-3 The firm will wish to produce up to the point where its combined MC rises to meet MR on the last unit sold. This means that MC will be approximately the same in all three plants, at the level at which the horizontally summed MC curves cut the market MR curve.

9A-4 The firm maximizes profits because it sells in each market to the point where MC = MR, and price elasticities (hence demand curves) differ. Thus the firm gets higher profit margins from the less-elastic market and greater volume in the more-elastic market, than it would by setting a single price for all buyers.

9A-5 At the time of writing, OPEC was no longer an effective cartel due to the independent pricing and output policies of its members and the availability of oil from non-OPEC suppliers. It has evolved into a price leader of sorts, with Saudi Arabia acting like a low-cost price leader.

9A-6 First degree price discrimination involves setting a different price for each buyer. Second degree price discrimination involves setting higher prices for those whose demand is more urgent. Third degree price discrimination involves setting different prices in different markets. The conditions required for price discrimination are separable markets (or buyers), differing price elasticities, and no price competition.

9A-7 The transfer pricing problem is to choose the transfer price such that the firm's overall profits are maximized. Any non-optimal transfer price may allow one division of the firm to maximize profits but the firm's profits would not be maximized.

9A-8 The delivered price increases at a decreasing rate because the cost of transportation has a fixed component (on and off-loading costs) and a variable component (relating to distance).

The variable cost per mile is likely to be constant, while the loading costs per mile decrease as the distance increases.

9A-9 It can reduce production costs, and/or improve the efficiency of its transportation service, in order to reduce its delivered prices. Given its costs, it could reduce prices and accept a lower profit margin. Finally, it could attempt to shift its demand curve using other strategic variables.

9A-10 Cross-hauling occurs when two suppliers' trucks pass each other while each is on it's way to a customer who lives nearer the other firms' factory. It will happen if one firm has a cost advantage, if products are differentiated, to maintain supplier contacts with more than one firm, and due to the buyer's ignorance of the other firm's existence.

Chapter 10

10-1 It is profit maximizing to use a rule-of-thumb pricing procedure whenever the incremental costs of search and data analysis are expected to exceed the revenues forgone by not having the desired information. That is to say, if the cost of additional information exceeds the value of that information, the firm should proceed without the information.

10-2 No, because the price, and the elasticity at that price, are uniquely determined. Higher prices have higher elasticity values. To "solve for" price given an elasticity and cost data effectively violates the connection between each price and its unique elasticity value. We assume that MC = AVC.

10-3 Search costs cause the profit curve to shift down, such that there is a series of prices for which profits will be higher without search, as compared to the optimal price after search costs have been incurred. The width of this range of prices depends on the elasticity of demand and the level of marginal costs, as well as the magnitude of search costs.

10-4 The markup will remain profit maximizing despite shifts in cost and demand curves if the demand shifts are isoelastic and ceteris paribus, or if both cost and demand curves shift upwards by the same proportion (in nominal terms).

10-5 The presence or absence of particular attributes determines the location of each product's ray in attribute space. The product must then be priced such that it extends the frontier just far enough for the marginal revenue of the last unit sold to fall to equality with the marginal cost of producing that unit.

10-6 Each product should be priced such that it maximizes its contribution to the EPV of the product line as a whole. The interdependencies in demand of the products must be considered, as well as the attribute content of the products and their prices relative to other firms' products and prices.

10-7 New products, and others for which very little quality information is available to the consumer such that price is the best indicator of quality; products for which search is expensive relative to the product's price; products for which quality is imperative; and products amenable to conspicuous consumption.

10-8 This firm would increase its total contribution by raising prices of all or most individual items, and then offering bundle prices that are less than the sum of the prices of the items that are included in the bundle. This would extract additional consumer surplus from many customers, although it would also alienate some customers, for a net gain in contribution.

10-9 If the costs of manufacturing, packaging, storing, and selling increase less than proportionately with volume, the product can be sold in larger bundles with discounts for quantity. The discounts should not be so deep that the marginal revenue per unit is less than the marginal cost per unit.

10-10 A firm would use promotional pricing to clear excess inventories, to gain market share, to enter a market or obtain new distributors, to meet competition, as a loss leader, or to remind buyers that the firm is a source of lower-priced goods.

Appendix 10A

10A-1 Horizontal price agreements are those between firms competing at the same level in the maufacturing-wholesale-retail sequence. Vertical price agreements are those between firms at different levels in this sequence.

10A-2 Any kind of market-sharing agreement may be found to constitute a price-fixing agreement, because market price tends to rise when supply is restricted, and tends to be higher when there is a monopoly supplier rather than two or more rival firms.

10A-3 No, the existence of meetings followed by coordinated price adjustments, written or reported statements, and any communications between firms concerning prices or market shares, may be sufficient evidence for a conviction.

10A-4 If firms _independently_ decide to adjust prices, and there is no evidence of a conspiracy to agree on prices, then price leading and following, or conscious parallelism, is not illegal.

10A-5   Price discrimination is allowable if the prices (i) reflect differences in costs; (ii) do not injure existing or potential competitors; (iii) simply meet the competition; and/or (iv) reflect the deteriorating marketability of the product.

10A-6   Predatory pricing is price discrimination for the purpose of destroying competition or eliminating a competitor. The firm's intent to achieve that purpose is the critical difference between vigorous price competition and predatory pricing.

10A-7   RPM is a vertical price agreement between manufacturer and wholesaler or retailer concerning the resale price of an item. Manufacturers may want RPM to protect their products' quality images, or to avoid price competition at any level.

10A-8   Resellers may support RPM because it tends to eliminate price competition at their level, and obviates their pricing problem. They might oppose it if they felt the RPM price was at an inappropriate level, or inhibited their competitiveness.

Chapter 11

11-1   It is best analyzed in the context of an established product market when it is basically similar to those existing products. In this context its price can be determined by the value of the additional attributes incorporated in the product.

11-2   With really new products there is virtually no information concerning the demand curve. An estimate of market demand may be very important to align productive capacity with market demand at the chosen price to avoid production or marketing problems.

11-3   Essentially, when it is EPV-maximizing to do so, as when (i) the firm's time horizon falls in the short run; (ii) the demand will be short-lived; (iii) entry barriers are very high; and (iv) the impact on quality perceptions is such that it is so.

11-4   It would be EPV-maximizing if the impact on quality perceptions was so great that the demand curve in future periods would be shifted outward by enough to more than compensate for the current profits forgone.

11-5   The sales maximizing (subject to a profit target) model is appropriate if entry is impossible or tolerable, otherwise one of the limit pricing models is appropriate. These will result in a relatively low price that allows substantial market penetration.

11-6   The limit price is a skimming price if barriers to entry are high, such that the price is high relative to costs, perhaps near to the profit-maximizing level. It is a penetration price if barriers to entry are low, and price is low relative to costs.

11-7 If the new product is a search good, post-entry profits will be relatively low, so limit pricing is indicated. But if it is an experience or credence good, post-entry profits may be relatively high, militating in favor of price skimming initially.

11-8 Price will decline due to entry of new firms, learning effects in production, economies of plant size, and ultimately because of declining market demand for the product.

11-9 The product life cycle hypothesis contends that market demand will increase but ultimately decline as it passes through the introductory, growth, maturity, and decline stages. The innovating firm's sales will increase if market demand grows faster than its share of the market declines.

11-10 The first-mover advantages are the initial monopoly profits and the higher profit margin in later periods due to this firm being "further down" its learning curve. Risks include bankruptcy, loss of capital invested and forgone alternatives, and damage to the firm's, or the manager's, reputation.

Chapter 12

12-1 Situations will include price quotes on various repair jobs and other one-of-a-kind or one-on-one pricing situations. Shopping around for consumer durables such as automobiles and appliances often leads to a competitive bid situation, as different sales people offer various discounts, trade-ins, etc.

12-2 Cost categories would include labor and materials both for initial construction and its later operation, and maintenance. Research may be necessary to find a suitable system. Public relations and legal expenses might be expected, and future earnings (goodwill) from other airports might be forthcoming.

12-3 One would proceed by converting the various possible levels of lawsuit costs to present value terms, estimating the probabilities of each cost level occurring, calculating the expected value of the (present valued) costs, and adding this expected net present value to the other incremental costs.

12-4 Goodwill should be regarded as the present value of future contributions to overheads and profits occasioned by the current decision. Since there will be a probability distribution of future contributions, the ENPV of these outcomes should be estimated and entered into the calculation of (net) incremental cost. Yes, you would be prepared to bid lower than otherwise since your (net) incremental costs will be lower.

12-5   The EPV criterion operates on the principle that over many trials the incidence of each outcome as a proportion of total outcomes will tend toward the probability values previously assigned to each outcome.   Some outcomes will be greater, some smaller, than the EPV, but over many trials the sum of the actual outcomes should approach the sum of the EPV's of the outcomes.

12-6   There are fixed-price, cost-plus-fee, or risk-sharing bids, with the risk of cost variation being borne by the seller, the buyer, or shared, respectively. The cost-plus-fee bid is the certainty equivalent of the fixed-price bid, and there is also a series of risk-sharing bids that the buyer will regard as equal.

12-7   If the markup percentage is chosen with an eye to balancing the probability of obtaining the contract with the profitability of the contract, the bid price may come quite close to the EPVC-maximizing bid price, and will economize on search costs.

12-8   Presuming that you want to win the contract, you would bid lower than ordinarily if you need the job badly due to (i) low capacity utilization and the desire to avoid associated problems and costs; (ii) goodwill considerations; (iii) aesthetic and political considerations; and (iv) knowledge of rivals' low capacity utilization or extraordinary desire to win the contract.

12-9   Value analysis attempts to explicitly evaluate each bid, in terms of both the price and the qualitative features of the bid. It is useful for making and defending the decision made, and allows the criteria to be explicitly stated and argued. It is analogous in concept to attribute analysis of consumer behavior, except that the tastes and preferences may reflect company policy or preferences rather than the decision maker's own preferences.

12-10   Collusive bidding is against the public interest because it tends to raise the price of the winning bid compared to what it might otherwise have been.   It hurts the customer who must pay more than otherwise with subsequent impact on utility or profits; it hurts those competing firms who would otherwise get more business and profits; and it hurts all other firms in the economy by restraining the forces of competition with subsequent adverse effects on the allocation of resources.

Chapter 13

13-1   _Ceteris paribus_ will be an appropriate assumption for a monopolist or for any firm that is small relative to its market, since no reaction from rivals would be expected. An oligopolist might expect _ceteris paribus_ to apply in a situation of limited information flow between sellers, but usually would not.

13-2   A minimum level of advertising and promotional efforts may be required to attract or hold the consumer's attention, or counteract rivals' advertisements. Also, a minimum level of expenditure may be required to get into certain types of media which in turn are indispensible for an increase in sales.

13-3   First, the marginal non-buyer is likely to be increasingly reluctant to purchase our product. Second, it is likely to cost more to advertise to more distant customers. Third, higher levels of advertising may provoke a negative reaction from some people.

13-4   Expand advertising expenditure to the point where the increment to total contribution is just equal to the increment to advertising expenditures. Alternatively, expand it to the point where marginal revenue is just equal to incremental production and selling costs.

13-5   Increased advertising shifts the demand curve outward, causing a higher price to be profit maximizing.   Given diminishing returns to advertising, this process is continued until the last dollar spent on advertising adds only one dollar to contribution.

13-6   Since they make decisions in isolation from each other and are unable to continuously monitor each other's decisions, they are faced with the dilemma of being forced to act to protect themselves, knowing that if they do, they are likely to be worse off than they otherwise would be.

13-7   No. Apart from other strategic variables which might be manipulated, the quantity of advertising expenditure may bear no relationship to the quality of the advertising and promotional activity produced.

13-8   Ascertain consumer tastes and preferences and how well the campaign is directed at the target consumers, and use past behavior or pre-testing to estimate the impact the campaign will have on consumer tastes and preferences, on consumer information, and ultimately on their purchasing behavior.

13-9   No, since the EPV of future contributions due to this period's advertising may be greater than the excess of short run advertising cost over short run incremental revenues.

13-10   The residual impacts of advertising accumulate to cause brand loyalty to existing brands. To overcome this loyalty the entrant must be prepared to spend a higher proportion of revenues on advertising compared to the existing firms. Since brand loyalty could be expected to exist without advertising, product differentiation barriers could exist without advertising.

Chapter 14

14-1   Competitive advantage is the goal, and it means superior and sustained profitability. Competitive strategy is the means to that end. Competitive advantage is compatible with maximizing the EPV of net worth, given uncertainty and search costs.

14-2   Can it be a cost-leader without inducing vigorous price competition? Does it have the necessary technology to produce at low cost? Is its product conducive to a cost leadership strategy? Does it already have a reputation for low prices and good value?

14-3   Price elasticity tends to be relatively high because search goods are easily matched by rivals and consumers will be aware of more substitutes. Advertising elasticity tends to be low because repetitive informative advertising is redundant and persuasive advertising is ineffective for search goods.

14-4   The firm should produce basic products incorporating all the features expected, but no more than are expected for the price, and should consider launching several different brand names of the product if this will expand total sales.

14-5   Price leadership, if this role is vacant or can be usurped, and promotional pricing on a periodic basis. Informative advertising, utilizing relatively small advertising budgets.

14-6   Peters and Waterman's two essential ingredients can be viewed as elements of a differentiation strategy. Service and product quality are attributes of the product, and continued technical development allows the firm to continually find new features to differentiate its product.

14-7   Is there a viable market niche currently being neglected? Does the firm have the technology to achieve its objectives? Can it position itself as a supplier of quality, specialized goods, given its recent history? Is its product conducive to a differentiation strategy?

14-8   The firm must produce goods and services that more closely reflect the buyer's tastes and preferences. Thus product lines will be more extensive, product bundles will be offered, new features will be incorporated whenever possible and profitable, and particular attention will be given to quality control.

14-9   As a new entrant, or a smaller firm, the firm may find a focus strategy the best alternative. Profit opportunities may be greater for any firm in a particular niche, rather than attempt to compete on the entire spectrum of products and regions that comprise the national market.

14-10   There are thousands of correct answers for this one. To a large extent your lists will reflect regional awareness of firms and their competitive strategies.

Chapter 15

15-1   A project is acceptable if the NPV of the revenue stream is positive when discounted at the opportunity discount rate. The IRR criterion is to accept a project if its internal rate of return exceeds the opportunity discount rate. Since the NPV can only be positive if the IRR exceeds ODR, the two criteria must always agree on the accept-reject decision.

15-2   The initial cost, estimates of future costs and revenue streams, their probability distributions, and the opportunity discount rate.

15-3   Different depreciation methods have different impacts on net cash flow after taxes. "Accelerated" depreciation methods increase the NCFAT as compared to the straight line method, and different "accelerated" methods increase NCFAT by more or less.
15-4   As the firm demands progressively more funds, the cost of these will increase as the lenders recognize the increasing risk of default associated with lending the next block of funds.

15-5   The payback criterion may be appropriate when the time horizon is relatively short. Also, the payback criterion will rank projects the same as the IRR criterion if projects are long-lived and have uniform revenue streams after the initial investment cost. Thus, if the IRR criterion agrees with the NPV criterion, then so too will the payback period.

15-6   The average rate of return does not consider the present value of the revenue stream, and tends to obscure important cashflow information by averaging revenues over the life of the project.

15-7   The IRR may rank projects differently due to the implicit assumption that the earlier receipts may be reinvested at the IRR. In practice it may be impossible to reinvest these funds in any new projects or securities which have a return as high as the IRR, whereas investments at the opportunity rate are always available. The IRR calculation is useful, where people are accustomed to thinking in terms of rates of return, as an additional piece of information to the NPV calculation.

15-8   The profitability index criterion may be in conflict with the NPV criterion where there are differences in the magnitudes of the initial costs and the revenue streams, and in the time pattern of the revenue streams.

15-9   It changes the decision rule for limited capital budgets. When projects are indivisible, the NPV rule indicates skipping over those you can't afford and implementing those you can.   If projects are divisible the PI criterion will rank the projects in order of their relative efficiency of generating NPV, and thus the PI criterion should be followed.

15-10   The degree of uncertainty of future costs and revenues increases, the further into the future we attempt to forecast. The payback-period criterion chooses the project which minimizes the length of time to recoup its initial investment, and thus puts minimal reliance on the accuracy of future estimates.

Chapter 1.

Q1. purpose...pedagogical...explanatory...predictive.

Q2. opportunity discount.

Q3. daily.

Q4. planning period.

Q5. probabilities of the potential outcomes.

Q6. full...incomplete.

Q7. $425,680.

Q8. present...net present worth.

Q9. $46.30.

Q10. $239.05.

Chapter 2.

Q1. product.

Q2. the net present value multiplied by the joint probability of that outcome occurring.

Q3. standard deviation of the probability distribution of potential outcomes.

Q4. potential outcome...deviations...joint probabilities of occurring...variance...square root.

Q5. utility...disutility...nothing.

Q6. standard deviation...expected net present value.

Q7. the largest minimum outcome.

Q8. the certain return that would make the decision maker indifferent between that return and the gamble.

Q9. is (i) based on EPV data, which is (ii) obtained from search taken to the optimal point, and (iii) is found by the application of the appropriate criterion, and (iv) is taken at the optimal time, and (v) is suitably qualified by sensitivity analysis.

Q10. the decision alternative that appears optimal would remain so under any other set of reasonable assumptions.

Chapter 3.

Q1. combinations of two variables that provide the same level of utility.

Q2. predictive.

Q3. the ratio of marginal utility to price...equal...budget... spent.

Q4. higher...lower...negatively...intersect...convex.

Q5. amount of Y that the person will give up...an extra unit of X...total utility.

Q6. negative...increase(decrease)...increases(decreases).

Q7. (i) reduced price(s); (ii) increased incomes; and (iii) improved perceptions of the product(s).

Q8. a possible shift of the efficiency frontier...a shift of the indifference curves.

Q9. attainable indifference curve...consumers.

Q10. rates of substitution...attributes...products...similar.

Appendix 3A.

Q1. quantity demanded...relative prices...income effect...real income...the price of a product.

Q2. positive...negative...reinforce.

Q3. decrease...increase...decrease. (Presuming it is not a Giffen good).

Q4. negative...outweighs...negative.

Q5. other things were not equal. (Mother's Day is in May).

Chapter 4.

Q1. price...advertising _and/or_ promotion...product design _or_

258

quality....place of sale <u>or</u> distribution strategy.

Q2.   tastes and preferences...perceptions of the product.

Q3.   False. (For the conventional expression P = a + b Q.)

Q4.   P = 2,000 - 0.25 Q.

Q5.   in...positive.

Q6.   the proportion of income absorbed by the price...the number of close substitutes available.

Q7.   luxury good.

Q8.   P = 16.667 - 0.0667 Q.

Q9.   discrete <u>or</u> not very small...average...range.

Q10. negative...positively...are not. (Profits <u>may</u> be maximized in the case of kinked demand curves, discussed in Ch. 9.)

Chapter 5.

Q1.   current values for the parameters in the demand function... future values of both the parameters and the variables in the demand function.

Q2.   <u>any three of</u> non-representative samples, interviewer bias, poor questionnaire design, intentions may not continue to actions, interviewer malfeasance, improper data treatment.

Q3.   the squared deviations of the Y observations from the predicted values of the Y variable are minimized.

Q4.   distortion of the respondent's answers due to the presence
of   the interviewer.

Q5.   the influence of uncontrolled determinants of demand must be accounted for.

Q6.   many situations during the same period of time...a single situation over many periods of time.

Q7.   the dependent variable...variations in the independent variables.

Q8.   proportion of total variation in the dependent variable that is explained by variations in the independent variables.

Q9. the coefficient be at least twice the size of its standard error of estimate.

Q10. the residuals are not random with respect to any of the independent variables...the independent variables are correlated with each other.

Appendix 5A.

Q1. use past values of the variables to predict future values ...considering foreseeable changes in the variables.

Q2. coefficient of determination...significant at high level of significance.

Q3. the use of predicted values in the prediction of subsequent values.

Q4. minimizes the sum of the squared deviations of the observations from the predicted values.

Q5. ratio of the observation in any period to the moving average centered on that period.

Q6. three.

Q7. cyclical...irregular.

Q8. averaging...experts...business periodicals...the Wall Street Journal, Fortune and Business Week magazines (for example).

Q9. it tends to exhibit turning points prior to the turning points of the series we wish to predict.

Q10. of the series being observed that are rising at any time.

Chapter 6.

Q1. a period in which at least some fixed inputs constrain the output level.

Q2. short run situations available at any point of time.

Q3. after some point, as progressively more units of the variable inputs are added to the fixed inputs, the marginal product of the variable inputs will diminish.

Q4. falling...falling.

Q5.   falling...falling faster than AVC is rising <u>or</u> falling while AVC is virtually constant.

Q6.   marginal product of the variable inputs is constant <u>or</u> marginal cost is constant...divisible.

Q7.   use inventories...contract out...ask customers to wait.

Q8.   The SAC curves associated with progressively larger plant sizes shift downward to the right.

Q9.   marginal cost begins to exceed short run average costs.

Q10. the percentage reduction in unit costs when output is doubled.

<u>Appendix 6A.</u>

Q1.   positive...also positive.

Q2.   equal to the negative ratio of the marginal products, <u>or</u> the marginal rate of technical substitution, <u>or</u> the amount of one input that can be withdrawn when one unit of another is added, such that output remains constant.

Q3.   the least-cost input combinations for every output level when all inputs are variable.

Q4.   the same amount of...substitute away from labor toward other inputs.

Q5.   labor cost per unit is lower, labor productivity may be higher, and capital cost is probably similar.

<u>Appendix 6B.</u>

Q1.   outputs...constant rate...profit margin.

Q2.   maximum quantities of either variable that can be produced given any value of the other variable.

Q3.   the amount of a fixed input that remains available.

Q4.   the value of an additional unit of a fixed input.

Q5.   slack variables into...m - n...each remaining variable... objective function...corner.

Q6.   utilize the inputs such that the value of the remaining (unutilized) inputs is minimized.

Chapter 7.

Q1.   residual accruing to the owners of the firm's assets...the excess of total revenue over the total opportunity costs of all inputs.

Q2.   vary directly with the output level...exclude.

Q3.   it happens to equal the opportunity cost of the funds tied up in the asset.

Q4.   that equals the replacement cost of the item.

Q5.   total revenue...total cost...the opportunity cost of all inputs.

Q6.   more than they could in any alternate employment...risk.

Q7.   the difference between profit and contribution to overheads and profit is a constant, namely fixed costs.

Q8.   quality control...production and delivery schedule.

Q9.   outlays which the firm is obligated or committed to make.

Q10. the contribution that would otherwise be made by product A to the payment of the resources in question, and to overheads and profit.

Appendix 7A

Q1.   total revenue...total cost curves...relevant range.

Q2.   whether or not that volume is attainable at the price level chosen.

Q3.   price...total cost curve.

Q4.   total fixed cost...contribution margin.

Q5.   profit...output.

Q6.   incremental.

Chapter 8.

Q1. average rate at which TC changes with respect to output over the range of outputs being considered.

Q2. time series...functional form...highest coefficient of determination.

Q3. and subtracting three times the standard error of estimate to the predicted value of total variable costs.

Q4. physical production function or the input requirements of each output level...transforms the input-output data to cost-output data by multiplying the inputs by their prices.

Q5. different plants probably have different and older technologies, as well as different input prices and productivities.

Q6. economies of plant size, at least initially (assuming the cost-output data is from different plant sizes).

Q7. measurement error.

Q8. firms typically experience substantial economies of plant size at first, followed by constant returns to plant size, with little evidence of diseconomies of plant size.

Q9. factor prices and factor productivities.

Q10. increasing...labor and management inputs.

Chapter 9.

Q1. the number of sellers...the degree of product different-iation.

Q2. the market forces of supply and demand...marginal cost with marginal revenue or price.

Q3. the market is small relative to the economies of plant size available such that monopoly is inevitable.

Q4. it is one of many firms and is small relative to the market.

Q5. the kinked demand curve model...the price leader/follower models...the limit price models.

Q6. smaller firms may earn pure profit and expand and new firms may enter the industry.

Q7.   the lower price inhibits entry...larger current sales lead to greater repeat business...larger current sales lead to greater future sales of complementary items.

Q8.   not allow the potential entrant to make normal profit in EPV terms over its time horizon.

Q9.   minimal barriers to entry and exit.

Q10. pursue the attainment of satisfactory levels or targets in one or more variables, rather than to attempt to maximize an objective function.

Appendix 9A.

Q1.   marginal cost in each plant rises to the level to which marginal revenue in the market has fallen.

Q2.   Side payments.

Q3.   want to buy the product sooner rather than later.

Q4.   separable markets or buyers...differing demand elasticities between markets or buyers...no price competition.

Q5.   demand is less elastic.

Q6.   net marginal revenue (of the selling division)...marginal production cost...marginal production cost.

Q7.   lower than.

Q8.   their distance from the supplier.

Q9.   reducing delivered price as a result of reduced production costs...reducing price as a result of reduced transportation costs.

Q10. buyers' preference to buy from more than one seller as an insurance policy...search costs preventing consumer awareness of the lowest delivered price or managements' awareness of cross hauling... product differentiation.

Chapter 10.

Q1.   the contribution forgone due to the "wrong" price is less than the search costs avoided.

Q2. fifty.

Q3. e = [-AVC/(P - AVC)] - 1.

Q4. search costs are greater...elasticity of demand is higher...
     marginal costs are lower. (This was a tough one - see fn.10,
     p.419, and figure out why a lower MC increases the range.)

Q5. iso-elastic...nominal...real.

Q6. the attributes of the firm's product compared with the
     attributes of the rival firms' products, given the prices of
     rivals' products.

Q7. contribution to the firm's overheads and profit.

Q8. too high.

Q9. consumer surplus.

Q10. high...search...transportation...inventories.

Appendix 10A.

Q1. there is evidence of a conspiracy to fix prices, such as
     meetings or communications concerning prices.

Q2. meetings of decision makers where prices were discussed...
     communications between firms concerning prices...evidence of
     market-sharing agreements.

Q3. different costs...nobody is injured...match rival's price
     reduction...deteriorating marketability of the product.

Q4. did so without intending to destroy competition or to harm a
     competitor.

Q5. all manufacturers set the same resale prices and enforced
     the observance of these prices.

Q6. the use of their product as a loss leader may harm the
     quality perception when consumers make price-quality
     associations.

Chapter 11.

Q1. a future period...surmountable...price-quality inferences.

Q2.   price skimming...future profits will be minimal in any case.

Q3.   price skimming.

Q4.   maximizes sales subject to a profit constraint...limits the entry of new firms.

Q5.   penetration pricing...price skimming.

Q6.   the learning effect...economies of plant size...reduced... price skimming strategy.

Q7.   introduction...growth...the number of new firms expands faster than the market demand does.

Q8.   initial monopoly profits...higher contribution margins in later periods.

Q9.   new entrants can learn faster, by avoiding mistakes the initiating firm was seen to make.

Q10. best serves the firm's objective function or maximizes the EPV of the firm's profit stream over its planning period.

Chapter 12.

Q1.   single...suppliers or sellers...uncertainty.

Q2.   the risk of cost variation.

Q3.   initial bid price or the target cost and profit margin... buyer's...cost under-run...cost over-run.

Q4.   they are essentially search costs that are sunk by the time the firm considers the choice of the actual bid price level.

Q5.   present period explicit costs and revenues...opportunity costs and revenues...future costs and revenues.

Q6.   the contribution at that bid price...the probability of success at that bid price.

Q7.   cost-plus-fee...total utility as the fixed price bid.

Q8.   increase...bid higher than they usually would (to cover their increased costs).

Q9.   (i) it is achieving its targets and (ii) it does not have the technology and (iii) it is not considering diversification and (iii) it is not necessary to bid to maintain a relationship with the buyer.

Q10. desired attributes and weights...scrutiny and discussion.

Chapter 13.

Q1. price elasticity tends to be relatively low while advertising elasticity tends to be relatively high.

Q2. the marginal consumer will be increasingly difficult to attract, and repeated information reaches fewer new people.

Q3. outward...diminishing.

Q4. output...advertising...reciprocal of the contribution margin.

Q5. increment to total revenue...the increment to advertising and production costs.

Q6. the increased advertising by each firm reduces the effectiveness of the other's advertising.

Q7. advertising is a desirable forum for competition...there are time lags involved...these leave them vulnerable to being doublecrossed.

Q8. uncertainty regarding the advertisement's effectiveness.

Q9. the revenue implications extend beyond the present period.

Q10. raising the cost structure of entrants, who must spend large amounts on promotion to counteract the accumulated effects of the existing firms' past advertising.

Chapter 14.

Q1. superior and sustained profitability or profits that are above the industry average on a continuing basis.

Q2. its product has unique features...it is incapable of achieving cost leadership.

Q3. the learning effect in production, economies of plant size, and pecuniary economies in purchasing.

Q4. can more easily emulate the firm's product...can easily

verify product quality and will be aware of more substitutes.

Q5.   cover the bases...trim the fat...that can be essentially
      similar under a variety of brand names.

Q6.   price leadership...promotional pricing...information about
      the products quality attributes, price, and place of sale.

Q7.   difficult and/or temporary...easier and/or more longstanding
      due to the difficulty of evaluating and emulating these
      attributes.

Q8.   can be higher than otherwise...be inferred to be of a
      similar level to the firm's existing products.

Q9.   persuasive...quality...price...large.

Q10. confines its attention to a market segment and attempts to
      provide those buyers with the highest-quality product.

Chapter 15.

Q1.   residual or difference...ratio.

Q2.   internal rate of return...opportunity discount rate.

Q3.   opportunity revenue...it allows the firm to avoid taxes.

Q4.   that reduces the EPV of the future net cash flows to
      equality with the initial cost of the project.

Q5.   lenders will recognize that the borrower's risk of default
      increases as it's financial leverage increases.

Q6.   it ignores cash flows that occur after payback is attained,
      and the conditions for equivalency are unlikely.

Q7.   the revenue stream is uniform...the project (and the firm's
      time horizon) are infinitely long-lived.

Q8.   reinvested at the internal rate of return.

Q9.   relative efficiency...dollar of outlay...size-disparity.

Q10. neutrality...neutral.

COMPUTER COURSEWARE MANUAL

Introduction   270

The Benefits of Using the Computer Courseware   270

How to Use the Lotus Templates   272

    - hardware and software needed
    - retrieving Lotus files
    - moving the cursor and entering data
    - erasing data ranges
    - the escape key
    - filing a revised worksheet
    - printing a copy of your worksheet
    - viewing graphs of your data

The Lotus Templates   274

    - a brief description of each template
       with excerpts of some

How to Modify the Templates, or Make your Own   285

    - protecting and unprotecting the worksheet
    - inserting and deleting columns and rows
    - copying and moving data and formulas
    - relative vs. absolute addresses
    - values vs. labels
    - adjusting column width
    - inserting formulas
    - @ functions

The Fortran programs   287

    - EPV program
    - MULTREG program

Introduction.

    This manual introduces you to, and explains how to use the courseware files that are available on floppy disk for your use at home or at school on a personal computer.

    What is courseware? It is a series of programs, written using a particular software, that will run on your computer hardware. It is called courseware because it is specific to a particular course, in this case Managerial Economics, although you will find this courseware useful in other courses and for other purposes as well. The courseware provided here includes over twenty templates usable with the Lotus 1-2-3 spreadsheet software, or any other software that will read Lotus files.

    What are templates? Each one is an established format for the analysis and solution of a particular problem or type of problem. They contain words to guide you when you enter the data and to explain the results. They contain formulas which are embedded in the cells of the spreadsheet and which automatically make calculations whenever you input new data values.

    The courseware also includes two more-complex programs written in the Fortran programming language (by my colleague Dr. Andrew Stollar) to run on MS-DOS (Micro-Soft's Disk Operating System). These programs can handle larger data sets and more complex problems, but their use is relatively simple. You simply follow instructions and enter the data, and leave the hard work to the computer.

    Your instructor can get the courseware files on request from the publisher, Prentice-Hall, and you can copy these to your disk for use at home or in the computer laboratory. You will need an IBM (or compatible) personal computer, and a copy of the Lotus 1-2-3 software package (or other software that reads Lotus files.)

    Is this courseware necessary to understand the Managerial Economics course material? No, you can proceed without it, as we all did before the personal computer became more readily available. But this computer hardware/software/courseware package will save you time and help increase your understanding of the material. Use it if you can.

The Benefits of Using the Computer Courseware

    1. The courseware will help you better understand the course material, since the templates set up the end-of-chapter problems in a way that will enhance your understanding of the central issues involved in the problems and their solution.

270

2. The courseware greatly reduces the "number crunching" you would have to do. As you know, number-crunching can be time-consuming, tedious, and frustrating (when arithmetic errors creep in). The computer is perfectly suited to this task, however, and does the job quickly and accurately. Your time is valuable. You could be spending it to learn more, to get better grades, to earn more money, or to enjoy yourself!

3. The templates greatly facilitate sensitivity analysis of your results. Spreadsheet analysis is renowned for its "what if" capability. For example, what if interest rates were higher, would that change the result? By how much? What if the demand estimates are too optimistic, would the venture still be profitable? With the templates you simply insert the new data and instantly see the new results. This "what if" capability is what we call sensitivity analysis, and being able to do it accurately, thoroughly, and quickly is the major benefit of this courseware.

4. Finally, using these courseware files will help you to become familiar with, and increase your knowledge of, the use of Lotus 1-2-3 software (which is the industry standard) and spreadsheet analysis in general (which is an amazing productivity booster). It will increase your computer literacy and personal productivity, which in turn will make you more marketable as you start and pursue your career.

Are there any arguments against using this courseware? There are two that seem to arise every semester in the three years we have been using it. First, people say "I can't afford the start-up time required to learn how to use a computer or Lotus". Taking the longer view, you can't afford not to! A few hours invested in familiarizing yourself with Lotus early in the semester will pay you back with hundreds of hours saved in the future, not to mention your greater productivity. In any case, Lotus is easy to learn. There are tutorial disks that teach you on-screen how to use it, and the user's manual is very helpful when you run into a problem. In any case, using previously set-up templates requires minimal understanding of Lotus - you can learn as you go.

The second, much more serious problem is when students say "I thought I understood the material until I had to do the problem in the midterm exam without the computer". The templates can lull you into a false sense of security, since all you have to do is enter the data and write down the results. It is critical to understand the methodology of the solution - which number is multiplied by what number to find the answer? Why? To avoid this problem, I advise my students to work out the first problem in each set by hand, using a calculator, then use the template to check their method and their arithmetic, to do sensitivity analysis, and to do any additional problems.

How to Use the Lotus Templates

To use the templates you need a personal computer that is IBM or IBM-compatible and that has sufficient random access memory (at least 256K) to run Lotus 1-2-3. You will need a copy of the Lotus 1-2-3 software, either version 1 or 2. If it is your first time with Lotus, the tutorial disks are well worth a quick session, and you should keep the Lotus Manual nearby in case you want to try anything more ambitious.

First, you should turn on the computer, and load Lotus. This procedure will vary with your hardware, so you may need to seek assistance from your computer center personnel. Lotus is ready when you see the screen finally settle on a blank worksheet, with letters A,B,C, and so on, across the top to identify the columns, and numbers 1,2,3 and so on, down the left side to identify the rows. Each column/row coordinate, such as E4, is known as a cell. Within each cell you can put words, numbers, or formulas. With these templates, however, you only have to worry about entering data, unless you want to modify the templates.

To access the templates, put your courseware disk in the "default" disk drives (where the computer will look for files), or tell the computer where it should look for the files. Use the command signal, the slash, /, to bring up the menu of commands. Then, type FD to see which is the default file directory. If you wish to change this to, say, disk drive A, type A: then press the Enter, or Return key, and the READY sign will reappear. The /FR command will then bring a list of all worksheet files (templates) that are on your disk. Using the cursor control (the keys with the arrows on them) move the bright block to the file you want, then press the Enter key. Within moments, the selected template will appear on the screen.

Each template begins with a brief explanation of what it does, and tells you where to enter the data. To enter the data, move the cursor (the bright block or flashing indicator) to the cell you want, using the cursor control keys. Then, simply write over the existing data by typing in the numbers and pressing the Enter key. The computer will immediately recalculate the answers, but these will be nonsensical until you have entered all the new values. You will notice that the numbers in some cells glow more brightly than the numbers and words in other cells. This is because they are "unprotected" cells into which data can be entered. Make sure that you completely revise the data set to properly reflect the problem at hand.

If you want to erase the data value that is in a cell, use the /RE command, when that cell is highlighted by the cursor, then press the Enter key. To erase several cells at once, press

/RE, and type in the range of cells to erase, such as B14..B23 (ten cells in the B column), or A2..C6 (a rectangular piece of the worksheet). Alternatively, define the range by "anchoring" the bright area to one corner by pressing the . key (the period), and use the cursor to define the width and depth of the range to be erased. Then press the Enter key.

If you make a mistake, you can escape from that mistake by pressing the escape (ESC) key. This backs you out of the commands that you had entered, one at a time.

To file a revised template to the memory on your disk, give it a name that is different from the template file name. This will leave the original template undisturbed on your disk and file another version of the template on your disk. Name the new template by the problem name or number to help you easily identify it again. To file the template, use the /FS command, type in the name of the new file, and press the Enter key. Later you will notice that this new file now appears on the menu of files when you use the /FR command to retrieve a file.

To print a template, or any part of it, use the /PPR command and then define the print range, such as A15..H45, either by typing in those cell addresses or by anchoring the cursor at one corner and using the pointers to define the range to be printed. Then press Enter, then A (to align the printer to the top of the page) then G (for Go). The printer should then start printing, if it is turned on and properly connected! Press Q to quit the print mode and return to the ready mode.

To see a graph of any pair of data ranges, one plotted against the other, use the /G command to enter the graphics mode, and follow the instructions implicit in the menu choices given. The X-range will form the horizontal axis of your graph, and the A, B, and other ranges identified will be plotted against the X variable and measured on the vertical axis. After defining the ranges, use the Options menu to label your graph, then press V to view the graph. In many of the templates this has already been done, and the simple command /GV will let you view the picture. Some of the templates contain macro-command statements that allow more than one graph to be stored and retrieved easily. In the COSTFUN template, for example, the total cost curves are invoked by pressing the ALT (or CTRL) and T keys simultaneously, while the average cost curves are found by pressing ALT and A keys together.

There is a "help" file called 123HELP on the courseware disk that you should retrieve and consult if you have a problem with the Lotus files.

The Templates

I shall now introduce the templates in the order that you would use them if you were proceeding through the text chapters in sequence, indicating the place in the text where you would first benefit from the template.

ENPVA: Expected Net Present Value Analysis [Chapter 2]
This template calculates the expected net present value of an uncertain series of cashflows, where there are three possible outcomes in each of two years subsequent to the initial year. The cashflows are assumed to occur in lump sum at year end. Below is an excerpt from the ENPVA template, with the input cells (where you enter the data pertinent to the specific problem you wish to solve) identified by the **bold print**.
....
Opportunity discount rate is assumed to be   10 percent.
Cashflows are assumed to occur in lump sums at year end.

Yr0 $000	Demand1 probs.	Yr1 $000	PVYr1 0.9091	Demand2 probs.	Yr2 $000	PVYr2 0.8264	NPV $000	Joint prob	ENPV $000
				0.4	**200**	165.29	101.65	0.12	12.198
	0.3	**150**	136.36	**0.4**	**150**	123.97	60.33	0.12	7.239
				0.2	**100**	82.64	19.01	0.06	1.140
				0.4	**200**	165.29	56.20	0.20	11.239
−200	**0.5**	**100**	90.91	**0.4**	**150**	123.97	14.88	0.20	2.975
				0.2	**100**	82.64	−26.45	0.10	−2.644
				0.4	**200**	165.29	10.74	0.08	0.859
	0.2	**50**	45.45	**0.4**	**150**	123.97	−30.58	0.08	−2.446
				0.2	**100**	82.64	−71.90	0.04	−2.876

Expected Net Present Value ($000s)   27.686

Standard Deviation   ($000s)   44.369

Coefficient of Variation   1.603

Maximum Expected Outcome ($000s)   101.653

Minimum Expected Outcome ($000s)   −71.901
....

Note that the template calculates the project's ENPV, standard deviation of the joint probability distribution, and coefficient of variation, and selects the largest and smallest outcomes from the NPV column. These statistics are then used to compare this project, or decision alternative, with one or more others. ENPVA greatly facilitates sensitivity analysis, since the opportunity discount rate, the initial cost, and the year 1 and 2 probability distributions, can each be changed to see "what if" a more optimistic, or more pessimistic, view were to be taken. You simply type in the new data values and note the changes in the solution values.

ENPVB: Expected Net Present Value Analysis - Daily Cash Flows
[Chapter 2]
This template is similar to the preceding one except that it is for daily cash flows rather than year-end cash flows. Note that the daily discount factors must be looked up in Appendix B, Table B-3, of the text and inserted in the template in the cells just under those that say PVYr1 and PVYr2. (The formula for daily discount factors is very long and complex and is not embedded in the template).

INFO: The Value of Additional Information [Chapter 2]
INFO calculates the ENPV of the decision if one could always choose the most profitable alternative given prior knowledge of the state of nature. It looks like Table 2-9 in the text on page 57, but it also calculates the value of information by subtracting the full-information ENPV from the best ENPV obtainable with the information held.

DEMFUN: Demand Function, D and MR Curves, and Elasticities
[Chapter 4]
An excerpt from DEMFUN will show what it can do. Again the input data is shown in **bold print**.
. . . .

	Quantity intercept	Own Price	Independent variable #2	Independent variable #3	Independent variable #4
Independent variable	4.50	4.39		168	182
Regression	2468.5	−1931.6		168.2	−18.8

Quantity demanded at current price: 19,858.62   units

Demand Curve: P = 14.78091 −0.00051 Q

Marginal Revenue   MR = 14.78091 −0.00103 Q

ELASTICITIES			OTHER CALCULATIONS		
Price elasticity	e =	−0.43770	Enter MC = AVC =	$	2
Indvar2 elasticity	e2 =	0.062759	Enter TFC =	$	0
Indvar3 elasticity	e3 =	1.422938	Thus, TVC =	$39717.24	
Indvar4 elasticity	e4 =	−0.17229	TC =	$39717.24	
Indvar5 elasticity	e5 =	0	TR =	$89363.79	
Indvar6 elasticity	e6 =	0	and Profit =	$49646.55	

. . . .

Thus DEMFUN calculates the quantity demanded, and the elasticities for each of the independent variables, given the demand function coefficients and the current values of the independent variables. Expressions for the demand curve and the marginal revenue curve are also generated, and the impact on the firm's total revenues and profits can be seen by varying price. Note that there may be up to six independent variables in the demand function.

ELAST: Arc and Point Price Elasticity [Chapter 4]
This template calculates the arc and point price elasticities of demand, and generates expressions for the demand and marginal revenue curves, following the input of two price-quantity observations. It also calculates new values of quantity demanded when a new price is entered, and shows the revenue-maximizing price, output, and total revenue.

MAXPRICE: Profit and Revenue Maximizing Price and Output Levels [Chapter 4]
MAXPRICE takes as input an expression for the demand curve and for the total fixed and total variable cost curves, and generates the profit-maximizing and revenue-maximizing prices and output levels. Here is an excerpt from MAXPRICE:

....

P = 14.78091 −0.515 Q (Note Q represents thousands of units)
MR = 14.78091 −1.030 Q

TFC = 0
TVC = 0 + 2 Q + 0 Q^2 = $24817.30

PROFIT-maximizing output: 12.40865 thousands of units
Profit-maximizing price: $ 8.39045 per unit

TR = Profmax price times profmax quantity $ 104114.20
TC = TFC + TVC @ 12.40865 thousand units $ 24817.30
Maximum Profits $ 79296.90

MC = 2 c/f MR = 2
AVC = 2 and SAC = 2 at that output .

REVENUE-maximizing output: 14.35039 thousands of units
Revenue-maximizing price: $ 7.39045 per unit

Maximum Revenue $ 106055.90
TC = TFC + TVC @ 14.35039 thousand units $ 28700.79
Profit given Revmax price $ 77355.11

MC = 2 c/f MR = 1.5E-16 i.e. zero
AVC = 2 and SAC = 2 at that output.

....

276

ESTDEM: Estimated Demand Curve and Maxprice, given Elasticity
[Chapter 4]

ESTDEM calculates expressions for the demand and marginal revenue curves, given your input of the current price, quantity demanded, and an estimate of the price elasticity. Here is an excerpt.

. . . .

Enter current price in cell G4	P =	8 (dollars)
Enter current quantity in cell G6	Q =	32 (units)
Enter estimated price elasticity in G8	e =	-3
Enter marginal cost per unit in G10	MC =	4 (dollars)

(assuming a constant MC = AVC)

ESTIMATED DEMAND CURVE	P = 10.66666 -0.083333 Q
ESTIMATED MARGINAL REVENUE	MR = 10.66666 -0.166666 Q
PROFIT-MAXIMIZING PRICE	P = 7.333333 AND VOLUME Q = 40
REVENUE-MAXIMIZING PRICE	P = 5.333333 AND VOLUME Q = 64

If you do not know the price elasticity, is your current price profit maximizing?

Enter current price in cell G29	P =	8 (dollars)
Enter current quantity in cell G31	Q =	32 (units)
Enter MC = AVC in cell G33	MC =	4 (dollars)

NULL HYPOTHESIS: If your current price IS the profit-maximizing price, the MC = MR at the current output level, and the implied value of price elasticity (at the current price level) is: -2 This implies that if your price was reduced by 10 percent, for example, your quantity demanded would increase by 20 percent.

Do you think this elasticity value accurately describes the probable reactions of your customers to a change in the price level? If so, then the current price is profit-maximizing, to the best of your knowledge. If you think the actual price elasticity is somewhat LOWER (in absolute terms), then your current price is lower than the profit-maximizing level. You may wish to raise your price a little, and observe the impact on profits. If you think the true elasticity is HIGHER than that, your price is currently too high. Reduce it and see what happens to profits.

. . . .

BESTFIT: Line of Best Fit, R-squared, and Confidence Intervals
[Chapter 5]

This template calculates the line of best fit to a collection of up to ten X-Y observations, using the simple least squares method as in the text, page 170. A graph can be viewed of the data points and the line of best fit. The coefficient of determination, the standard errors of estimate and of the coefficients, and the 95% confidence interval for the predicted value, are also calculated.

MOVINGAV: A Four-period Moving Average Forecasting Model
[Appendix 5A]
MOVINGAV calculates a four-period moving average of the observations, using up to six preceding periods, and uses this to provide a (recursive) forecast of the Y values in the next two periods, t + 1 and t + 2.

EXPOSMOO: Exponential Smoothing Forecasting Model [Appendix 5A]
This template allows you to find the optimal value of the weight that is used in an exponential forecasting model. You adjust the weight until the sum of the squared deviations of the predicted values from the actual values is minimized. The model then predicts the Y value in the t + 1 time period.

PRODFUN: Production and Cost Data [Chapter 6]
PRODFUN calculates total, average, and marginal cost values from a simple production function with one variable input. You enter each input level and the corresponding output level, and the price of capital and labor units, and the cost data appears instantly. Graphs of the TP, MP, TVC, TC, AVC, SAC, and MC curves can be viewed with a few simple keystrokes explained on the template. Here is an excerpt from PRODFUN:
....

Input units	0	1	2	3	4	5	6	7
Output (TP)	0	100	160	218	272	302	320	335
Marginal product	0	100	60	58	54	30	18	15

Total Fixed Costs per period TFC = $ 80000

Cost per unit of the Variable Inputs $ 10000

TVC	0	10000	20000	30000	40000	50000	60000	70000
TC	80000	90000	100000	110000	120000	130000	140000	150000
AVC		100	125	137.61	147.05	165.56	187.50	208.95
AFC		800	500	366.97	294.11	264.90	250	238.80
SAC		900	625	504.58	441.17	430.46	437.50	447.76
MC (at midpoint)			166.66	172.41	185.18	333.33	555.55	666.66

....

PRODFUN2: Deriving Cost Curves from a Production Function
[Chapter 6]

This template calculates the TFC, TVC, TC, AVC, SAC, and MC given an estimated production function of the cubic form:

$$Q = a + bK + cK^2 + dK^3 + eL + fL^2 + gL^3$$

Enter the values of the coefficients a through g, as well as the cost of K and L per unit, and set the plant size (K) equal to some number, and the cost data is generated in a form similar to that in the lower part of the PRODFUN template, and is excerpted here.

Output	TVC	TFC	TC	AVC	AFC	SAC	MC (at) midpoint
1000	1000	2500	3500	1	2.50	3.50	
							0.75
2000	1750	2500	4250	0.88	1.25	2.13	
							0.50
3000	2250	2500	4750	0.75	0.83	1.58	
							0.50
4000	2750	2500	5250	0.69	0.63	1.31	
							0.75
5000	3500	2500	6000	0.70	0.50	1.20	
							1.00
6000	4500	2500	7000	0.75	0.42	1.17	
							1.50
7000	6000	2500	8500	0.86	0.36	1.21	
							2.00
8000	8000	2500	10500	1.00	0.31	1.31	
							3.00
9000	11000	2500	13500	1.22	0.28	1.50	
							4.00
10000	15000	2500	17500	1.50	0.25	1.75	

COSTFUN: Deriving Cost Curves from an Estimated Cost Function
[Chapter 6]

COSTFUN calculates TVC, TC, AVC, SAC, and MC given the input of an estimated total variable cost function of the form:

$$TVC = a + bQ + cQ^2 + dQ^3$$

The TFC value, and ten output levels that represent the relevant range, are then entered and the cost values are displayed in a form similar to that in PRODFUN. Graphs of the total and per unit cost curves can then be viewed using simple commands.

PLANTSIZ: Choice of Plant given Uncertain Demand   [Chapter 6]

This template allows you to choose between any two plant sizes, given a probability distribution of quantity demanded (at a particular price) and the SAC values from those plants at each of the output levels, as shown in the following excerpt.

QUANTITY DEMANDED		PLANT A		PLANT B	
Output	Probability	SAC	Exp.Value	SAC	Exp.Value
500	0.05	3	0.15	5	0.25
1000	0.15	2.5	0.375	3	0.45
1500	0.25	2	0.5	1.75	0.4375
2000	0.35	2.75	0.9625	1.5	0.525
2500	0.15	3.5	0.525	2	0.3
3000	0.05	4.5	0.225	3	0.15
1775	Expected Values		2.7375		2.1125
601.5	Standard Deviations		0.6249		0.8605

CONTRIB: Contribution Analysis [Chapter 7]

CONTRIB calculates the EPV of the contribution to overheads and profits of a proposed decision, after you have entered all incremental costs and revenues, and the opportunity discount rate, in the appropriate cells.

ENGINEER: Estimating Cost Curves using the Engineering Technique [Chapter 8]

ENGINEER calculates values for all the cost curves, given a production function with up to six variable inputs. You enter the physical inputs of each variable input for each output level, as well as the prices of the inputs and the total fixed costs per period. Following is an excerpt from the ENGINEER template. Note that you can also view graphs of the cost curves.

Enter the Total Fixed Costs here: TFC = $ 3000 per period

Output levels:		1000	2000	3000	4000	5000	6000
Input name	Input cost ($)	Input Units required for each Output Level					
Labor	10	400	700	880	990	1450	2850
Materials	5	100	200	300	420	560	720
Var.O/head	0.05	4000	9500	16000	30000	43000	63000
Other1	0	0	0	0	0	0	0
Other2	0	0	0	0	0	0	0

COST DATA OUTPUT:

Q	1000	2000	3000	4000	5000	6000

TFC	3000	3000	3000	3000	3000	3000
TVC	5000	9000	12000	15000	22000	39000
TC	8000	12000	15000	18000	25000	42000
AFC	3	1.5	1	0.75	0.6	0.5
AVC	5	4.5	4	3.75	4.4	6.5
SAC	8	6	5	4.5	5	7
MC (at midpoints of quantity ranges)		4	3	3	7	17

CUBICOST: Linear, Quadratic, and Cubic Cost Curves [Chapter 8]

This template is usable only if you have version 2 of Lotus 1-2-3, which does regression analysis. If you do not, you may use the MULTREG Fortran program to do exactly the same analysis. Total Variable Cost (or Total Cost) and output data is entered, and you decide whether to regress TVC as a linear, quadratic, or cubic function of Q. By comparing the regression statistics (the R^2 in particular), you can decide which functional form provides the best fit to the data, and which, therefore, should be used as your predictive model of the total variable costs.

PRIDISCR: Price Discrimination between Two Markets [Appendix 9A]

This template calculates the profit-maximizing prices and outputs in each of two separate markets for the price discriminating firm, given your input of the two demand curve expressions and the total cost curve equation. The following excerpts will demonstrate its capability.

MARKET #1
Demand Curve $P_1 =$ 100 -15 Q_1
Marginal Revenue $MR_1 =$ 100 -30 Q_1

MARKET #2
Demand Curve $P_2 =$ 60 -2.5 Q_2
Marginal Revenue $MR_2 =$ 60 -5 Q_2

Total Costs   TC =   150 +   20 TotQ +   0.1 TotQ^2
Marginal Cost MC =   20 +   0.2 TotQ

Set MR_1 and MR_2 equal to that same level and find:
$$Q_1 = 2.598726$$

and $Q_2 =$ 7.592356

Substitute into demand curve expression to find:

$P_1 =$ 61.01910

and $P_2 =$ 41.01910

Total Cost at 10.19108 units is $ 364.2074

Revenue Mkt1	2.598726 units @	61.01910	= $	158.5719
Revenue Mkt2	7.592356 units @	41.01910	= $	311.4317
		Total revenue	= $	470.0036
PROFIT per period			= $	105.7961

Price elasticity at price P_1:   -1.56535
Price elasticity at price P_2:   -2.16107

. . . .

MARKUP: Markup Rates to Maximize Profits [Chapter 10]
This template calculates the markup that is implicit in the difference between the firm's current price and its marginal cost levels. The price elasticity required for that markup rate to be profit-maximizing is also shown. If you think the elasticity is different, enter your estimate, and the template calculates the profit maximizing price and output levels based on your estimate. Finally the potential increase in contribution (if your estimate is correct) is calculated. See the excerpt below.

. . . .

Your current price is $ =   8.95 per unit
Your marginal cost is constant at $ =   4 per unit
The current MARKUP RATE is thus   123.75 percent.

The IMPLIED PRICE ELASTICITY (for this
to be the profit-maximizing markup rate
and price level) is   -1.80808

Your ESTIMATED PRICE ELASTICITY is   -1.25

Enter current sales volume   Q =   120 units

Your estimated demand curve is   P = 16.11 -0.05966 Q
and   MR = 16.11 -0.11933 Q

Estimated profit-maximizing output is   101.4804 units
Estimated profit-maximizing price is $ 10.555 per unit
Estimated optimal markup rate is   151.375 percent

Total contribution at optimal price would be $ 614.4641
Total contribution at existing price is $ <u>592</u>
Potential Increase in Contribution $ <u>20.4641</u>

. . . .

ADVERT: Optimal Advertising Expenditures [Chapter 13]

ADVERT calculates the profit-maximizing level of advertising (and other promotion) expenses, given a sales-advertising function and data on the firm's price and average variable costs. Consider the following excerpt.

. . . .
Current Advertising Budget, A, in $'000s, is: 1000
Current price is $ 16 per unit, and AVC = MC =   8 per unit
Total Fixed Cost is $ 80000 excluding advertising expenditures
(continued over....)
The Sales-Advertising function has been estimated as:
    Q =   110386.3 + 298.674 A - 0.10537 A^2

Thus current sales volume should be: 303690.3 units.

The Optimal Advertising Expenditure level is $ 824.115 (000s)
At present advertising level, Total Profit is $ 629522.4
At optimal advertising level, profit would be $ 655599.8
. . . .

CAPBUDGE: Capital Budgeting Analysis of Alternate Proposals
[Chapter 15 (and Chapter 1 as well)]

This template calculates the present value, the internal rate of return, the profitability index, and the payback period, for each of two investment projects, using year-end discount factors. Note that the projects can generate cash flows for up to ten years.

. . . .
PLAN A   PLAN B
Opp. Disc. Rate (%)   17   Opp. Disc. Rate (%)   14

Cash flows after taxes   Cash flows after taxes
          Nominal   PV   Nominal   PV
Year 0   -50   -50   Year 0   -40   -40
Year 1   15   12.8205   Year 1   5   4.3859
Year 2   20   14.6103   Year 2   8   6.1557
Year 3   20   12.4874   Year 3   15   10.1246
Year 4   20   10.6730   Year 4   20   11.8416
Year 5   50   22.8056   Year 5   70   36.3558
. . . .
TOTALS   75   23.3968   TOTALS   78   28.8637

To calculate the Internal rate of return, increase the opportunity discount rate in the following table until the total PV is zero.
. . . .
IRR is   32.5381 percent   IRR is   31.075 percent
. . . .
Profitability Index 2.467925   Profitability index 2.721592

283

```
. . . . . . . . . . . . . . . . . . . . . . . . . . . . . . . . . . . . . . . . . . . . . . . . . . . . .
Payback period -                    Payback period -
     Nominal   3.75 years                Nominal      4.6 years
     PV terms  4.95 years                PV terms     5.21 years
. . . . . . . . . . . . . . . . . . . . . . . . . . . . . . . . . . . . . . . . . . . . . . . . . . . .
```

How to Modify the Templates, or Make your Own

To modify a formula or change some of the words on a template you will need to open up the protected cells first. Use the **/WGPD** command to "unprotect" the entire worksheet, or the **/RU** command to unprotect a particular cell or range of cells. But be careful. The protection feature is designed to prevent you from inadvertently erasing data or formulas. After you have made the changes, protect the cells again by the using **/WGPE** or the **/RP** command. Position the cursor on the cell you want to revise. The EDIT function key [F2] allows you to modify any entry, using the cursor control to move to the place where you want to make the change. Otherwise, simply write over the existing formula or words with the new material, and finally press the Enter key.

To insert a new column or row into the worksheet, use the **/WIC** or the **/WIR** command, after positioning the cursor where you want the new column or row. If you want a single new column or row, simply press Enter. Otherwise, use the pointers to indicate how many extra columns or rows before pressing Enter. Similarly, to delete a column or row, use the **/WDC** or **/WDR** command.

To make a column wider or narrower, place the cursor in the desired column, use the **/WCS** command, and then enter the number of spaces you want the column to cover.

To copy data, words, or a formula from one cell or range of cells to another, use the **/C** command. Define the range to be copied and press Enter. Identify the cell, or the top left hand cell in the new range, where it is to be copied to, and press Enter again, and the contents will be copied from one place to the other. To move data, words, or a formula to another range and leave the initial range empty, use the **/M** command.

When copying or moving formulas that refer to values in a particular cell you have to use either relative or absolute cell addresses. A formula placed in cell C12 using relative addresses might be, for example, +C9/A9. The computer looks in the cell that is three rows above C12 (that is, C9) and divides that value by the value in the cell three rows above and two columns to the left of C12 (that is, A9). If you were to move this formula to cell C14, the computer would then look in the cells that have the same address relative to C14, namely cells C11 and A11, and find the quotient of those two values. This may be what you want to do, of course. Other times you will want to anchor the formula to a particular cell, or absolute address.

Absolute addresses are written by using the $ sign prior to the column letter and/or the row number. Suppose you sum the values in cells A8 through A16 by entering @SUM(A8..A16) in cell

A17. Then you want to show in column B the proportion of the total that each component represents. In cell B8, type +A8/A17, and press Enter. Then use the /C command to copy that formula from cell B8 to the range B9..B16. The copy command will automatically change A8 to A9, A10, and so on, but will keep A17 as the denominator because of the $ sign that precedes the 17. Similarly, the $ sign before the A locked the address into column A, although it made no difference in this case.

When entering data or words into a Lotus worksheet, the computer immediately recognizes numbers as "values" that can be used in computations, and letters as "labels" that cannot. If you want to mix numbers and letters in a label or word, such as 13A, you will have to tell the computer that it is a label by typing the ' (single quotation mark) character first, and 13A will appear at the left of the cell into which it is entered. Alternatively, the " (double quotation mark) character will align this or any other label flush right, and the ^ (circumflex) character will center the label in its cell.

To enter formulas in a cell, identify data values by the cell address in which they will be found, make sure you use enough brackets to allow the machine to do the computations in the appropriate mathematical order. For example, if we want to add the values in cells B8 and G17, type +B8+G17. Alternatively, you could type (B8+G17). Note that the initial plus sign or bracket alerts the computer that you mean a value, not a label. Similarly, if you want to multiply the numbers in A4 and C7 and divide the product by the square of the value in G6, you would write (A4*C7)/(G6^2).

Lotus has many built in formulas and computation commands, which are triggered by the @ character. For example, @SUM(A2..A8) will add the values in those cells. @AVG(A6..H6) will find the mean value of the values in this row of cells. @STD(H35..H90) will find the standard deviation of those values. @SQRT(E42) will calculate the square root of the value in cell E42, and so on. There is a wide variety of mathematical, statistical, financial, logical, and other @ functions that greatly facilitate building a template to suit special applications.

Lotus 1-2-3 is an extremely powerful tool for analysis and computation. I encourage you to read the Lotus Reference Manual and discover the wide range of tasks that Lotus can handle. I also encourage you to experiment, and to set up templates to save time with all kinds of things, like your income taxes and your household budget, for example. After a while you will wonder how you ever got along without Lotus to help you.

The Fortran Programs

Also available are two Fortran programs, written by Dr. Andrew Stollar, which are capable of handling more complex problems. These programs are relatively easy to use, since they are menu-driven. You select what you want to do from a series of menus, and simply follow directions.

The first program, EPV, calculates the expected-present-value of a decision alternative or investment project, and is not limited to two-year time horizons and only three possible outcomes in each year, as are the ENPV templates. Thus, EPV can handle complex decision problems with many cashflow possibilities in each period and time horizons stretching over several years.

The second program, MULTREG, includes a multiple regression program, but it also handles other types of statistical analysis. If you have access to version 2 of Lotus 1-2-3, you will not need MULTREG for the multiple regression, since Lotus version 2 has that capability incorporated. Other statistical capabilities of the MULTREG package may be useful to you however.

The two Fortran programs are run from MS-DOS (which stands for Microsoft Disk Operating System) by typing the name of the program when the MS-DOS prompt appears. That is, when the prompt "A>" appears on the screen at the left-hand margin, one simply enters MULTREG or EPV to load the program into the computer memory so that it can be run. Note that these are not Lotus files and cannot be accessed from within Lotus. These two programs are provided on a separate disk to allow space for you to create data files and file them on the same disk, and retrieve them as required.

MULTREG requires a computer with 256K whereas EPV requires only 128K. If your computer can run Lotus 1-2-3, then it can run both of these Fortran programs, assuming it has MS-DOS (or PC-DOS in the case of IBM hardware).

In MS-DOS you can see a directory of the files on your disk by entering DIR at the prompt. If there are too many files for a single screen, enter DIR /P to see them one page at a time. Other MS-DOS commands you may find useful are DEL, which will delete a file. Type DEL FILENAME (substitute the actual name of the file you wish to delete) at the prompt to delete any file. To copy a file from one directory to another, say, from directory (disk drive) A to directory (disk drive) B, type COPY A:FILENAME B: and the file will be copied from the disk in drive A to the one in drive B. Use this procedure to make backup copies of your files in case your (main) disk is damaged.

EPV - the Expected Present Value Program

EPV calculates the expected present value of up to three alternative decisions or investment projects. You can enter the data and save this data to a named file for later use or re-use. You may change any or all input values and re-run the EPV program. You can send output to the screen for perusal, or to the printer for a permanent record. You can then ask for more or less output data and have both screen and printer output.

To access this program, enter EPV at the prompt. The program will be loaded and the first menu will appear on the screen. At this point you will be asked to state how many projects you wish to compare, how many years each one will be considered over, and how many states of nature there are in each year. Take notice of the limits on these, individually and in aggregate.

You will be able to print out the results of your analysis. Specify what output you want, and whether it is to be printed or simply viewed on the screen, when asked at the beginning of the program.

EPV allows you a variety of discounting options, and you can either leave the options set at the default values or change them to suit the problem at hand. You can change the discounting option to pursue "what if?" questions, such as "what if the cash flows arrive on a daily basis rather than at year end?"

You can either create a new data file within EPV, or retrieve a data file that had been created earlier. To create a data file, simply follow directions and enter the data in the order requested by the program. If you make an input error, you will be given a chance to change the entry later. Simply continue entering data at each prompt, and then go back and fix errors when asked if you want to change any values.

When you have created a file, you will be given the opportunity to save it, and you should do so, using a specific file name that you will find easy to remember. Note that file names must not be longer than 12 characters. If you enter a longer name the program will abort and you will have to enter the data all over again!

A separate file called EPVHELP may be found on your disk. This explains the various choices you have to make in EPV, concerning what output will be printed, whether it will simply be sent to the screen or to the printer, and so on. If you get stuck, take a look in EPVHELP and you will, hopefully, find the solution to your problem.

MULTREG: Multiple Regression and Statistics Program

MULTREG offers several options, including multiple linear regression analysis, confidence intervals for the predicted values, general statistics (including correlation and covariance matrices), and data file and variable manipulation.

To access this program, enter MULTREG at the prompt and you will see the list of the options come to the screen. If you choose HELP at this point you will get a more detailed explanation of the options available. You can also choose to have these printed out for easy reference.

In the multiple regression option, default output includes the ordinary least squares coefficients, standard errors, t-statistics, sums of squares for variance analysis, F-statistic, R^2 (adjusted and unadjusted), Durbin-Watson statistic, mean of the dependent variable, the mean absolute deviation, and the Theil inequality coefficient. Optional output includes printout of data set, variance-covariance matrix, predicted values and residuals, and so on.

In the general statistics option, output includes means, standard deviations, coefficient of variation, medians, skewness coefficient, maximums and minimums, correlation and covariance matrices, beta and partial elasticity coefficients, and so on.

In the confidence intervals option, output includes four confidence intervals each on the mean and on another specified value of the dependent variable. Tests for linear restrictions on model parameters are also allowed. Like the general statistics option, this option can be used with the regression option or independently of it.

Data file manipulation options include create a new data file; choose a data subset; transpose a matrix; transform to logarithms (base e or 10); insert dummies; insert variables (from disk or keyboard); delete variables; interchange variables; multiply/divide variables; power term; reciprocals; sort; merge two data files; change data values; print data set (to screen or printer); read new data file; and write data to disk.

In the regression option you will be able to enter data and create a file, or retrieve a previously entered data file for analysis. When creating a data file, note that file names must not be longer than 12 characters, either numbers and letters, with an optional .DAT ending to remind you that it is a data file.